PROMOTING EQUALITY

PROMOTING EQUALITY

CHALLENGING DISCRIMINATION AND OPPRESSION

SECOND EDITION

NEIL THOMPSON

Foreword by Audrey Mullender

Consultant Editor: Jo Campling

First published 2003 by
PALGRAVE MACMILLAN
Houndmills, Basingstoke, Hampshire RG21 6XS and
175 Fifth Avenue, New York, N. Y. 10010
Companies and representatives throughout the world

PALGRAVE MACMILLAN is the global academic imprint of the Palgrave Macmillan division of St. Martin's Press, LLC and of Palgrave Macmillan Ltd. Macmillan® is a registered trademark in the United States, United Kingdom and other countries. Palgrave is a registered trademark in the European Union and other countries.

ISBN 0–333–99353–5

This book is printed on paper suitable for recycling and made from fully managed and sustained forest sources.

A catalogue record for this book is available from the British Library.

Library of Congress Catalog Card Number: 2003040545

11 10 9 8 7 6 5 4 3 2 1
13 12 11 10 09 08 07 06 05 04 03

Printed and bound in Great Britain by
Creative Print & Design (Wales), Ebbw Vale

Er cof am ewythr John,
dyn arbennig iawn

CONTENTS

LIST OF FIGURES

FOREWORD

It is always good to see a really useful text updated, so that it can continue serving its purpose with a new generation of readers. This book is certainly a case in point.

Some considerable time before the words 'difference' and 'diversity' became widespread in sociology, Neil Thompson was working and writing to promote equality. Furthermore, his location in the human services has always made his approach far more than a description and analysis of what is wrong – moving, rather, into an active framework for tackling discrimination and oppression in practical ways. The fact that he encompasses complex sociological theory, explaining postmodern concepts of power along the way, is a definite bonus for students, teachers and practitioners who recognize that thinking has presented new challenges but who cannot always quite grasp how this is relevant to their own work in an applied discipline or profession. This book shows that it is possible to think and to act, to understand and to progress – surely the fundamental challenge to anyone who seeks to be a change agent in contemporary society.

The first edition of this book proved useful beyond the human services, as, in this post-Macpherson world, we came to realize that racism and other forms of oppression are endemic in all our public (and private) institutions and that it is down to all of us to take action to combat them. Disability discrimination is now stronger than it was five years ago, when this book first appeared, reaching into educational and other settings and posing a new set of challenges. There is talk of bringing all anti-discriminatory work together into one policy, one Commission, one effort for change. So there are additional external drivers now for developing an overarching anti-oppressive strategy, to add to the internal desire, on the part of professionals and their managers, to 'get it right' for the full range of patients, service users and customers. Having this one readable and helpful book available to satisfy this need is a boon.

Real change is a slow process. Neil Thompson's work has never been about easy rhetoric. It is about making us stop and think, re-examine our day-to-day work and alter the way we have traditionally done things if it has created obstacles to the accessibility or appropriateness of the services we offer. The most damaging phrase in the English language is 'political correctness'. It has been employed constantly, in a slick backlash reaction against just the kind of thought and effort that Neil Thompson shows is needed to create a fairer context for the organization of all health, social care and related services. It cannot be 'correct' to ignore these imperatives and it is certainly not only for political reasons that people want to engage with these vital issues. Whatever our motivation – altruistic, humanitarian, moral, or the pursuit of good, old-fashioned fairness and equity – this is a book to challenge the easy dismissal of good intentions and to ensure that we translate them into demonstrable improvement.

AUDREY MULLINDER
Professor of Social Work
University of Warwick

PREFACE TO THE FIRST EDITION

The need to take seriously issues of inequality, discrimination and oppression continues to be a pressing one, as human services workers each day come face to face with the negative effects of such problems. This book will not provide easy answers or formula solutions, but is intended to be of value in terms of the theoretical analysis presented and the constant links between the theory base and the realities of day-to-day practice. It is presented not as a comprehensive theoretical exposition, nor as a 'cookbook' of recipes as to how to practise in ways that seek to challenge inequality and disadvantage. Rather, it represents an attempt to integrate theory and practice by exploring a range of theoretical issues and relating these to the practice context – with a view to contributing to high-quality practice informed by clear principles and an appreciation of the complexities involved.

Practitioners, managers, educators and policy-makers in the human services face a number of challenges, due to the demanding nature of responding to human problems in a range of settings and contexts. Having to take account of the need to promote equality and recognize the significance of discrimination and oppression in people's lives is therefore an additional pressure in what already tend to be highly pressurized work situations. However, my argument here is that this additional challenge should be seen as a core element of good practice, for to practise without addressing issues of inequality is to run the risk of exacerbating the situation – reinforcing existing patterns of disadvantage. A central theme of the book, then, is the importance of addressing issues of inequality, discrimination and oppression in all aspects of theory, policy and practice in order to make sure that our efforts are part of a process of promoting equality, rather than one of adding to or intensifying existing burdens of oppression.

Staff in the human services are in a pivotal position as far as discrimination and inequality are concerned. Whether we are nurses, social workers, teachers, youth workers, police or probation officers, housing officers, counsellors, advisors or members of any other branch of the human services, we are likely to work with people who are discriminated against in one or more ways, and our actions could be of benefit to them in dealing with the challenges their circumstances present, *or* the steps we take could have the opposite effect of further marginalizing and disempowering already disadvantaged groups, for example by reinforcing negative stereotypes. Human services practice can be empowering or it can, in itself, be a form of oppression. This book is intended as an aid to people involved in the human services to appreciate the significance of these issues and to be better equipped to play a part in making sure that practice contributes to empowerment, and not to oppression.

NEIL THOMPSON

PREFACE TO THE SECOND EDITION

The five years since I wrote the first edition of this book have seen a significant growth of interest in matters of inequality and the related concept of diversity. The theory base has continued to grow, practice initiatives have developed, training courses have proliferated and there appears to be considerable commitment to taking seriously the challenges of inequality and diversity, in certain quarters at least. These are positive developments but, of course, the work that remains to be done to get these issues firmly on the agenda is none the less of major proportions. While there is room for at least a small amount of cautious optimism, there is certainly no room for complacency.

During those five years I have worked as a trainer and consultant with a wide range of organizations, trying to help them tackle the complex yet important issues of promoting equality and valuing diversity. In that work I have encountered a range of responses – a great deal of enthusiasm and commitment (particularly from people who had felt hemmed in by dogmatic approaches which had left them feeling attacked and undermined, rather than educated and motivated to support change – see Chapter 5); a lot of anger about how people had been treated badly on courses they had attended in the past; some discomfort about how complex and sensitive the issues are; a degree of resistance to exploring those complexities and sensitivities; and occasionally, a degree of complacency ('I've been on a course on discrimination before so I make sure I never discriminate against anyone'). I am pleased to say that, while the initial responses are sometimes problematic, the vast majority of people I have worked with have gone away with a much more positive and committed attitude towards promoting equality once they have a good understanding of the basis of discrimination and oppression, why they are important problems to be tackled and how we can begin to do so. This book is intended to be part of developing that understanding – trying to help people understand that discrimination and oppression are much more common than most people realize, and, moreover, that they are also very detrimental to not only the people 'on the receiving end', but also the organizations which allow such problems to persist, and indeed for society as a whole.

In this second edition I have revised, updated and, in places, extended the points I put forward in the first edition. I have incorporated new ideas and have developed my own thinking along the way. However, the basic message of the book remains the same, as do the theoretical and moral-political foundations on which my work is based.

The first edition focused primarily on the work of staff and managers in the helping professions or 'human services'. However, I have received a great deal of feedback since the publication of the first edition that a large number of people outside of these professional groups have also found the book helpful, informative and an important source of 'food for thought'. This edition has therefore been broadened in its scope. While still offering a great deal to people working in the human services (nursing and health care; social work and social care; probation and community justice work; advocacy and advice work; counselling; youth and community work; and so on), it will also appeal to anyone who works with people and their problems, broadly defined (local government workers of various kinds, managers and supervisors in a variety of settings, for example). Indeed, this book should be of value to anyone who wishes to engage with the very real but very important challenge of promoting equality and valuing diversity.

NEIL THOMPSON

ACKNOWLEDGEMENTS

Many people were supportive of my efforts to produce the first edition of this book, and I continue to be grateful to them for that. I would therefore like to express once again how indebted I am to Colin Richardson, Fellow of Keele University, John Bates of North East Wales Institute, Beth Humphries of the University of Lancaster, Brid Featherstone of the University of Huddersfield and Jane Boylan and Bernard Moss of Staffordshire University.

I must also express my gratitude to Professor Audrey Mullender for being so kind in providing the Foreword for both editions. Jo Campling deserves both thanks and credit for her continued support, as does Susan Thompson for the major contribution she makes to all of my work in one way or another. Once again I am indebted to Judy Marshall for the excellent quality of her editorial work and to Catherine Gray and Jo Digby at the publishers for their unstinting support.

I would also like to thank the various people I have worked with in a training and/or consultancy capacity since the publication of the first edition of this book. They have provided me with such fertile soil for learning and immense job satisfaction in their predominantly positive responses to the messages I have been trying to put across in that work and indeed in this book.

NEIL THOMPSON

INTRODUCTION

A basic premise of this book is that contemporary western societies are characterized by inequality. For those of us involved in working with people and their problems, this presents a fundamental challenge, in so far as decisions made and actions taken can play a significant role in either moving towards a greater degree of equality or reinforcing existing inequalities. This is because 'people work' so often involves the exercise of power, frequently with relatively powerless people. Thus, the worker can play a pivotal role with regard to people's experience of the discrimination and oppression arising from inequality.

This, then, is the central theme of this book – the crucial role of the 'people' worker in promoting equality, rather than reinforcing or exacerbating the inequalities that already exist in society and in people's lives. The traditional approaches that have tended to pay little or no attention to issues of inequality, discrimination or oppression will be shown to be seriously flawed and, as a consequence, the source of harmful practices that can leave people feeling alienated, devalued and disempowered.

Some may argue that inequality is an inevitable part of professional practice and of society more broadly – and will therefore see any attempt to tackle inequality as doomed to failure. While some degree of inequality may well prove to be unavoidable, this is not to say that substantial progress cannot be made in terms of reducing inequality and alleviating its negative effects. However, it is not simply a matter of reducing or cushioning inequality, there is also the important question of seeking to ensure that professional practice does not increase such inequality or amplify its harmful or destructive consequences.

The people who require assistance from professional helpers are often from disadvantaged social groups, and the fact that they are in need of such assistance may disadvantage them further. That is, the illness, crisis, loss or other problem that brought them into contact with a professional worker is likely to make them more vulnerable than would otherwise be the case. The disparity of power between the helper and the person being helped can therefore be a very significant aspect of the relationship and interactions between them. This disparity creates considerable potential for the abuse and misuse of that power. By abuse I mean the deliberate use of such power to harm or exploit others. Misuse, by contrast, is the term I use to refer to the unintentional or unwitting role of power in maintaining inequalities and disadvantage. While deliberate abuse may be less common, I shall be arguing that the misuse of power, stemming from a lack of awareness and understanding, is unfortunately all too prevalent.

This is an important point that merits further emphasis. The discrimination and oppression associated with inequality should not be seen as simply arising from the actions of a prejudiced or bigoted minority. For example, sexism is not simply the result of the prejudice of 'male chauvinists', nor does racism arise solely from the actions of right-wing extremists who actively support racial division and disharmony. The reality of discrimination is far more complex, with its roots in psychology, sociology, economics and politics. Inequality, discrimination and oppression are largely sustained by *ideology*, the power of ideas. Consequently, if we are not aware of the subtle workings of ideology, we are likely to find ourselves practising in ways that unwittingly reinforce existing power relations and thereby maintain the status quo with its inherent inequalities.

Ideology, and the related concept of discourse, will therefore be central themes in the arguments presented here. This is because discriminatory ideas become embedded in everyday 'common sense' and are rarely questioned or challenged. Many examples of this process will be provided in the chapters that follow. We shall see how traditional approaches that do not examine ideological assumptions run the risk of unwittingly contributing to oppressive inequalities. It is for this reason that this book addresses important questions of ideology. Without developing an understanding of how ideology and discourse serve to maintain existing power relations, students, practitioners and managers will be less well equipped to achieve high-quality standards of practice that are fair, equitable and geared towards greater equality and an increased range of life chances.

The core arguments underpinning this book can be summarized as follows:

1. The contemporary social order is characterized by a range of social divisions (class, race, gender, age, disability and so on) that both embody and engender inequality, discrimination and oppression.
2. These inequalities, and the ideologies that support and sustain them, are generally taken for granted and subtly influence our actions and attitudes.
3. Unless we develop an understanding of inequality and the ideologies underpinning it, we are likely not only to fail to address discrimination and oppression, but also to reinforce or even exacerbate them.
4. Issues of equality must therefore be central to working with people and their problems. To offer help and assistance without taking into account inequality is a very risky undertaking indeed. Good intentions and kindhearted actions can, and often do, cause a great deal of damage if they are not premised on an understanding of, and sensitivity to, the inequalities that already exist and the potential for making them worse.

The basic approach can be captured in one sentence: good practice must be anti-discriminatory practice. As I have argued previously:

> practice which does not take account of oppression and discrimination cannot be seen as good practice, no matter how high its standards may be in other respects. For example, an . . . intervention with a disabled person which fails to recognize the marginalized position of disabled people in society runs the risk of providing the client with more of a disservice than a service.
>
> (Thompson, 2001a, p. 11)

In order to develop these arguments more fully, the book is organized into seven chapters. The first explores the theoretical foundations, the conceptual framework on which each of the subsequent chapters is built. Although this is, of necessity, a theoretical chapter, it is also closely linked to practice, as I see theory and practice as two sides of the same coin (Thompson, 2000a). Chapter 2 focuses on one particular aspect of the theory base that has a central role to play, namely power. This is a topic that has received a great deal of attention in terms of theoretical analysis. This chapter reviews our theoretical understanding of power and considers the implications for practice that flow from this.

It is important to acknowledge that the first two chapters encapsulate a great deal of theoretical material that may deter some readers from reading on. However, it should be noted that the remaining chapters build on this theory base, and help to place it in the context of practice, thus making it easier to assimilate some of the complex issues presented in the first two chapters. In this respect, the first two chapters should not be seen in isolation, but rather as part of the whole, as elements from each chapter should cast light on material in the others, and therefore help to knit together the elements of understanding from across the various chapters. In short, if you find the first two chapters very heavy-going, do not despair – the remaining chapters should help to develop your understanding and thereby make you feel more confident about your grasp of the underlying theory base.

Chapter 3 covers discrimination and oppression and explores the variety of ways in which these destructive processes can manifest themselves. This involves focusing on particular forms of oppression such as sexism, racism, ageism and disablism, and examining the ways in which they combine and interact as dimensions of human experience. Health is the topic explored in Chapter 4. Here the emphasis is on two main sets of issues: inequalities in health and the significance of the concept of health in constructing and maintaining ideologies of discrimination and oppression. This chapter raises significant questions for *all* 'people' workers and not simply for health care workers.

Chapter 5 is entitled 'Learning from the past', and this refers to the attempts made over the years to address inequality and its attendant problems. There is much that we can learn from earlier developments in theory, policy and practice in terms both of mistakes made and of progress achieved. Inequalities do not occur in a vacuum. They operate within, affect, and are affected by, an organizational context. Chapter 6 is therefore concerned with the ways in which organizational factors interrelate with issues of inequality.

Chapter 7 is the concluding chapter and seeks to draw out the practice implications of the theory base developed in the earlier chapters by developing a set of strategies for promoting equality. It is recognized that there can be no simple or straightforward solutions to the problems of inequality. Progress in reducing or alleviating inequality is likely to depend on overcoming a range of obstacles, resistance and setbacks. It is therefore important to ensure that our efforts are based on sound well-thought-out strategies that are geared towards maximizing our chances of success. This chapter therefore examines possible ways forward. In this way the strong emphasis on practice in this concluding chapter seeks to draw out some of the implications of the theoretical analyses explored in the earlier chapters.

The world we live in is an extremely complex one that presents major challenges for any individuals or groups that seek to change the status quo. What we must recognize, then, is the need to find a constructive balance between the extremes of cynicism and defeatism on the one hand, and a naïve idealism on the other. Finding, and maintaining, that balance can be a difficult and demanding task. This book will not alter that fact. It should, however, help to cast light on the important issues that underpin and inform equality practice. In this way, it is to be hoped that the book can make a positive contribution to an emancipatory practice that challenges discrimination and oppression.

THEORETICAL FOUNDATIONS

Introduction

The term 'foundations' in the title of this chapter has been deliberately chosen for two reasons:

1. It reflects the need to have a firm footing on which to base our analysis, our plans and our actions. It is in this sense that theory *underpins* practice.
2. It emphasizes the fact that theories of inequality, discrimination and oppression are still at a relatively early stage in their development, particularly in terms of how they can be applied in practice. There is a great deal of theory building that remains to be done.

The discussion of theory is not an intellectual exercise for its own sake, but rather a means of clarifying theoretical issues with a view to guiding and informing practice. As Sayer (1992) acknowledges, theorists often work on the premise that: 'there's nothing so practical as a good theory' (p. 50).

This chapter begins to get to grips with the concept of equality by asking the thorny but none the less very important question of: What is equality? From this we move on to consider how discrimination and oppression are related to inequality. This discussion is developed further by exploring the application of 'PCS analysis', a concept I introduced in an earlier work (see Thompson, 2001a). This refers to the need to recognize that discrimination operates at three separate but interconnected levels – the personal, cultural and structural. The important themes of ideology and discourse are also considered as fundamental elements in a theory of promoting equality. Finally, the theoretical issues discussed are woven together under the heading of what I shall call 'emancipatory practice'.

The chapter covers a range of important issues and introduces a number of important theoretical concepts. It may therefore prove difficult to assimilate all the information on first reading, but many of the concepts and themes featured are revisited in subsequent chapters, giving readers the opportunity to develop their understanding of the ideas presented. Therefore if you struggle with this chapter (and perhaps to a lesser extent, Chapter 2), do not despair – they are both 'heavy-going' chapters in terms of the theoretical ground that they cover, but they serve the purpose of laying the foundations for the remaining chapters and so the discussions there should help to cast light on the ideas presented here. You may find it helpful to re-read this chapter after you have completed the other chapters.

What is equality?

Equality is a word that means different things to different people. This is due, in no small part, to the fact that it is a *political* term. Like 'democracy' and 'freedom', equality is a term used by different political groups or affiliations to promote their own particular values or interests. In this sense, equality is an *ideological* concept. As we shall see below, ideology involves the power of ideas being used to reinforce and legitimize existing power relations. The task, then, is not to find the 'true' meaning of the word 'equality', but rather to clarify the way it is being used in the context of this book.

Equality, in the sense I am using it here, is not to be confused with uniformity. Being equal does not necessarily mean being the same. Indeed, I shall be arguing later that a better understanding of difference and diversity is an important part of promoting equality. As Lister (1997) argues:

> Equality and difference are not incompatible; they only become so if equality is understood to mean sameness. In fact, the very notion of equality implies differences to be discounted or taken into account so that, despite them, people are treated as equals for specific purposes. Equality and difference are, therefore, better understood as simultaneously incommensurate and complementary rather than antagonistic. The opposite of equality is inequality. To posit it as difference disguises the relations of subordination, hierarchy and consequent disadvantage, which underlie the dichotomy, and serves to distort the political choices open to us.
>
> (p. 96)

We shall examine in more detail below the relationship between inequality and difference when we explore the important role of diversity.

Turner (1986) argues that: 'The modern notion of equality cannot be divorced from the evolution of citizenship' (p. 21). This is an important point, as it draws our attention to the links between equality and rights. Conversely, inequality can be seen to involve an undermining or denial of rights.

In a classic text of social policy, Marshall (1963) describes three sets of rights, as Mishra (1981) explains:

> Marshall's analysis is chiefly concerned with the development of citizenship rights and its impact on social inequality. These rights, according to Marshall, consist of three different elements – civil, political and social. The first refers broadly to guarantees of individual liberty and equality before the law; the second to political enfranchisement – the right to vote and to seek political office; the third, a good deal less specific than the other two, comprises a 'modicum of economic welfare and security' and the 'right to share to the full in the social heritage and life of a civilized being according to the standards prevailing in the society'.
>
> (p. 27)

This passage touches on a number of important issues:

- Social rights owe a great deal to the provision and effectiveness of a system of human services.
- The notion of sharing 'to the full in the social heritage' begins to account for the marginalization associated with inequality – that is, socially disadvantaged groups are pushed to the margins of mainstream society.
- 'Standards prevailing in the society' suggests that social rights are not absolute – they have to be understood in the context of the society concerned.

Taking this a step further, it can be argued that one important implication for working with people and their problems is the need to recognize:

- The significant role of health, welfare and related practices relating to 'people problems' in terms of rights, citizenship and equality;
- The process of marginalization as a key element in the development and maintenance of inequality;
- An understanding of the social context as a basic requirement for good practice.

Turner (1986) speaks of equality as both a value and a principle:

> Basically, I conceive equality as a value and as a principle, as essentially modern and progressive. Of course, the debate about equality has gone on for centuries but the special feature of modern societies is that we no longer take inequality for granted or as a natural circumstance of human beings. Under conditions of modern social citizenship, it is inequality not equality which requires moral justification.
>
> (p. 18)

The reference to 'modern and progressive' is one that brings Turner's views into conflict with the postmodernist conceptions of society to be discussed in Chapter 2. However, his basic point is that contemporary societies place a certain amount of value on equality (even though this may not be manifested as fully as it could be). An important implication of Turner's comments is that equality is something that societies can and do strive for – inequality is not accepted as natural or inevitable. It is something that can be removed or at least decreased if appropriate steps are taken. It is a goal for us to aim for.

One well-known approach to promoting equality is that of equal opportunities (EO). The equality of opportunity approach is based on the desire to achieve a fair starting point for people – a level playing field – so that some people are not disadvantaged in terms of employment, access to services, housing and so on. While this has a lot of merit as a strategy, it has also been criticized for its narrow focus on individual issues without addressing broader structures of power and inequality. It is a philosophy of equality that emphasizes opportunities rather than outcomes – which may be anything but equal as a result of the broader issues of culture and structure. It is therefore very consistent with individualistic and conservative approaches to equality but is limited in its scope for addressing the more complex issues of institutionalized discrimination and inequality (Cashmore, 1996; Marlow and Loveday, 2000). As Humphries (1996) comments:

> EO policies were based on the liberal assumption that inequality equals discrimination. In other words, the society was at root sound, with discrimination against some groups a superficial blemish which could be manipulated away – a wart on the face of the good community.
>
> (p. 3)

A new approach that is gradually challenging the EO approach for dominance is what has come to be known as the managing diversity approach (or, simply, the diversity approach). This differs from traditional EO approaches in two main ways. First, by concentrating on diversity (that is, social variety across and within groups of people) as a positive aspect of society – an asset to be affirmed and valued rather than a problem to be solved – it seeks to counteract the negative, defensive elements of EO that have unfortunately tended to develop. Second, it is broader than the traditional EO approach which tends to have a narrow, legalistic focus – that is, EO approaches tend to concern themselves primarily if not exclusively with those aspects of discrimination that are illegal in terms of the framework of anti-discrimination legislation. The development of the diversity approach, its strengths and weaknesses, will feature in the discussions below in later chapters.

Contrary to what some people seem to believe, diversity is not an issue that has replaced equality as a focus of concern and interest – rather it has added another dimension to attempts to promote equality. Equality is a complex and intricate matter that can be interpreted in a variety of ways. It is not my intention to enter into an in-depth exposition of its subtleties. Rather, I shall simply emphasize that equality, as the concept is used in this book, can be seen as primarily a question of equality of human rights – particularly social rights as they relate to social justice. In this context, working in occupations that help people deal with their problems can be seen to be, in part at least, a process of addressing inequalities and promoting social justice.

What are discrimination and oppression?

At its most basic level, discrimination is simply a matter of identifying differences, and can be positive or negative. For example, in driving a car, being able to discriminate between lanes of traffic is a very important and positive attribute. However, negative discrimination involves not only identifying differences but also making a negative attribution – attaching a negative or detrimental label or connotation to the person, group or entity concerned. That is, it is a question of certain individuals or groups being discriminated *against*. As we shall see in Chapter 3, such discrimination does not occur at random – it follows clear social patterns in terms of class, race, gender, age, disability, sexual orientation and other such social divisions.

When such negative discrimination occurs, the resulting experience is generally one of *oppression*, which can be defined as:

> Inhuman or degrading treatment of individuals or groups; hardship and injustice brought about by the dominance of one group over another; the

negative and demeaning exercise of power. Oppression often involves disregarding the rights of an individual or group and is thus a denial of citizenship.

(Thompson, 2001a, p. 34)

Discrimination and oppression are therefore closely related concepts. Their interrelationship is a complex matter and it is not my intention to explore it in any detail here, but see Chapter 3 for a fuller analysis. However, it is worth noting that discrimination is a major contributory factor in relation to oppression. That is, a fundamental source of oppression is the set of processes by which certain social groups are discriminated against and thereby disadvantaged. The discussion below of PCS analysis attempts an explanation of how and why discrimination occurs and thereby leads to oppression.

Discrimination and oppression can be seen to be linked to inequality in a number of different ways:

- *Economic* The differential distribution of financial resources and rewards is a key factor underpinning poverty and social deprivation (Chapter 3 – see also Jones and Novak, 1999), and also plays a part in other forms of discrimination.
- *Social* The extent to which a person is integrated into society and enjoys its esteem, rewards, privileges and opportunities depends to a large extent on his or her 'social location' – that is, his or her status in terms of social divisions, such as class, race and gender.
- *Political* Access to power is not evenly distributed in society and once again relates to social divisions, the various dimensions of social organization. Questions of power and the implications of power relations are the major focus of Chapter 2.
- *Ethical* Banton (1994) argues that: 'The best protections against discrimination are those in the hearts of people who believe discrimination is wrong' (p. 36). Challenging discrimination is therefore a question of morality and thus of values.
- *Ideological* Grabb (1993) argues that inequality is maintained by, among other things, a mechanism of ideological control: 'It entails the control of ideas, knowledge, information, and similar resources in the establishment of structured inequality between groups or individuals' (p. xix).
- *Psychological* This can be subdivided into three aspects – cognitive, affective and conative, or, to put it more simply, thoughts, feelings and actions:

  – *Cognitive* Thought patterns can be seen to vary according to social divisions. For example, there are significant differences in the use of language across genders and ethnic groups, with the speech patterns of dominant groups being seen as superior or more prestigious (Cameron, 1998; Guirdham, 1999; Scollon and Scollon, 2001; Thompson, 2003).

– *Affective*   Emotional responses are also rooted in social divisions. For example, responses to loss can be seen to vary between men and women (Riches, 2002; Thompson, 1997a).

– *Conative*   Behavioural norms follow distinct patterns in terms of class, ethnicity, gender, age and so on.

In each of these three cases, there tend to be clear social expectations as to how members of a particular group or social category should think, feel and act, with strong sanctions against those who fail or refuse to comply with these expectations (see Practice Focus 1.1).

◀ **PRACTICE FOCUS 1.1** ▶

Sally was an experienced bereavement counsellor who enjoyed her work, even though it could be quite upsetting at times. However, the aspect of her work she found most demanding was her role in counselling men. She often found that there were significant barriers that many men had to overcome before they were able to talk freely about their feelings of loss – barriers brought about by masculine notions of toughness and emotional robustness. Sometimes it made her quite angry to think that such stereotypical expectations could cause additional pressures and difficulties at a time when they were very vulnerable, distressed and hurt. She had to be very careful to ensure that her annoyance about this did not affect her work with specific clients.

Existing inequalities are maintained through processes of discrimination that have the effect of allocating life-chances, power and resources in such a way as to reinforce existing power relations. It is through this interactive process between discrimination and inequality that the status quo tends to be maintained – with the net result that dominant groups benefit, while subordinated groups experience a degree of oppression. This contributes to a cyclical process in which the social and cultural order is reproduced – see the discussion of 'autopoiesis' in Chapter 6.

The main processes of discrimination that give rise to oppression will be discussed in some detail in Chapter 3 and so I shall say no more about them at this point.

PCS analysis

In order to develop our understanding of discrimination and the oppression that arises from it, it is important to recognize that it operates at three separate but interrelated levels: personal, cultural and structural (hence the term PCS analysis). Each of these levels is important in its own right, but so too are the interactions between them.

The personal level

One's thoughts, feelings and actions at an individual level can have a significant bearing on inequality and oppression. This is particularly the case when the individual concerned is in a position of power – for example, someone who has control over the allocation of resources (a very significant issue in so many work settings).

Discrimination at the personal level frequently manifests itself as prejudice. This involves forming a judgement and refusing to alter or abandon it, even in the face of considerable evidence that contradicts and undermines it. Often, such prejudicial judgements are based on *stereotypes*, a concept I shall discuss in more detail below.

Prejudice can be open and explicit or covert and implicit. An example of the former would be a teacher who once told me that she did not like homosexuals and saw them as a threat to the moral order. Many other people, by contrast, can be just as prejudiced without realizing that they are doing so. For example, a participant at a case conference commented that the parents concerned were 'quite intelligent for a black family'. When challenged that this was a racist remark, she became very upset and argued vehemently that she 'would not dream of being racist'. None the less, her assumption that black people were less intelligent than white people clearly revealed a degree of underlying racial prejudice.

Although it cannot be denied that prejudiced attitudes and behaviours do exist, we have to be careful to avoid the mistake of attaching too much significance to the personal level. Individual behaviour needs to be understood in its broader context if we are to have more than a partial and distorted view of the situation. The **P** level of prejudice and individual attitudes and actions is only one part of the overall picture.

Vivian and Brown (1995) are critical of a personality-based approach to understanding discrimination:

> The problem, very simply, is that an analysis of individual personalities cannot account for the large-scale social behaviour that normally characterises prejudice and intergroup conflict more generally. If it were true

that prejudice derived from a disorder in personality, then we would expect the expression of prejudice or discrimination within groups to vary as much as the personality of members comprising the group. But in fact the evidence seems to indicate that prejudice within groups is often remarkably uniform.

(p. 59)

A reliance on personal explanations of discrimination is problematic in a number of ways, not least the following:

- It provides an excuse: Comments such as 'I'm not racist' or 'I'm not prejudiced' can be used as a refusal to consider the impact or significance of discrimination and oppression. It neglects, for example, the fact that discrimination can often be unintentional (a point to which I shall return below).
- It ignores wider issues: To see discrimination simply as a matter of personal prejudice is to ignore a significant range of cultural, social, political and economic factors.
- It 'blames the victim' (Ryan, 1971): By focusing on the individual level, we fail to recognize that discrimination is not one-dimensional – it affects different people in different and overlapping ways. An overemphasis on the personal level disguises the fact that a person can be both victim and perpetrator of oppression. For example, a black woman can experience both racism and sexism and yet still be ageist and disablist.

In order to go beyond the personal level, we need to consider the cultural context in which individuals operate. Although each individual is to some extent unique, we also have to recognize that individual beliefs, values and actions owe a great deal to prevailing norms and expectations. That is, the **P** level is embedded within the **C** level, as Figure 1.1 illustrates.

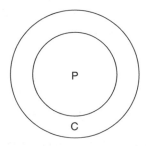

Figure 1.1   The personal embedded within the cultural

The cultural level

Culture is an important sociological concept which describes sets of patterns shared across particular groups. As Kendall and Wickham (2001) comment:

> 'culture' refers to the way of life of a group (including, possibly, a society), including the meanings, the transmission, communication and alteration of those meanings, and the circuits of power by which the meanings are valorised or derogated. By analogy, 'Cultural Studies' involves the study of a group's way of life, particularly its meanings (including its morals and its beliefs), with an emphasis on the politics of the ways those meanings are communicated. Cultural Studies must concern itself with the control of meanings and their dissemination, that is, with circuits of power and with forms of resistance.
>
> (p. 14)

Cultural patterns can be identified through such factors as humour and language. Humour can tell us a great deal about what is valued in a culture, as well as what is feared or rejected. Humour often involves the use of 'demons', people or things that are pilloried and scape-goated, with the effect of emphasizing that they do not belong within that particular culture. In this respect, humour is used to set down boundaries, thereby defining the parameters of that particular cultural formation.

Language can be seen to fulfil a similar role. It is an integral part of how culture 'operates' as a social force. That is, language both reflects cultural norms, assumptions and patterns and contributes to their maintenance and their transmission from generation to generation. In this way, language acts a vehicle for transmitting discriminatory ideas and values (Thompson, 2003).

One of the factors that binds together language and culture is the tendency to produce what Berger and Luckmann (1967) refer to as the 'taken-for-grantedness' of everyday life. Both lead to thoughts and actions that become routine and unquestioned, the 'wallpaper' in the background of everyday existence. Consequently, both language and culture can have the effect of conveying meanings beyond those intended, often without the person concerned even being aware that the process is taking place. In this respect, language and culture have much in common with ideology, a concept I shall discuss in more detail below.

Culture is an important concept in relation to discrimination and oppression in a number of ways:

- Its role as a boundary marker can be used to exclude or marginalize other groups. It can be used to create 'us–them' situations.
- Culture is, in itself, a site of discrimination. For example, racism is premised on the belief in the superiority of one culture over others (Ahmed, 1991).
- Cultural assumptions are often of a discriminatory nature. For example, assumptions about older people are often unduly negative and patronizing (Thompson, 1995a).

A significant feature of culture is the way in which members of a particular cultural group become so immersed in its patterns, assumptions and values that they do not even notice they are there – they become part of the 'taken-for-grantedness of everyday life'. This can be both positive and negative. It is positive, in so far as it contributes to 'ontological security', a sense of rootedness and psychological integration – an important element of mental well-being. It allows us to pursue our everyday activities without having to question every aspect of everything we do. We have to take a great deal for granted if we are to prevent an overload of sensory information. (The concept of 'ontological security' is an important one to which we shall return below.)

The more negative side of this cultural taken-for-grantedness is the potential for ethnocentrism. This is a term that refers to the tendency to see the world from within the narrow confines of one culture, to project one set of norms and values on to other groups of people. An ethnocentric outlook can be a major contributory factor to racism in so far as it:

- fails to recognize significant cultural differences and their importance for the people concerned; and
- is based on the false premise that one culture is superior to others.

The tendency towards ethnocentrism is therefore an important danger to be wary of at the cultural level. Indeed, we can go a step beyond this to argue that we need to be wary of unquestioned assumptions in general. We need to guard against the dangers of what I have previously referred to as 'egocentricity':

> Anti-discriminatory practice entails recognising the significance of difference and diversity and thus avoiding too narrow a perspective. The term 'egocentricity' can therefore be used to describe the inability, or unwillingness, of an individual to go beyond his or her own perspective. Thus,

for men to appreciate the significance of sexism and to contribute to anti-sexism, they must begin to see what the world looks like through women's eyes. To see everything simply from a masculine perspective can lead to too narrow a view and a failure to appreciate the experience of oppression.

(Thompson, 1995b, p. 25)

An understanding of the cultural level is therefore necessary both to contextualize the personal level and to show its limitations as an explanation of discrimination and oppression. However, the cultural level also has limitations as an explanatory framework, and it too needs to be seen in a broader context – the cultural level is embedded with the structural level, as Figure 1.2 illustrates. Kendall and Wickham (2001) draw links between culture and what they call 'ordering': '"Culture" is one of the names given to the different ways people go about ordering the world and the different ways the world goes about ordering people' (p. 24). This refers to how social structures intertwine with cultural patterns and formations – a point which introduces the importance of understanding the social structures of the S level.

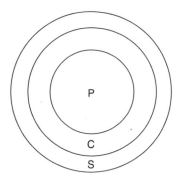

Figure 1.2   The cultural embedded within the structural

The structural level

Just as individual actions at the **P** level are circumscribed by the cultural context in which they occur, cultural factors also owe a great deal to the social structural level which underpins and envelops them. The **S** level comprises the macro-level influences and constraints of the various social, political and economic aspects of the contemporary social order. That is, cultural patterns do not exist in a vacuum – they are in constant interaction with:

- *Social factors*: issues relating to class, race, gender and other such social divisions.
- *Political factors*: the distribution of power, both formally (political structures, parties and so on) and informally (power relations between individuals, groups and so on).
- *Economic factors*: the distribution of wealth and other material resources.

Although I have presented these as separate sets of factors, they do, of course, overlap a great deal, each influencing, and interacting with, the other two.

A central theme that applies to all three aspects is that of power. Indeed, power is such an important concept with regard to inequality, discrimination and oppression that it merits a full chapter in its own right (Chapter 2). I shall therefore not explore its significance further at this point, except to emphasize that power is a key issue in understanding the macro-level structures of the S level.

The development of anti-racist thought provides a good example of the need to go beyond the cultural level and take on board issues that apply at the structural level. Multiculturalism is an approach to race relations that operates primarily at the C level. Donald and Rattansi (1992) are critical of multiculturalism for: 'identifying racism as the ideas in people's heads when it should be located in institutional structures' (p. 3) and they argue that:

> It is not individual beliefs and prejudices about 'race' that are the main problem . . . nor the contents of different traditions. What matters are the structures of power, the institutions and the social practices that produce racial oppression and discriminatory outcomes.
>
> (p. 3)

This is a point to which we shall return in Chapter 5.

In similar fashion, sexist assumptions and cultural patterns do not arise as a matter of coincidence – they are explained by reference to the need to protect vested interests, in this case to maintain men in positions of power and privilege (Walby, 1994). Structured inequalities are part and parcel of the social order and play a part in maintaining that order. As Grabb (1993) comments:

> The study of social inequality is really the study of . . . human differences. In particular, inequality refers to differences that become socially structured, in the sense that they become a regular and recurring part of how people interact with one another on a daily basis. Structured

inequality involves a process in which groups or individuals with particular attributes are better able than those who lack or are denied these attributes to control or shape rights and opportunities for their own ends. One major factor in this process is that the advantaged groups or individuals tend to obtain greater access to the various rewards and privileges that are available in society. These benefits, in turn, serve to reinforce the control over rights and opportunities enjoyed by the advantaged factions, in a cyclical process that structures and *reproduces* the pattern of inequality across time and place.

(p. xi)

The processes by which such structured inequalities are reproduced are an important topic of study within social theory, and so I shall explore them in more detail below under the heading of 'structuration theory'.

◀ **PRACTICE FOCUS 1.2** ▶

Tim had worked in a variety of settings in different parts of the country. He therefore had a wide range of experiences to draw upon. What this breadth of experience had taught him was that, although individual people are very different, there are also significant common themes that can be detected – cultural and structural patterns. Tim's earlier studies of sociology helped him to understand that discrimination and oppression have a lot to do with these cultural and structural commonalities. He was able to realize that discrimination was much more than a simple matter of personal prejudice. This broader perspective allowed him to develop a much better understanding of inequality and equipped him much better for practising in ways which promoted equality and valued diversity.

Giddens (1990) argues that there are four sets of factors that characterize institutionalized relations of power in contemporary society. As Held (1992) comments:

In Giddens's view, there are four main institutional aspects to modernity: (a) capitalism (the system of production of commodities for markets, in which wage labour is also a commodity); (b) industrialism (the application of inanimate sources of power through productive techniques for the transformation of nature); (c) coordinated administrative power focused through surveillance (the control of information and the monitoring of the activities of subject populations by states and other organizations); and (d) military power (the concentration of the means of violence in the hands of the state). These four institutional dimensions of modernity are irreducible to one another, for the form and logic of each one are quite different from those of the others.

(p. 32)

For present purposes, (a) and (c) are the important issues to consider:

- Capitalism involves the exploitation of one group of people (the proletariat) by another (capitalists) for the sake of economic advantage and power. This combines with, and draws upon, other forms of exploitation and oppression such as sexism (Bryson, 1999; Connell, 2002), racism (Culley and Dyson, 2001a), ageism (Marshall and Rowlings, 1998) and disablism (Oliver, 1990; Oliver and Sapey, 1999). The structural level therefore involves multiple forms of oppression (see Chapter 3), although it is sadly not uncommon for these matters to be oversimplified and treated in a reductionist way.
- Administrative power lies in the hands of many groups, not least people who often play a pivotal role in the lives of those who are vulnerable by virtue of crisis, distress, illness or other such factors. The disciplinary power of surveillance is an important theme that will be explored in Chapter 2.

Both these sets of issues are closely linked with the concepts of ideology and discourse, and it is to these that we shall be turning shortly. However, before doing so, there is one final point in relation to PCS analysis that I wish to emphasize, namely the danger of confusing or conflating the levels. Unfortunately I have come across instances of people using PCS analysis to argue, for example, that all white people are racist or all men are sexist. The argument tends to be presented as follows: Because we live and work in a society which is discriminatory at the cultural and structural levels, then individuals within that society must, by definition, be prejudiced and thus discriminatory. However, as we shall see in the pages that follow, this is a gross oversimplification which commits the theoretical 'sins' of reductionism (reducing a complex, multilevel explanation to a single-level one), determinism (neglecting the important role of human agency) and reification (treating a diverse group of people as if they formed a homogeneous whole) – see Thompson (2000a) for a discussion of theoretical adequacy.

Ideology and discourse

Ideology and discourse are two important concepts that have much in common – and both have a significant bearing on inequality, discrimination and oppression.

Ideology is a term that has been used in different ways by different theorists over the years (McLellan, 1995). Here I shall be using it in what is now perhaps its most common usage, namely to refer to sets of ideas, beliefs and assumptions in general and, more specifically, to those that reflect existing power relations.

Such ideologies provide frameworks for making sense of the social world; they enable us to construct meanings and maintain a relatively coherent thread or perspective – what is sometimes referred to in technical language as a '*Weltanschauung*', a world-view. In this respect, ideology can be seen as inevitable. Our thoughts, actions and interactions pass through the filter of one or more ideologies – we inevitably have to take a great deal for granted in our everyday lives, to rely on sets of assumptions that underpin, guide and constrain how we conduct ourselves.

We can divide ideologies into two main categories: dominant and countervailing. A dominant ideology is one that represents and reinforces the position of one or more powerful groups. For example, patriarchal ideology supports the dominant position of men (Herrmann and Stewart, 1994). The ideas, beliefs and assumptions that characterize patriarchy help to maintain its position of dominance as a social force.

A countervailing ideology, by contrast, is one that does not enjoy such dominance and is, in fact, in opposition to one or more dominant ideologies. For example, feminism is an ideology (or set of related ideologies) that opposes, challenges and seeks to undermine the dominance of patriarchy. Consequently, we can see that ideologies often compete; they can enter into conflict, each trying to discount or discredit the other. As ideology is closely linked to power, struggles over power can often be seen as ideological struggles – power and control are commonly contested at the level of ideas and values rather than physical force (although the use of force is often available as a back-up if required).

Although ideologies often conflict with each other, this is not to say that they are necessarily internally coherent. Indeed, it is not uncommon for ideologies to encompass a range of contradictory or logically incompatible ideas – the power of ideology need not rest on rational argument.

In fact, ideology gains its ability to shape thoughts and actions through its ability to 'get under one's skin', to become so ingrained that we do not question its existence or effects. In this respect, ideology operates as a form of 'camouflage'. It becomes such an important part of the 'taken-for-grantedness of everyday life' that we do not generally recognize that it is there. It is for this reason that ideological assumptions often manifest themselves as 'common sense', 'natural' or 'obvious' – that is, as beyond question. Billig (2001) comments as follows:

> An ideology comprises the ways of thinking and behaving within a given society which make the ways of that society seem 'natural' or unquestioned to its members (Eagleton, 1991). In this way, ideology is the common-sense of the society. Through ideology, the inequalities of that society will appear as 'natural' or 'inevitable'. Thus, ideology comprises the habits of belief, which, for example, in former terms, made it appear 'natural' that women should not be full citizens, or which, in our day, make it appear obvious that the street-sweeper be paid a fraction of the company director's remuneration. These ideological habits can be deeply rooted into language, and thereby, into consciousness.
>
> (pp. 217–18)

This process of 'camouflage' is sometimes described in terms of Althusser's (1971) concept of 'interpellation'. This refers to the way in which an ideology 'hails' the individual and 'recruits' him or her. Interpellation therefore involves 'winning people over'. In this way, ideology plays a part in identity formation – ideologies have strong influence on how we see ourselves, how we construct our sense of self. This relates closely to the concept of 'ontological security' which I shall discuss in more detail below.

The concept of discourse has come to be used in ways that overlap to a large extent with ideology in the sense in which it has been used here. It is therefore important to clarify how the term is used and how it differs from ideology. Abercrombie *et al.* (1994) define discourse as 'a domain of language-use that is unified by common assumptions' and they go on to refer to Foucault's description of:

> discourses of madness – ways of talking and thinking about madness – which have changed over the centuries. In the early medieval period, the mad were not seen as threatening but almost as possessing an inner wisdom. In the twentieth century the discourse of madness emphasises the condition as an illness in need of treatment. In the intervening centuries there have been other discourses of madness, treating madness and the mad in quite different ways.
>
> (p. 119)

A discourse, then, is a 'way of talking and thinking' about particular aspects of social life. Although this is very similar to ideology, discourse is more closely focused on language. An important aspect of understanding discourse is the related notion of 'text', as Burr (1995) explains:

> anything that can be 'read' for meaning can be thought of as being a manifestation of one or more discourses and can be referred to as a 'text'. Buildings may 'speak' of civic pride, like the town halls and factories of the industrial revolution, or of a yearning for the past as in the recent trend towards 'vernacular' building. Clothes and uniforms may suggest class position, status, gender, age or sub-culture and as such can be called texts. Given that there is virtually no aspect of human life that is exempt from meaning, everything around us can be considered as 'textual', and 'life as text' could be said to be the underlying metaphor of the discourse approach.
>
> (p. 51)

Discourse is therefore an important concept in understanding discrimination and oppression, as discourses constrain and shape the way we think, speak and ascribe meaning. Many such discourses are discriminatory and therefore contribute to oppression. For example, medical discourse presents disability as a form of individual pathology, thereby disempowering and marginalizing disabled people (Oliver, 1990, 1996). Conversely, promoting equality can be seen to depend on constructing and supporting emancipatory discourses.

The position of discourse as a key theme in social theory owes a great deal to the works of the French theorist, Michel Foucault.

Foucault drew very close links between discourse and power, and it is at this level that the concepts of ideology and discourse overlap to a large extent – both are concerned with power and symbolic representations. However, the two terms have very different historical backgrounds.

Ideology, as it is currently understood, has developed from the narrower marxist conception of 'false consciousness', a set of ideas that serves to conceal the exploitative nature of capitalism from the proletariat. The problem with this conception of ideology is that it hinges on a distinction between truth and distorted ideas. That is, it assumes that there is an absolute truth that underpins social experience, an assumption that is seriously open to challenge, particularly from the point of view of social constructionism (Burr, 1995).

It is this narrow sense of ideology as an alternative to 'the truth' that Foucault rejects. The broader conception of ideology, though, as *any* set of ideas, beliefs and assumptions, is much closer to the idea of discourse, especially as used by Foucault. As Hall (1996) comments:

the term 'ideology' has come to have a wider, more descriptive, less systematic reference, than it did in classical Marxist texts. We now use it to
refer to *all* organized forms of social thinking . . . It certainly refers to the
domain of practical thinking and reasoning (the form, after all, in which
most ideas are likely to grip the minds of the masses and draw them into
action), rather than simply to well-elaborated and internally consistent
'systems of thought'. We mean the practical as well as the theoretical
knowledges which enable people to 'figure out' society, and within those
categories and discourses we 'live out' and 'experience' our objective
positioning in social relations.

(p. 27)

It is beyond the scope of the discussion here to develop further the
debate about the interrelationships between ideology and discourse. It
will therefore suffice to note that it is the area of overlap between ideology and discourse that is of significance in my explorations of the
theoretical foundations of inequality, discrimination and oppression.

To summarize, ideology and discourse are concepts which:

- describe clusters of ideas and assumptions that help shape our
  understanding of the world;
- form the basis of the frameworks of meaning we develop to make
  sense of our lives;
- are closely linked to the concept of power; and
- have a significant bearing on inequality, discrimination and oppression.

It is this final point that I now wish to explore further.

Burr (1995) makes the important point that ideas are not 'ideological' in their own right – it is the way they are used:

A version of events, or a way of representing a state of affairs, may be
true or false, but it is only ideological to the extent that it is used by relatively powerful groups in society to sustain their position. Thus ideas in
themselves cannot be said to be ideological, only the uses to which they
are put. The study of ideology is therefore the study of the ways in which
meaning is mobilised in the social world in the interests of powerful
groups.

(p. 82)

Existing power relations are therefore maintained and reinforced by
certain ideas operating ideologically.

A common theme in this respect is the use of biological explanations as a means of legitimating the status quo. This can be illustrated in the following ways:

- *Racism* is based on the premise that there are biologically distinct 'races', some of which are inferior to others (Sardar *et al.*, 1993).
- *Sexism* often manifests itself in the argument that a woman's place is in the home because of her 'biological role' as a mother and thereby confusing childbearing with childrearing – see Chapter 3 (Gittins, 1993).
- *Disablism* involves seeing only a person's physical impairment and not recognizing his or her strengths, or the social processes that have an oppressive effect on disabled people (Swain *et al.*, 1993).
- *Ageism* arises from the tendency to see older people in unduly negative terms, to overemphasize the significance of physical and mental decline in old age (Thompson, 1995a).
- *Heterosexism* rests on the assumption that heterosexuality is biologically given or 'natural', while gay, lesbian or bisexual relationships are seen as 'abnormal' (Fuss, 1991).

These examples show that biological arguments are frequently used as a powerful means of legitimating social relations, particularly those that involve the dominance of some groups over others. However, the ideological nature of such biological explanations is demonstrated by the fact that such arguments quickly collapse when subjected to critical analysis – their power is ideological rather than rational. For example, Saunders (1993) focuses on biological explanations of gender differences and shows their lack of validity in three ways:

> First, there is the failure of the various assumed relationships between biology and behaviour to 'stand up' in cross-cultural comparisons. We know, for example, that the assumed correlation between hormonal levels at certain periods in the female menstrual cycle and emotional states such as tension, anxiety, or irritability does not exist in many other cultures (see Bardwick, 1971: 27–33). This indicates that hormonal fluctuations during hormonal cycles are, to a large extent, *learned* rather than innate behaviour.
>
> (p. 265)

That is, biological explanations focus on what is deemed to be common to all humanity and are therefore easily undermined by reference to cultural or other differences.

From this, she goes on to comment on the:

tendency to ignore or downplay the impact of cultural patterns on a particular sex difference. Margaret Mead, for example, found that in Arapesh culture, the lack of emphasis on strenuous work for either sex decreased the differences in somatotype – particularly muscular build (Mead, 1935). In other words, there is some social capacity to affect sex differences through cultural practices.

(p. 265)

Biological factors are therefore not absolute, and need to be understood within the broader context of complex interactions with cultural and other factors.

Finally, Saunders argues that: 'a taxonomy of particular biological sex differences in no way serves as an explanation for the differential social evaluation of these differences' (p. 265). This third argument is perhaps the most important one, in so far as it reflects a very common process underpinning discrimination and oppression, namely the tendency to attach significance to particular differences and assign different levels of value accordingly. For example, differences in skin colouring can be given considerable social significance, at great cost for certain groups whose skin colour is devalued, while other biological differences in terms of eye or hair colouring are given little or no significance. This echoes Burr's point, mentioned earlier, that it is not the basic ideas in themselves that are ideological, but rather the way in which they are used to sustain relations of power and inequality through a process of legitimation – making certain ideas and assumptions appear 'legitimate' and therefore beyond question.

This is closely linked to the idea of diversity which is based on the principle of valuing differences between people rather than seeing them as the basis of unfair discrimination – a topic to which we shall return below.

◀ PRACTICE FOCUS 1.3 ▶

Barry was a well-meaning and considerate person who did not wish anyone any harm. However, when it came to issues of equality, he refused to make any changes to his behaviour. He dismissed such matters as 'left-wing nonsense'. He believed that racial and sexual inequalities were 'natural' biological differences and were therefore not a problem. He was not able (or not willing) to recognize the ways in which such attitudes played a part in maintaining relations of inequality or to acknowledge the problems of oppression that arise as a result of racism, sexism and so on. Unfortunately, he also brought this attitude to his work, a fact which often caused friction between him and the people he was trying to help, due to his tendency to adopt a judgemental attitude towards them.

Sustaining such relations is an example of *hegemony*, an important concept in understanding ideology. Hegemony refers to 'dominance', the ability of a set of ideas to become a dominant force. Clegg (1989) explains that: 'Hegemony involves the successful mobilization and reproduction of the *active* consent of dominated groups' (p. 160). The term implies that dominance is maintained more by the power of ideas than by coercion. Ideologies become internalized and tend to influence us without our recognizing it.

John Thompson (1994), in his discussion of ideology and modern culture, identifies a number of processes through which ideology operates, including the following:

> *naturalization* A state of affairs which is a social and historical creation may be treated as a natural event or as the inevitable outcome of natural characteristics, in the way, for example, that the socially instituted division of labour between men and women may be portrayed as the product of the physiological characteristics of and differences between the sexes. A similar strategy is what may be described as *eternalization*: social-historical phenomena are deprived of their historical character by being portrayed as permanent unchanging and ever-recurring.
>
> (p. 140)

An example of naturalization would be the assumption that old age is 'naturally' a time of withdrawal or disengagement from social life (Cumming and Henry, 1961). This, then, would be an example of ageist ideology – the portrayal of older people in unduly negative terms. The other end of the age spectrum provides an example of eternalization, namely the social construction of childhood. The concept of childhood has changed and developed over time, and is not 'eternal' (Archard, 1993). However, the assumption that children must necessarily occupy a powerless position with little or no emphasis on rights (Dalrymple and Burke, 1995; Thompson, 2002b) is an historical (ideological) product, rather than an inevitable 'eternal truth'.

These are important examples, as they illustrate that ideological assumptions underpin many of the issues that human services workers face on a day-to-day basis. This in turn emphasizes the need to develop an awareness of, and sensitivity to, the workings of ideology and discourse, particularly as they play such an important role in legitimating power relations and their attendant inequalities, discrimination and oppression.

Anti-essentialism

The earlier discussion of biological explanations as legitimations of inequality provides a good example of 'essentialism'. This is a term that refers to the tendency to ascribe our behaviour to 'essences' or fixed qualities. Such essences take different forms but all have the effect of justifying the status quo and acting as an obstacle to positive change:

- *Biology* Women are seen as the weaker sex; black people are seen as intellectually inferior (Richardson and Robinson, 1993; hooks, 1992).
- *Personality* Selfhood is seen as fixed and immutable: 'I can't help being the way I am' (Thompson, 1992a; 2003).
- *Destiny* Many people believe that their lives are governed by a predetermined destiny.

Although these are not the only examples of essentialism, they should be sufficient to illustrate this important concept. Essentialism acts as an ideological legitimation for inequality. Structures of discrimination and oppression are held together to a certain extent by essentialism due to its inherent resistance to change. Existing inequalities and structures of power therefore owe a great deal to essentialism for their continuation. Consequently, *anti*-essentialism can be seen as a prerequisite for promoting equality.

A key aspect of essentialism is 'bad faith', the denial of responsibility for our own actions. Bad faith is:

> a form of self-deception in which we deny or seek to avoid our freedom. We claim that our actions are beyond our control and we seek comfort and reassurance in some form of determinism, whether it be biological, psychological, environmental or even religious.
>
> (Thompson, 1989, p. 30)

The concept of bad faith is a vitally important one in terms of understanding the theoretical foundations of promoting equality. This is because:

1. Bad faith 'legitimates' existing inequalities – it denies that we are able to promote change and regards injustice as natural or unchangeable.
2. The denial of freedom at the personal level undermines the potential for freedom at the structural or sociopolitical level.

The first of these points is particularly relevant to working with people and their problems, as the problems encountered are often not unconnected with issues of personal responsibility and bad faith. Consider, for example, the matter of child abuse: it is not uncommon for sex offenders to deny responsibility for their actions, to be unwilling to face up to the consequences of their abusive behaviours (Morrison *et al.*, 1994; Thompson, 1992b).

The second point is significant in broader, macro-level terms. Bad faith involves relying on a form of essentialism in which we refuse to accept the possibility of change – we construct a view of ourselves as individuals who are dominated by forces beyond our control. This inherent conservatism at the **P** level thereby acts as a barrier to change at the **C** and **S** levels. As I have argued previously:

> Existential freedom – the process of self-creation – is a prerequisite for political liberty. To deny the former is to foreclose the latter and thus render authentic social work impossible.
>
> If, as the determinists would have it, we have little or no control over our own action, political praxis is rendered meaningless as collective action would equally be beyond our reach.
>
> (Thompson, 1992a, p. 188)

The argument can equally be applied to working with people and their problems in general, rather than specifically to social work.

◀ PRACTICE FOCUS 1.4 ▶

Sandra was a determined worker who did not give up easily and worked very hard to help people resolve their difficulties. However, when she worked with Pauline, a woman who had experienced domestic violence, she eventually had to give up and resign herself to the fact that Pauline was not prepared to accept that she could live independently without having to rely on a very violent man. Pauline believed she was 'too weak' an individual to live independently, that it wasn't her nature to cope with matters without her partner. In this way, her bad faith was condemning her to likely further incidents of violence. Sandra felt powerless to help protect her, so deeply ingrained was Pauline's belief that she could not change and therefore had to accept her fate of violence. However, Sandra could also recognize the way in which she and some of her colleagues also tended to rely on similar forms of bad faith at least part of the time.

Authentic practice can therefore be seen as an important aim to pursue. 'Authentic', in this sense, is used as the opposite of bad faith.

Authenticity involves being prepared to accept the challenge of facing up to the sometimes harsh reality that we are responsible for our actions, without relying on essentialist notions that the ways in which we act and interact are fixed, predetermined or beyond our control. Authenticity does not imply that we have *full* control over the circumstances that we find ourselves in – that would be an equally naive oversimplification that denies or neglects wider cultural or social forces and their profound influences.

Essentialism is therefore partly explained by the ontological concept of bad faith (ontology is the study of being and is therefore an important part of existentialism). However, another important concept to consider is that of 'ontological insecurity', as used by Laing (1965) and Giddens (1991). Ontological insecurity refers to a lack of 'existential wholeness', or the ability to deal with the day-to-day demands of human existence we each face in our lives. As Giddens (1991) puts it: 'To be ontologically secure is to possess . . . "answers" to fundamental existential questions which all human life in some way addresses' (p. 47). A lack of such security can manifest itself as a fractured or disrupted self. Giddens refers to Laing's (1965) discussion of this subject:

> The ontologically insecure individual, [Laing] points out, tends to display one or more of the following characteristics. In the first place she may lack a consistent feeling of biographical continuity. An individual may fail to achieve an enduring conception of her aliveness . . . Secondly, in an external environment full of changes, the person is obsessively preoccupied with apprehension of possible risks to his or her existence and paralysed in terms of practical action . . . Thirdly, the person fails to develop or sustain trust in his own self-integrity. The individual feels morally 'empty' because he lacks 'the warmth of a loving self-regard'.
>
> (1991, pp. 53–4)

Ontological security and essentialism can be seen to be closely associated in some respects. Essentialist notions of fixity and immutability can be recognized as props that are used to guard against the risk, threat and contingency that are part and parcel of human life. An absence of ontological security is therefore implicated in the maintenance of patterns of inequality in so far as a fear of change makes for an inherently conservative approach to social life.

◀ PRACTICE FOCUS 1.5 ▶

Lawrence had experienced mental health problems since his teens and had been a hospital in-patient on a number of occasions. At times, he felt very insecure and had delusions that his body was literally in the process of falling apart. Medication had, over the years, played a part in trying to deal with this problem but had not been entirely effective. What did seem to help was the counselling he received from Shobu, as this was geared specifically towards issues of ontological security, drawing on the principles of existential counselling. By recognizing the problem as being one of ontological security, Shobu was able to address the issues more directly.

Ontological insecurity is, of course, not the only factor involved in maintaining inequality. It is, however, an important one in so far as it affects the personal, cultural and structural levels:

- *Personal* Identity, self-worth and psychological well-being owe a great deal to the development of ontological security. As Giddens (1991) comments:

> A person with a reasonably stable sense of self-identity has a feeling of biographical continuity which she is able to grasp reflexively and, to a greater or lesser degree, communicate to other people. That person also, through early trust relations, has established a protective cocoon which 'filters out', in the practical conduct of day-to-day life, many of the dangers which in principle threaten integrity of the self.
>
> (p. 54)

Confidence, self-esteem and personal resilience – factors important in mitigating and challenging inequality – are closely associated with ontological security.

- *Cultural* A culture's characteristic patterns of shared meanings, values and assumptions both support and are supported by a degree of ontological security. In attempting to maintain a relatively stable sense of self, we draw heavily on the cultural forms we find all around us and those into which we have been socialized. In this way, cultural norms and patterns become enmeshed with aspects of personal identity and selfhood. Ontological security is therefore an important issue at those points where the **P** and **C** levels interact.

- *Structural* Forms of structural disadvantage can have the effect of providing a narrowly circumscribed form of ontological security. For example, sexism has a tendency to produce a set of narrowly defined expectations with regard to how women and men should think, feel and act. Such expectations can be seen to be oppressive and constricting in so far as they exclude a range of opportunities and life chances. However, despite these costs, there are benefits that need to be acknowledged – particularly the ontological security that can be gained from having roles that are relatively clearly defined. The stability that this offers thereby acts as an ideological underpinning of the structures of oppression – the oppressions of sexism, racism and so on offer a degree of ontological security which, in turn, serves to maintain such structures by drawing on the inherent conservatism of such security and stability.

Ontological security therefore has a complex and ambivalent relationship with inequality. A lack of such security may be associated with psychological breakdown. However, at the other extreme, an over-rigid identification with stereotypical norms provides a degree of security, but at the expense of contributing to the maintenance of patterns of inequality by discouraging any challenge or threat to the status quo and the power relations upon which it rests (Figure 1.3).

In order to promote equality we need to develop forms of ontological security that are sufficiently robust to equip us to deal with the existential pressures and challenges that we face, while remaining sufficiently flexible to resist and counter the stultifying tendencies that derive from dominant forms of oppression. Ontological security has the potential to play a part in countering discrimination and oppression if the extremes of insecurity and rigid stability can be avoided. This is a theme to which we shall return in later chapters.

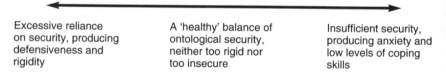

| Excessive reliance on security, producing defensiveness and rigidity | A 'healthy' balance of ontological security, neither too rigid nor too insecure | Insufficient security, producing anxiety and low levels of coping skills |

Figure 1.3   The ontological security continuum

Dialectical reason

Dialectical reason is a method of understanding complex social phenomena in terms of interaction, conflict and change. It is a form of reason that goes beyond traditional understandings of everyday events and processes. It is commonly associated with marxism but is not exclusively aligned with that particular form of theory.

Proponents of dialectical reason argue that traditional approaches present too narrow and limited an account and therefore need to be superseded by the dialectic:

Conventional logic is *analytical*. That is, it involves breaking situations down into their component parts so that a complex matter can be understood in simpler terms. Such an analysis, by its very nature, produces a snapshot rather than a moving picture. It is therefore ill-equipped to account for conflict, change and development . . . Dialectical reason does not contradict or invalidate analytical reason, it goes beyond it. Analytical reason breaks things down into their component parts, and this is an essential first step in the process of understanding. It is, however, only a first step and needs to be followed by *synthesis* – the linking together of those parts into a coherent whole. This process of synthesis, or . . . totalization, is the hallmark of dialectical reason . . . The basis of dialectical reason is conflict. The dialectic refers to the process by which conflicting forces come together and produce change.

(Thompson, 2000a, p. 68)

Issues of inequality, discrimination and oppression can be seen to be characterized by interaction, conflict and change (or resistance to change), and so dialectical reason is an important part of the theoretical foundations of promoting equality. It will therefore feature at various points in the chapters that follow.

An important point to emphasize with regard to the dialectic is that it refers to a continuing process, a perpetual series of interactions. One common misunderstanding is that the syntheses produced by dialectical interaction are, in some way, final outcomes or end results. This view of the dialectic fails to recognize the *dynamic* nature of dialectical reason – it refers, by definition, to a continuous process of change. This is a point to which I shall return in Chapter 2 when I address the postmodernist critique of the dialectic.

Structuration theory and beyond

Ontology, the study of reality, is an important set of issues to consider with regard to promoting equality due to the fact that social reality relates both to personal issues such as selfhood and loss (Thompson, 2002a) and to broader sociopolitical issues of power, discrimination and oppression. The relationship between the personal and the sociopolitical is a long-standing concern of social theorists. A consideration of social theory can therefore help us to develop our understanding of this important area. Some aspects of social theory will be addressed in Chapter 2 but, for present purposes, I wish to explore one particular element, that of 'structuration theory' – an approach associated with the leading contemporary sociologist, Anthony Giddens.

Giddens (1984) is critical of interpretive sociology with its overemphasis on the individual, but also berates structural theories that pay almost exclusive attention to wider social factors. Structuration theory is an attempt to bring these two sets of factors together, to understand individual and social factors *in relation to each other*. He argues that:

> The basic domain of study of the social sciences, according to the theory of structuration, is neither the experience of the individual actor, nor the existence of any form of societal totality, but social practices ordered across space and time. Human social activities, like some self-reproducing items in nature, are recursive. That is to say, they are not brought into being by social actors but continually recreated by them via the very means whereby they express themselves *as* actors.
>
> (p. 2)

'Social practices ordered across space and time' refers to the actions of individuals and groups understood in their social, cultural and historical context. A key element of this theory, therefore, is the attempt to understand social reality in terms of both *structure* – the significance of social divisions and other aspects of social organization – and *agency* – the exercise of choice. While many forms of social theory address either structure or agency, structuration theory is characterized by a focus on structure *and* agency and the ways in which they are intertwined.

In this respect, structuration theory has much in common with existentialism (Thompson, 1992a), a philosophy which:

> aims to understand human existence in terms of freedom and responsibility, and the problems and complexities we encounter when we exercise such freedom (in the form of choices and decisions) and take responsibility for the consequences of our actions. It seeks to locate such freedom (the fundamental freedom of being responsible for ourselves) in the wider social context of the structure of society, in terms of social constraints and influences, for example class (Sartre, 1976), race/ethnicity (Sartre, 1948) or gender (de Beauvoir, 1972).
>
> Existentialism emphasizes the dialectical interaction of individual factors (my choices, values, actions) and wider sociopolitical factors (the oppressions of sexism and racism). It is not a case of working out which dimension is more important, the personal or the social, but rather a matter of understanding existence as a constant interplay of the two, a dynamic process simultaneously personal and social.
>
> (Thompson, 2000a, p. 73)

◀ **PRACTICE FOCUS 1.6** ▶

Tina was a nurse who had recently transferred to a children's ward after many years of working with adults. One of the first thing she noticed when she transferred was the early age at which boys and girls started to display gender-specific behaviour. As a parent who had tried to avoid bringing up her children in line with sexist stereotypes, she found it depressing to note how strong were social pressures to conform to stereotypical gender expectations, even for preschool children. This situation puzzled her for quite some time. She was beginning to wrestle with an understanding of the complex issues of structure and agency.

An important concept in this regard is that of the dialectic of subject-ivity and objectivity. This refers to the interaction of the internal world of subjective experience with the external world of nature, social structure and other people. The point to emphasize is that social reality needs to be understood not in abstract terms as *either* subjective *or* objective, but rather in concrete terms as a perpetual interaction of subjective and objective factors, each influencing the other (Figure 1.4). The common thread that links structuration theory and existen-tialism is that of social constructionism. This is a term used to describe theoretical approaches that are critical of traditional models of society which fail to recognize the significance of perception and meaning. Burr (1995) comments that:

> Social constructionism insists that we take a critical stance towards our taken-for-granted ways of understanding the world (including our-selves). It invites us to be critical of the idea that our observations of the world unproblematically yield its nature to us, to challenge the view that conventional knowledge is based upon objective, unbiased observation of the world. It is therefore in opposition to what are referred to as posi-

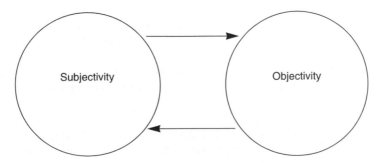

Figure 1.4   The subjective-objective dialectic

tivism and empiricism in traditional science – the assumptions that the nature of the world can be revealed by observation, and that what exists is what we perceive to exist. Social constructionism cautions us to be ever suspicious of our assumptions about how the world appears to be.

(p. 3)

Social constructionism rejects the tendency to see social factors as 'given', natural or absolute. Such factors are *socially constructed* – they arise as a result of social processes and the interaction of social forces. Personal identity or selfhood is a good example of a socially constructed phenomenon that is commonly perceived as a given, predetermined entity over which we have little or no control. Structuration theory, by contrast, shows identity to be a social construct, owing much to the interaction between structure and agency. As Giddens (1991) comments:

> The self is not a passive entity, determined by external influences; in forging their self-identities, no matter how local their specific contexts of action, individuals contribute to and directly promote social influences that are global in their consequences and implications.
>
> (p. 2)

As Giddens implies, identity is continually forged in and by social interactions, rather than predetermined by biological or other factors. In this respect, the micro-level process of identity formation and maintenance closely parallels the macro-level processes involved in the reproduction of social structures and relations. Social structures (including power and domination, as we shall see in Chapter 2) are continually reproduced through routine social practices, through taken-for-granted thoughts, feelings and actions which both *reflect* and *reinforce* existing social relations and divisions:

- Routinized social practices are strongly influenced by, and channelled through, dominant norms and cultural patterns and therefore *reflect* the status quo.
- The tendency to maintain such patterns of routinized practices thereby serves to perpetuate social structures and relations – it *reinforces* the status quo.

Once again we are engaged with questions of ideology and discourse – the subtle ways in which ideas, assumptions, values and social practices maintain the social fabric with all its attendant structures and systems. Ideological processes can therefore be seen as an integral part of structuration. They are aspects of the **C** level which stands between, and interacts with, the **P** and **S** levels of agency and structure respectively.

A further important concept is that of 'duality of structure'. This refers to the fact that: 'the rules and resources drawn upon in the production and reproduction of social action are at the same time the means of system reproduction' (Giddens, 1984, p. 17). That is, the actions of individuals and groups not only produce the specific outcomes of those actions (agency), but also contribute more broadly to the continuity of social systems (structure). What is needed, then, is an appreciation of both structure and agency – it is not a matter of 'either–or'. As Giddens (1984) comments:

> All competent members of society are vastly skilled in the practical accomplishment of social activities and are expert 'sociologists'. The knowledge they possess is not incidental to the persistent patterning of social life but is integral to it. This stress is absolutely essential if the mistakes of functionalism and structuralism are to be avoided, mistakes which, suppressing or discounting agents' reasons ... look for the origins of their activities in phenomena of which these agents are ignorant. But it is equally important to avoid tumbling into the opposing error of hermeneutic approaches and of various forms of phenomenology, which tend to regard society as the plastic creation of human subjects.
>
> (p. 26)

This is an important passage that incorporates three very significant points:

- Day-to-day social activities involve a great deal of knowledge and skill. Agency is not simply a matter of caprice – choices or decisions made at random. It is rooted in the complexities of social system but is not *determined* by them.
- Functionalist and structuralist theories have tended to present a distorted picture of social reality by *under*emphasizing the role of agency, by concentrating on social structures to the almost total exclusion of issues of choices, intentions, wishes, fears and aspirations. This is an example of determinism.
- Some forms of hermeneutical or phenomenological theory (that is, those which emphasize the importance of perception and meaning) have tended to *over*emphasize the role of agency, failing to recognize the powerful role of social structure in shaping, enabling and constraining the actions of individuals and groups. This is another example of reductionism.

In these respects, the notion of 'duality of structure' is consistent with both social constructionism in general and existentialism in particular. It also has much in common with the 'realist' theories of writers such as the sociologist Bhaskar:

> Bhaskar argues that human action does not create society but either maintains or changes it in some way – this is the sense in which the two are not independent of each other. Societies do not 'determine' agents, but they survive and change only through acting individuals. Bhaskar suggests a 'transformative' model of human action: societies provide the raw material, human beings act on it, and societies come out at the other end. The crucial property of human action . . . is that it is *intentional*; it aims at achieving something . . . [H]uman beings not only monitor their action (i.e. know what they are doing) but monitor the monitoring – they can reflect on what they know, assess it, make judgements and choices. In this respect they are crucially different from societies, which are structures of social relationships.
>
> (Craib, 1992, p. 20)

Although a more detailed analysis of structuration theory, realism, social constructionism and existentialism would no doubt identify subtle yet significant differences, for present purposes there is sufficient common ground to justify building later discussions in this book on the key concepts of agency and structure. These, then, will be recurring themes in the chapters that follow.

One of the main benefits of structuration theory is that it provides a coherent way of understanding the interplay of personal factors (agency) and the sociopolitical context (structure). In this respect it goes beyond both psychologism (the tendency to focus on the individual and to neglect wider social factors) and sociologism (the tendency to focus on wider social structures and lose sight of the individual). Structuration theory is premised on the dialectical interplay of these two domains – the personal domain of agency and the sociopolitical domain of structure – and therefore succeeds very well in integrating the two dimensions of human reality.

However, in concentrating on these two areas, it neglects a third – namely the cultural level. In my view, the weakness of structuration theory is that it presents the relationship between agency and structure as a direct one – a direct dialectical interplay. However, this leaves insufficient scope for the central role of culture (as the domain of shared meaning and symbolic systems) as a mediator between the two. That is, it neglects the central role of culture in:

1. *Shaping how the structural domain is experienced by individuals, groups and communities.* It is through sets of meanings (at the cultural level) that the structural domain influences us (through the ideological use of discourses). For example, I am likely to respect the authority of, say, a police officer not only because he or she has the power to arrest me, but also because an important part of my socialization was an acceptance of a culture that taught me to value and respect law and order.

2. *Maintaining social structures through processes of legitimation.* The (structural) wheels of power keep turning because they are oiled by the systems of meaning which support them and make them seem 'normal' or 'natural'. For example, the predominance of men in managerial positions can be seen to owe much to the discourses of masculinity and managerialism which play a key part in reproducing the status quo of a structure in which positions of power belong primarily to men – the male-dominated structure is 'normalized' by a culture which constructs it as 'natural'. See the discussion of 'autopoiesis' in Chapter 6.

What we have, then, is not simply a dialectic between agency and structure (which in itself generates a very complex psychosocial reality), but rather two sets of dialectical interactions: agency–culture and culture–structure (see Figure 1.5), which make for an even more complex matrix of interactions – in effect, a 'double dialectic' of agency, culture and structure.

The relationship between the individual and culture has a vast psychological and microsociological literature, although not necessarily from a dialectical frame of reference. However, when it comes to the interplay between culture and structure, there is less of a theory base to draw upon. Rubinstein (2001) makes the important point that: 'Structure and culture are drawn on to explain action, but their "interpenetration" is missed' (p. ix).

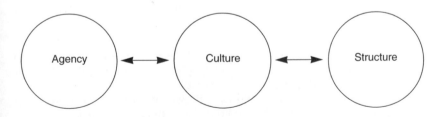

Figure 1.5   The double dialectic of agency, culture and structure

What PCS analysis presents, then, is an extension of structuration theory to attempt to integrate a mediating cultural level between the established domains of agency and structure. The implications of such an undertaking are beyond the scope of the present work, but it is none the less important to note that what is needed is a theoretical perspective which builds on structuration theory, but integrates this with some of the insights of cultural studies within a framework which addresses all three levels: personal, cultural and structural.

Emancipatory practice

A central premise on which this book is based is that the practice undertaken in working with people and their problems is pivotal with regard to discrimination and oppression. That is, such practices can either condone, reinforce or exacerbate existing inequalities or they can challenge, undermine or attenuate such oppressive forces. Consequently, it needs to be recognized that we 'walk a tightrope' with regard to inequality, and therefore have to be prepared to deal effectively with the challenges that arise if existing discrimination and oppression are not to be inadvertently strengthened.

In view of this, a form of practice that explicitly addresses inequality, discrimination and oppression needs to be developed. Indeed, a basic argument to be developed throughout the book is that practice needs to operate within a discourse that is overtly geared towards promoting equality and valuing diversity in order to ensure that inequalities are positively addressed.

Giddens (1992) draws a distinction between life politics and emancipatory politics. The latter refers to: 'individual and collective demands for freedom and justice and the struggle against barriers that prevent the possibility of leading an antonomous life' (Cassell, 1993, p. 33). The former, by contrast, relates to: 'how power can be used to arrange the world in a way which permits self-actualisation' (Cassell, 1993, pp. 33–4).

There is a strong parallel here with a distinction I have previously drawn between existential freedom and political liberty:

> Existential freedom – the process of self-creation – is a prerequisite for political liberty. To deny the former is to foreclose the latter and thus render an authentic social work impossible.
>
> If, as the determinists would have it, we have little or no control over our action, political praxis is rendered meaningless as collective action would equally be beyond our reach. Where social workers accept a voluntaristic, humanistic approach, politics cannot be excluded. Workers

and clients are circumscribed by the broader socio-political factors. Social work practice, when seen in this context, is part of a dialectic between individual and collective concerns, between existential freedom and political liberty. The two are necessarily intertwined.

(Thompson, 1992a, pp. 188–9)

(The references to social work in this passage can readily be applied to the broader framework of working with people and their problems in a variety of contexts.)

Political liberty parallels emancipatory politics in so far as both refer to the sociopolitical context in which power and the related issues of inequality, discrimination and oppression are very much to the fore. The potential for creating change in the broader systems and structures is a key issue here. To ignore that potential is to adopt a defeatist attitude and to become part of the problem rather than part of the solution. On the other hand, to be unrealistic about that potential can be a significant stressor and can undermine the validity of any emancipatory project by overemphasizing the part individuals can play in promoting social change (see Chapter 5).

Existential freedom parallels life politics in so far as both are concerned with the process of self-creation. Deterministic theories that reject human agency can be seen to act as a barrier to emancipatory politics (challenging discrimination and oppression) and life politics (countering bad faith and alienation).

The challenge of promoting equality needs to incorporate both life politics and emancipatory politics, as both have an important part to play in countering discrimination and oppression (Figure 1.6):

Figure 1.6   Emancipatory vs life politics

- Emancipatory politics involves identifying and addressing barriers to equality and social justice. This applies to a much broader field than the helping professions – the whole of the sociopolitical sphere of human existence, in fact – but none the less *includes* 'people work'. Indeed, as such work so often involves vulnerable or disadvantaged groups and individuals, it can be seen to be of particular significance within the overall picture of promoting social justice.

- Life politics involves identifying and addressing barriers to self-actualization. A key aspect of this is *empowerment* – the process of supporting individuals and groups in exercising as much control over their own lives as possible. This has the potential benefits of not only improving the quality of life of the persons concerned but also contributing more broadly to the process of challenging oppression (Ward and Mullender, 1993) through the raising of emancipatory awareness, the assertion of rights, identification of injustices and deprivations and so on.

From this it should be clear that the two forms of political praxis, although distinct, are closely interrelated and influence each other in subtle but important ways.

As I shall discuss in more detail in Chapter 5, it is important to be realistic about the extent to which professional practice can play a major role in producing social change at a macro-level. However, being realistic entails avoiding both overambition *and* defeatism. As Wineman (1984) comments: 'Mainstream politics rest on the reality of unimaginably destructive concentrations of power. Radical politics rest on a refusal to despair; rest on stubborn faith in contrary possibilities' (p. 248).

This is an important point to note. However, we should also note that radical approaches have been criticized for their narrowness (Pearson, 1975; Thompson, 1992a), for their failure to go beyond emancipatory politics and to take on board Giddens's concept of life politics. The emancipatory practice to be discussed in this book is to be seen as radical in the sense of wishing to tackle problems and issues *at the root*, rather than in terms of their surface manifestations. However, it also needs to be recognized that radical practice in the narrow sense in which it is often conceived does not form an adequate basis for a genuinely emancipatory practice.

Emancipatory practice involves helping to set people free from:

- discriminatory attitudes, values, actions and cultural assumptions;
- structures of inequality and oppression, both within organizations and in the social order more broadly;
- the barriers of bad faith and alienation that stand in the way of empowerment and self-direction;

- powerful ideological and other social forces that limit opportunities and maintain the status quo; and
- traditional practices which, although often based on good intentions, have the effect of maintaining inequalities and halting progress towards more appropriate forms of practice.

The development of such an emancipatory practice, one that truly promotes equality and values diversity, is a challenge that faces everyone in the human services. One important step in that direction is a fuller understanding of the concept of power and its role in the balance between equality and inequality. It is for this reason that Chapter 2 is devoted to the topic of power.

Conclusion

This has been a wide-ranging chapter, in so far as it has covered a great deal of conceptual ground in a relatively short space. It has reviewed a range of theoretical issues relating to equality, discrimination and oppression and has argued for a multidimensional approach – one which is not satisfied with either a micro-level focus on the individual or a macro-level focus on the wider social sphere. It is not even satisfied with an approach which recognizes the importance of both these domains and the interactions between them (structuration theory), as even that neglects the importance of the cultural level of shared meanings which mediates between the domains of agency and structure. What is needed even to begin to do justice to the complexity of discrimination and oppression is an approach based on the 'double dialectic' of agency, culture and structure – in other words, PCS analysis.

It is important to remember that the chapter is entitled 'Theoretical foundations' – that is, it offers only a foundation on which to build. The remaining chapters accomplish some of that building but by no means all of it. We remain a long way from an adequate theoretical understanding of the intricacies and subtleties of promoting equality.

2

POWER

Introduction

Much has been written on the subject of power and it would clearly be unrealistic to attempt a comprehensive analysis within the space available in this chapter. I shall therefore limit myself to a consideration of what I see as a number of key issues in terms of power and its role in relation to inequality, discrimination and oppression. I shall begin by asking the basic question of: 'What is power?', before exploring theories of power; language, discourse and power; the relationship between power and oppression; and, finally, the key concept of empowerment.

What is power?

In addressing this question, it is important to recognize that the concept of power is a 'paradigmatic' one. That is, it is used in different senses within different paradigms or theoretical frameworks. As we shall see below, there are various models or conceptions of power. However, one common theme is that of the ability to influence or control people, events, processes or resources. It amounts to being able to 'get things done', to make progress in achieving one's ends. In this sense, power can be seen as something positive, something to be valued and welcomed. However, it would be naïve not to recognize that power is also a potentially very destructive force, something that can be used to exploit, oppress or abuse – a significant barrier to equality. As Giddens (1993a) comments:

> Power is an ever-present phenomenon in social life. In all human groups, some individuals have more authority or influence than others, while groups themselves vary in terms of the level of their power. Power and inequality tend to be closely linked. The powerful are able to accumulate

valued resources, such as property or wealth; and possession of such resources is in turn a means of generating power.

(p. 209)

Power is therefore a central feature of the struggle to promote equality. Indeed, the very term 'struggle' is a significant one, as it indicates that there are established structures and vested interests that are likely to stand in the way of progress. Promoting equality inevitably involves entering into conflict with the 'powers that be', the dominant social arrangements that help to maintain existing power relations. Consequently, we need to recognize that an understanding of the workings of power is an essential part of challenging inequality, discrimination and oppression. As Fawcett and Featherstone (2000) put it: 'For those concerned with challenging injustice, exploring and understanding power relations are central activities' (p. 17).

While power is clearly a fundamental concept with regard to promoting equality in general, it can also be seen as particularly important in relation to working with people and their problems. This is because such work very often involves people in relative positions of power seeking to aid or serve people in relatively powerless positions. Power in such situations manifests itself in terms of:

- control or influence over the allocation of resources;
- knowledge, expertise and skills (for example, negotiation skills);
- professional discourse and legitimation;
- statutory powers (the backing of the law and court system); and
- hierarchical power by virtue of status or position within an organization.

Power, then, is a complex phenomenon that applies in a number of ways and at a number of levels. In order to develop further our understanding of these issues, we need to explore some of the key concepts that can help cast light on this important topic.

Theories of power

There are a wide variety of theories of power, and so the discussion here will necessarily be selective. I shall begin by discussing issues that relate to agency before addressing those that are more concerned with structure.

One well-established theory of power is that of Lukes (1974) who introduced a three-dimensional model, as described by Hugman (1991) in terms of three sets of situations:

1. situations of observable decision-making, focused on key issues over which there is overt conflict concerning the subjective interests of the individuals or groups involved;
2. situations of 'non-decision-making' in which only some potential issues become explicit, where there is covert as well as overt conflict concerning the subjective interests of groups or individuals;
3. situations in which the social agenda is established (that is, potential and explicit issues are created), in which there is actual (overt and covert) and also latent conflict over both objective and subjective interests of individuals and groups. (pp. 30–1)

(1) represents the one-dimensional model in which there is a narrow focus on overt conflict and concrete decisions. Power is exercised in a relatively open way, easily observed. (2) goes beyond this to incorporate the second dimension of covert or hidden conflict and 'non-decisions' – the outcomes that arise as a result of certain issues not being addressed. (3) represents Lukes's third dimension and is concerned with the political agenda of which the two other dimensions form a part (Clegg, 1989).

An important element of the third dimension is that of 'interests' – for example, material interests that underpin the operations of power. Power is therefore linked to the broader social context and is not simply a matter of the power relations inherent in interpersonal interactions and everyday social practices. In simple terms, power relates to:

- What is done – decisions made, steps taken (Dimension 1);
- What is not done – decisions or actions avoided or subverted (Dimension 2);
- The context in which it is done – interests, broader social and political factors and ideas (Dimension 3).

Although this approach has been very influential in social science, there are many aspects of power it does not address. It can therefore form only part of our understanding of the workings of power.

Another important theory of power is that of Weber (1968). Abercrombie et al. (1994) argue that, for Weber, power:

> is the probability that a person will be able to carry out his or her own will in the pursuit of goals of action, regardless of resistance. He defined 'domination' in a similar manner as the probability that a command would be obeyed by a given group of people. This definition has the fol-

lowing characteristics: (1) power is exercised by individuals and therefore involves choice, agency and intention; (2) it involves the notion of
agency, that is, an individual achieving or bringing about goals which are
desirable; (3) power is exercised over other individuals and may involve
resistance and conflict; (4) it implies that there are differences in interests
between the powerful and the powerless; (5) power is negative, involving
restrictions and deprivations for those subjected to domination.

(p. 329)

It is worth exploring each of these five characteristics in a little more
depth:

1. *Choice, agency, intention*

Power is a feature of everyday actions and interactions, in so far as it
involves individuals making decisions and living with the consequences of those decisions. Such actions can be used to enhance the
power an individual holds or, alternatively, they can be used to 'give
away' power – a process of self-disempowerment which will be discussed in more detail below. This emphasizes that power is not an
absolute quality that a person either has or does not have. The amount
of power an individual can exercise therefore depends upon, among
other things, the choices he or she makes – in short, human agency.

◀ PRACTICE FOCUS 2.1 ▶

Pat was a community nurse working mainly with older people. She
was often concerned that some of the people she worked with had
become very dependent on her, often not making decisions for
themselves and relying on her for guidance on a wide range of
matters. She realized that they needed a lot of help from her physically in order to cope on a day-to-day basis, but worried that they
were relying on her for other matters too, as if they did not want to
take responsibility for themselves. She discussed this issue with colleagues and found that they too had come across this pattern. Pat
therefore decided to look into how she could discourage people
from 'giving away' control over their lives in this way, and to
encourage them to be as autonomous as possible.

2. *Agency and desirable goals*

Power can be linked to desired outcomes, attempts to achieve particular goals. In this respect, power has a *past* dimension (it represents
the historical outcome of previous actions and power relations) and
also a *future* dimension (it represents what the individuals concerned
are trying to achieve, the direction they are taking). This is captured in
the notion of the 'existential project' (Thompson, 1992a), the everyday

process through which we 'pro-ject' ourselves into the future – our actions are geared towards moving closer to our desired goals. Power does not, therefore, relate only to the present.

3. Resistance and struggle

The power to achieve one's own ends often involves the use of power over other people, or their use of power to resist, block, sabotage or counteract one's attempts. Power can therefore be seen to entail considerable potential for struggle. This is the key element in Foucault's theory of power – power is not a one-way phenomenon.

4. Differences of interest

Conflicts of ends, competition for scarce resources and related matters can all be significant factors in relation to power. An understanding of power therefore needs to incorporate the sociological dimension of *conflict*, recognizing the inherent tensions between individuals and between social groups. Power thus represents a potential, and in many ways actual, battlefield involving a range of conflicts of interests. In this respect, power is an inevitable feature of human existence, in so far as differences of interest are intrinsic to social life.

5. Negative restrictions

The exercise of power by one person or group is often experienced by others as domination, involving a set of negative restrictions or deprivations. Power therefore contains within it the potential for abuse and oppression – a point which has major implications in terms of discrimination and inequality. However, we should also note that power is not inevitably negative in its consequences. The positive potential of power is a theme to be developed further in this and subsequent chapters.

Theories of power that focus on agency have been heavily criticized by theorists who emphasize the structural properties of power. For example, marxist sociology locates power primarily in class relations as a result of the economic exploitation of the working class (the proletariat) by the owners of the means of production (the bourgeoisie). That is, power is seen as deriving from the capitalist structure in which one class group benefits from economic, social and political domination at the expense of the other. Marxist theory would therefore see agency-based approaches to power as inadequate as a result of their neglect of the structural context, specifically the context of class relations. The power that comes from wealth and position is an important factor that should not be overlooked.

Marxist theories, in turn, have been criticized for too narrow a focus on class-based power relations and a neglect of other forms of social division such as gender and race. For example, many anti-racist feminists base their analysis on the need to go beyond a class perspective by integrating issues of oppression related to gender and race (Segal, 1999). Similarly, Williams (1989) comments on the general tendency of social policy to neglect such factors:

> In general 'race' and gender are issues that have been neglected or marginalized in the discipline of social policy, particularly in terms of a failure, to, first, acknowledge the experiences and struggles of women and of Black people over welfare provision; secondly, to account for racism and sexism in the provision of state welfare; thirdly, to give recognition to work which *does* attempt to analyse the relationship between the welfare state and the oppressions of women and of Black people (and, historically, other racialized groups like the Irish and Jews); and fourthly, to work out a progressive welfare strategy which incorporates the needs and demands which emerge from such strategies and analyses.
>
> (p. xi)

Power should therefore be seen as a structural property in the broader sense – relating to the various ways in which society is structured – rather than simply a question of class dominance. This is an important point for, as we shall see in Chapter 3, there are also other aspects of structural social division – age, disability and sexual identity, for example – that are very significant in terms of power relations and the distribution of life chances.

From the roots of marxist theories of class, therefore, have grown a number of other approaches that focus on the structural dimension. Some such theories, however, have emphasized structure at the expense of agency. For example, the structuralist approach of writers such as Althusser (1976) explicitly rejects the human actor as a significant factor in social theory. This is what is sometimes known as the 'death of the subject' thesis. Craib (1992) explains it in the following terms:

> The idea being attacked is that people are the authors of their own thoughts and actions. It is assumed instead that people are the puppets of their ideas, and their actions are not determined by choice and decision but are the outcome of the underlying structure of ideas, the logic of these ideas. If, for example, I am a Christian, I do not speak about Christianity; rather, Christianity speaks through me; some structuralists reach the extreme of saying that people do not speak; rather, they are

> spoken (by the underlying structure of the language); that they do not read books, but are 'read' by books. They do not create societies, but are created by societies.
>
> (p. 135)

This rather extreme form of determinism makes the fundamental mistake of ignoring the role of agency in reproducing social structure. It reduces the structure–agency dialectic to a linear relationship in which structure simply determines human action. As Giddens (1993b) argues:

> Most sociologists, even many working within frameworks of interpretive sociology, have failed to recognize that social theory, no matter how 'macro' its concerns, demands a sophisticated understanding of agency and the agent just as it does an account of the complexities of society.
>
> (p. 5)

We are once again in the realm of structuration, the process – or set of processes – described in Chapter 1 by which social structures are reproduced in and by the everyday actions of social actors. Structuralist theories of power can therefore be seen to be one-sided and reductionist.

Sibeon (1991) argues from a similar perspective when he discusses the tendency towards reductionism inherent in theories that emphasize either micro or macro issues, rather than the interaction of the two:

> To attempt to account for 'structure' *in terms of* agency is (micro) reductionist . . . equally, to attempt . . . to 'explain' human agency *in terms of* structure is (macro) reductionist . . . Social life is not reducible to a single reductionist principle of 'micro' or 'macro' explanation. Neither is it possible to arrive at an 'accommodation' or 'compromise' based on a *synthesis* of both these forms of reductionism.
>
> (p. 24)

Similarly, Westwood (2002) argues that sociology is beginning to move towards what she describes as a 'quantum' approach, based not on 'either/or' dichotomies which oversimplify complex social realities, but rather on both/and formulations which seek to capture the diversity, complexity and depth of the social world. This is an approach consistent with existentialism, with a focus on appreciating the multidimensional nature of human reality rather than seeking, in bad faith, to reduce it to a single aspect.

In reaction to structuralist theories of power and social relations there emerged a broad school of thought that came to be known as 'poststructuralism'. A number of major theorists are associated with this approach, not least Lyotard, Derrida and Foucault, and a number of important themes can be discerned:

- the critique of metanarratives;
- the dispersal of power;
- genealogy as a form of theoretical understanding; and
- the importance of language.

I shall discuss each of these themes in turn.

The critique of metanarratives

Lyotard (1984) rejected what he terms 'metanarratives', the grand theories that have attempted to develop a comprehensive picture of social life and experience. He describes such theories as 'terroristic', in so far as they are said to suppress difference in their attempts to provide an overview. As we shall see, difference is a key word in the poststructuralist vocabulary, particularly in relation to the workings of power.

◀ PRACTICE FOCUS 2.2 ▶

> Alan was a probation officer who was very knowledgeable and skilled in the art of family therapy. He sought to understand all his work in terms of systems, particularly family systems. This approach became the basis of all his work, a 'metanarrative' by which he tried to make sense of the problems his clients faced, the contexts in which they occurred and the interventions he needed to take. Although this proved to be very effective with many of his cases, it was often not an appropriate approach for some people or certain circumstances. However, his commitment to family systems theory prevented him from seeing this, and he often persisted with a family therapy approach when a less 'uniform' approach would have been much more appropriate.

While Lyotard's critique does have its strengths, particularly in terms of pointing out the dangers of an overzealousness for a particular theoretical approach, his complete rejection of metanarratives can be seen to be both inaccurate and excessive. It is excessive in so far as a grand theory or metanarrative does not necessarily suppress difference. It is a potential danger inherent in such approaches rather than an inevitable feature of them. This is a point to which I shall return in Chapter 5.

Lyotard is also inaccurate, in so far as he fails to distinguish between different types of metanarrative and the diversity of thought and culture they represent. Ironically, then, Lyotard's approach is itself terroristic in that he relies on a form of 'Thought Police':

> In our view, a more promising venture would be to make explicit, criti-
> cally discuss, take apart, and perhaps reconstruct and rewrite the grand
> narratives of social theory rather than to just prohibit them and exclude
> them from the terrain of narrative. It is likely – as Jameson argues – that
> we are condemned to narrative in that individuals and cultures organize,
> interpret and make sense of their experience through story-telling modes
> (see also Ricoeur 1984). Not even a scientistic culture could completely
> dispense with narratives and the narratives of social theory will no doubt
> continue to operate in social analysis and critique in any case (Jameson
> 1984b: p. xii). If this is so, it would seem preferable to bring to light the
> narratives of modernity so as to critically examine and dissect them,
> rather than to simply prohibit certain sorts of narratives by Lyotardian
> Thought Police.
>
> (Best and Kellner, 1991, p. 173)

Despite these criticisms, Lyotard's work has proven to be a major influence on the development of postmodernism, a theoretical perspective to be discussed in more detail below.

The dispersal of power

One of the underlying principles of the structuralist approach to power is that such power is concentrated in certain areas of the social structure, within the ruling class, for example. Poststructuralism, by contrast, emphasizes the *dispersed* nature of power. For example, Foucault sees power as a feature of *all* social relations, a ubiquitous aspect of social life: 'What I am attentive to is the fact that every human relation is to some degree a power relation. We move in a world of perpetual strategic relations' (1988, p. 168).

In Foucault's terms, then, power is a much more complex and wide-ranging phenomenon than the relatively narrow conception of power associated with structuralist approaches. As Bell (1993) comments:

> For Foucault, therefore, the locus of power is dispersed. The state, for
> example, can only operate on the basis of power relations that exist
> within the social field, the 'polymorphous techniques of power' (1981:
> 11). For the theorist, the prescription is not to formulate 'global system-
> atic theory . . . but to analyse the specificity of mechanisms of power, to
> locate the connections and extensions' (1981: 145). It is these local tactics
> that work to support what may have appeared at first to be the source of

power (1980: 159). Thus one can speak of strategies of power only once one has traced the 'tactics', the micro-techniques of power.

(p. 31)

Power, according to Foucault, is not an absolute entity that people either have or do not have. Rather, it is a property of the interactions between individuals, groups and institutions. It therefore needs to be understood as a relatively fluid entity that is open to constant change and influence. Consequently, a generalized theory will not be sufficient to explain the subtle workings of power. Gergen (1999) makes apt comment when he argues that:

> power resides not in a structure or a person but in a set of relationships. *Power relations* may not only include physical artifacts, but may also be extended outward to the more general conditions of the culture.
>
> (p. 207)

In presenting this fluid version of power, Foucault's work can be seen to represent Lyotard's critique of metanarratives – it seeks to provide specific, historically grounded explanations of the mechanisms of power, rather than an overall, abstract and generalized theory.

In this respect, Foucault's approach is 'ideographic' in so far as it seeks to provide: 'interpretations of individual cases that capture their particularity and uniqueness' (Morrow, 1994, p. 56) rather than a 'nomothetic' approach which seeks to provide overall, invariant rules or scientific laws (see also Sibeon, 1996). An important theoretical tool Foucault used to provide such ideographic explanations was that of discourse, a concept we encountered in Chapter 1 and to which we shall return below under the heading of 'The importance of language'.

Westwood (2002) links Foucault's conception of power to the work of Nietzsche:

> Following Nietzsche (1844–1900), Foucault (1926–84) regards power not as negative or positive but as omnipresent and productive. However, there are different forms of power, from governance through state organisations and the management of populations to discipline through internal bureaucracies and institutional arrangements that come to bear on all citizens in modern societies.
>
> (p. 19)

Genealogy

Foucault's earlier work was described as 'archaeological' in so far as it sought to reconstruct the diversity of discourses that underpinned particular historical development, for example in relation to the development of empirically based medicine (Foucault, 1975) or the development of the human sciences (Foucault, 1972). His task was not to fit the evidence into a preconceived theoretical framework, but rather to explain specific pieces of evidence, much as an archaeologist would do in trying to piece together fragments of the past. This once again reflects Foucault's ideographic approach.

His later works, by contrast, he described as 'genealogical'. As Bell (1993) explains:

> By the time Foucault wrote THS [The History of Sexuality], his concerns were less with the search for rules, regularities and the formation of discourses and more with questions of the relationships between power, knowledge and discourse. During the period between The Archaeology of Knowledge and THS, Foucault's own understanding of what he was doing altered. Whilst it still contained important aspects of archaeology, the later approach, which he named 'genealogy', resulted from important changes in his understanding of his work. The interest Foucault had had in the rules which governed discourses disappears, and, although discourses are still the object of study and the level at which Foucault's analysis 'enters', the abstract and generalized approach to discourse of The Archaeology of Knowledge is replaced by a more 'grounded' interest in the ways that discourse is both built upon networks of power/knowledge and produces certain power effects.
>
> (p. 44)

This approach to history differs significantly from traditional history in so far as it concentrates on meticulous detail and documentation, and does not seek to unearth an underlying truth or historical 'reality'. Indeed, this is a feature of poststructuralism, a movement away from underlying structures to focus instead on the diverse fragments or details – the 'polymorphous techniques of power'. As Rabinow (1986) comments: 'Foucault is highly suspicious of claims to universal truths. He doesn't refute them; instead, his consistent response is to historicize grand abstractions' (p. 4).

Genealogy represents an attempt to piece together the fragmented detail of the complex machinations of power as manifested through discourses in much the same way as a genealogist maps out the interrelationships within a family tree. As such, it is a core element within the poststructuralist approach to power.

The importance of language

Structuralist approaches to language emphasize the underlying structures, or 'deep structures' that underpin our actions and interactions.

Poststructuralism, by contrast, focuses on the surface manifestations of language – the discourses that are so important in understanding the workings of power.

Language, in poststructuralist terms, is the site where meanings are shaped and contested, identities formed and challenged. As Burr (1995) comments:

> If language is indeed the place where identities are built, maintained and challenged, then this also means that language is the crucible of change, both personal and social. A person may feel trapped, restricted or oppressed by his or her identity as, say, 'mother', 'homosexual' or 'mental patient'. Postructuralist theory would see language as the major site where these identities could be challenged or changed. If our experience of ourselves and of our lives is only given structure and meaning by language, and if these meanings are not fixed but constantly changing, sought after and struggled for, then our experience is potentially open to an infinite number of possible meanings or constructions. What it means to be a 'woman', to be 'a child' or to be 'black' could be transformed, reconstructed, and for poststructuralists language is the key to such transformations.
>
> (p. 43)

The linkages between power and language are therefore very significant for poststructuralism, as indeed for other theoretical approaches. I shall therefore return to the question of language and power later in this chapter under the heading of 'Language, discourse and power'.

Poststructuralism owes much to the work of Foucault and it is worth considering two particular aspects of his theory of power, namely surveillance and resistance.

Surveillance: the panopticon

One of Foucault's interests was in the ways in which externally defined discipline becomes internalized as a form of self-discipline. An important part of this work was his analysis of the role of surveillance as a tool of power. In particular, he was interested in 'the panopticon', a form of disciplinary technology proposed by Jeremy Bentham (Foucault, 1977a). This describes a prison arrangement whereby a central tower allows surveillance of a range of levels and cells. Such an arrangement acts as an important metaphor for Foucault's understanding of surveillance. As Rabinow (1986) explains:

> The architectural perfection is such that even if there is no guardian present, the power apparatus still operates effectively. The inmate cannot

see whether or not the guardian is in the tower, so he must behave as if surveillance were perpetual and total. If the prisoner is never sure when he is being observed, he becomes his own guardian. As the final step in architectural and technological perfection, the panopticon includes a system for observing and controlling the controllers. Those who occupy the central position in the panopticon are themselves thoroughly enmeshed in a localization and ordering of their own behaviour.

(p. 19)

This is a significant passage with important implications not only for our understanding of power in general but also, more specifically, for the role of the maintenance of power relations in working with people and their problems. This is because such work can be seen to involve an element of surveillance (Abbott and Sapsford, 1988). For example, helping someone to deal with a drink problem is likely to involve monitoring levels of alcohol consumption – care and control are necessarily intertwined through the use of such 'surveillance' (Thompson, 2000b). These implications include:

- Individuals contribute to their own oppression through the internalization of disciplinary practices.
- Power relations operate within systems of ideas (discourses) and do not rely solely on the actions of individuals or groups.
- Those who wield power, including those of us engaged in 'people work', are also subject to disciplinary practices – the controllers are controlled.

All three of these points relate to issues that can be seen to be of major importance in understanding inequality, discrimination and oppression. They will therefore feature in arguments to be presented in subsequent chapters.

Resistance

Simplistic conceptions of power often present it as something which some people have, while others do not have it. The reality is far more complex, as Foucault was at pains to point out. For Foucault, power is a dualistic phenomenon – that is, it is both constraining and enabling (Westwood, 2002). It allows one individual or group to dominate others through 'discursive practices', the powerful ideas and assumptions rooted in particular discourses. However, power also manifests itself as 'resistance', the ability of individuals or groups to struggle against such domination.

As power operates primarily through discourse (ideas, assumptions, knowledge, frameworks of understanding), such dominance can be challenged through acts of *resistance*, through the use of counter-vailing power to undermine dominant discursive practices. As power is an ever-present feature of everyday life, opportunities for resistance are also ever-present.

Callinicos (1990) makes apt comment in this regard:

> Indeed, it is impossible to account for historical struggles and transfor-mations without an understanding of the powers which human beings have, by virtue of their shared nature and their position in social struc-tures, to change the course of events. It is in part because agents have the ability to choose between different courses of action that historical processes do not follow an inevitable path of progress.
>
> (p. 115)

This conception of power has important implications for practice in so far as the minutiae of day-to-day work can be seen, at every step, to offer opportunities for empowerment through the process of resis-tance. This is a theme that will be developed in later chapters.

◀ **PRACTICE FOCUS 2.3** ▶

Linda was a skilled and experienced worker who was highly respected by her colleagues. One of her skills was the ability to influence others, subtly but effectively. Over the years she had care-fully nurtured the ability to exercise power in her day-to-day inter-actions without entering into direct conflict with others. She was particularly adept at using these skills to resist pressures from above to work in particular ways that she did not like, and gener-ally seemed to get her own way on most things. She had clearly developed a good understanding of micro-level power relations and had become very skilled in the art of resistance.

Resistance is also a significant concept in so far as it acts as a bridge between poststructuralism, with its emphasis on discourse, and another theoretical perspective, that of postmodernism, with its emphasis on deconstruction and fragmentation.

Postmodernism and power

Postmodernism is not so much a theoretical perspective as a style of theorizing. It encompasses a wide diversity of theoretical positions and political viewpoints. Despite this diversity, my focus here will be on the common themes and concepts, as space does not permit an analysis of the differences of emphasis and perspective across this broad intellectual movement (see Hollinger, 1994, for a more detailed exposition of postmodernist thought).

Postmodernism has its roots in art, architecture and philosophy as well as social theory. It represents a critique and rejection of 'modernity' and its aims and assumptions. Modernity refers to the post-Enlightenment era in which society is assumed to be based on rationality, progress towards humanist goals and the development of universalizing, totalizing theory. As such, it was seen as a development from traditional, or 'pre-modern' times which were characterized by unquestioning religious faith, a focus on continuity and a mistrust of innovation. For postmodernists, we are now in (or are approaching) an era of 'postmodernity' in which the assumptions of modernity are breaking down.

Postmodernist theory can be seen as a range of attempts to understand the social changes taking place and to draw out their implications. Such theory has much in common with the poststructuralist theory already discussed in this chapter but the two cannot be fully equated. For example, the work of Foucault has been very influential in both camps, yet he explicitly rejected the label of 'postmodernist'.

Postmodernism, as I have indicated, represents a broad intellectual movement, and so it is difficult to pin down precisely. However, there are a number of recurring themes that are closely associated with the term, and so I shall outline each of these and consider their implications for a postmodernist conception of power.

Fragmentation

Postmodernists criticize modernist thinking for its 'universalizing and totalizing' tendencies and, in this respect, they reflect the poststructuralist critique of grand narratives. Postmodernism rejects attempts to develop an overarching framework or all-encompassing theoretical perspective. Consequently, fragmentation is an important theme of postmodernist thought.

Such fragmentation can be seen to apply in terms of:

- *theoretical understanding* The rejection of metanarratives in general and the dialectic in particular.
- *self or personal identity* For postmodernists, the self is characterized by fragmentation rather than unity or coherence.
- *the affirmation of difference* Building on Foucault's emphasis on difference, postmodernist thought attaches great significance to social and cultural differences.

In short, postmodernists criticize 'modernist' theorists for emphasizing totalities, commonalities and coherence at the expense of fragmentation and discord. As Callinicos (1990) puts it: 'One might then say that where Modernism experiences fragmentation as loss, Lyotard and the other prophets of the postmodern celebrate it' (p. 110).

The rejection of logocentrism

Logocentrism is a term that refers to:

> the claim to be able to achieve the *logos*, an *unmediated* knowledge of the world; a claim, which in Derrida's (1976) view, has informed philosophy since Socrates, and is a theme replicated in the variety of discourses which have sought to explain the world, be they philosophical, religious or scientific. 'Presence' – this unmediated knowledge – is an indicator of authenticity, of experience of reality, of – simply put – being able to speak 'the truth' about something or other . . . In scientific discourse, logocentrism inheres in the claim that scientific method makes reality accessible, without the intervention of any mediating process which might distort our perception.
>
> (Fox, 1993, p. 8)

Postmodernists are critical of attempts to discover 'absolute' truth or to establish a fixed, underlying reality. To a large extent, this parallels both the social constructionist perspective outlined in Chapter 1 and existentialist thought (Thompson, 1992a). What counts as 'truth' depends, of course, on power relations and the discourses that sustain them. Foucault referred to 'truth effects', by which he meant the ability of a discourse to 'create' a truth, to construct reality in such a way as to make it 'real' and 'true'. Logocentrism is therefore a naïve approach that neglects the significance of discourse, language and power.

The myth of progress

A central feature of modernity is the belief in progress towards humanist goals, driven by rationality and scientific advancement. By contrast, postmodernist thought regards this as a myth with no basis in reality. In place of this grand plan of human progress, postmodernism paints a picture of diversity, difference and fragmentation in which no clear path of progress can be discerned.

There are two important aspects to this. First, the notion of progress can be seen as logocentric, in so far as it implies an absolute reality unmediated by the interpretations or constructions people place on actions and events. What constitutes progress is a contested issue rather than an undisputed consensus.

Second, progress towards humanist goals implies what postmodernists would call 'closure', an ultimate goal or purpose that humanity can reach – Marx's notion of the 'end of history' would be a good example of this. This can be seen as a form of optimistic naïveté that distorts our understanding of human experience and social processes. It is for this reason that postmodernists are generally critical of the dialectic, a point to which I shall return below.

Subjectless history

The poststructuralist concept of the 'decentred subject' emerges in postmodernist thought as 'subjectless history'. History is construed in terms of 'discursive practices', the complex interactions of discourses. As Fox (1993) comments: 'In postmodern theory, subjectivity is the outcome of power, and the subject is no more than an effect of power, constituted in discourses of power/knowledge' (p. 163). That is, the subject is seen as the outcome of discursive practices, a product of history rather than a motor force of history.

This ties in with the theme of the myth of progress, in so far as history cannot be seen as the strivings of individuals towards emancipatory goals. Postmodernism therefore rejects the notion of the romantic hero.

Simulations

Contemporary society is characterized by 'hi-tech' global communication systems – the mass media, computerized information technology and so on. We have become an 'information society' in which access to, and control over, information are important sources of power. Information and representation/simulation are therefore seen as very significant issues.

This is particularly the case in the work of Baudrillard. As Hassard (1993) comments:

> Unlike in modern industrial society, where production was the cornerstone, in the postmodern society simulations structure and control social affairs. Models and codes precede reality and are reproduced unceasingly in a society where the contrast between the real and the unreal is no longer valid. As Baudrillard says, 'the real is not only what can be reproduced, but that which is already reproduced, the hyper-real' (1983b: 146). In this society, 'simulacra' – that is, copies or representations of objects or events – now constitute 'the real'.
>
> (p. 8)

Différance

This is a term introduced by Derrida to refer to the 'slippery' nature of reality as mediated by language and systems of meaning. As Fox (1993) comments:

> Briefly, *différance* concerns the fundamental *undecidability* which resides in language and its continual *deferral* of meaning, the slippage of meaning which occurs as soon as one tries to pin a concept down. *Différance* is unavoidable once one enters into a language or other symbolic mode of representation, in which signifiers can refer not to referents (the 'underlying reality'), but only to other signifiers. While trying to represent the real, one finds that the meaning which one is trying to communicate slips from one's grasp. We are left not with the reality, but with an approximation which, however much we try to make it 'more real', is always already deferred and irrecoverable.
>
> (pp. 7–8)

The complexities of language and discourse are therefore part and parcel of the operations of power, in so far as our relationship with the world is mediated by language (Thompson, 2003). This is a topic to which I shall return later in this chapter.

Postmodernism: an evaluation

Postmodernist theory has much to say about power and is, in many ways, a radical departure from earlier theoretical perspectives. However, the argument I shall be presenting here is that postmodernist thought is a 'mixed blessing', in so far as it offers what I see as some important insights but also suffers from some major flaws and inadequacies. I shall therefore comment first on the positive aspects of postmodernism before exploring some of the criticisms.

Strengths

A major strength of postmodernist thought is its thoroughgoing rejection of essentialism. That is, the notion of fixed essences, such as an unchanging personality or an immutable human nature, is not given any credence. As noted in Chapter 1, essentialism is a significant barrier that stands in the way of developing practice based on empowerment. The anti-essentialist stance of postmodernism allows and encourages the possibility of personal and social change.

A further strength of postmodernism is its focus on 'dedifferentiation'. This refers to the tendency to break down discipline boundaries and recognize commonalities across the social sciences, humanities, arts and so on, to move away from traditional, somewhat arbitrary divisions.

A movement away from such potential divisiveness can be seen to be particularly important for the helping professions which have their roots in diverse theoretical traditions including sociology, psychology, social policy and philosophy. There is much to be gained from breaking down such boundaries to allow a constructive cross-fertilization of ideas and insights. Similarly, each of the professional disciplines can usefully draw on the knowledge base of other disciplines if artificial boundaries can be removed. For example, it has been argued that social work education has much to learn from nurse education and management theory (Thompson and Bates, 1996) and, increasingly, nurse education is following a path that has been a major issue for social work education for many years – namely the tackling of discrimination and oppression (Baxter, 2001a; Culley and Dyson, 2001a).

The process of dedifferentiation can therefore be seen as a valuable one for developing and consolidating the knowledge base of the helping professions and facilitating the integration of theory and practice.

Foucault's notion of 'normalization' is also an important and valuable theme in postmodernist thought:

> By 'normalization', Foucault means a system of finely gradated and measurable intervals in which individuals can be distributed around a norm – a norm which both organizes and is the result of this controlled distribution.
>
> (Rabinow, 1986, p. 20)

Such norms are maintained (or 'policed') through surveillance, the subtle workings of Foucault's panopticon. Again this is a particularly significant issue for practice, in so far as the potential for oppressive forms of surveillance and 'normalization' is ever-present. As Rojek *et al.* (1988) comment:

> Foucault and other commentators have remarked on the paradoxical nature of humanist caring. In determining the needs and rights of citizens, humanists are said to install new and extended patterns of surveillance and control which unavoidably limit the freedom of the individual.
>
> (p. 115)

◀ **PRACTICE FOCUS 2.4** ▶

Jan was a health visitor on the outskirts of a large city. Although children at risk of child abuse formed only a tiny proportion of her caseload, she recognized that they took up a lot of her time and energy – it was something that worried her quite a lot. In particular, she was concerned that, although her role in monitoring certain children's welfare and safety was very important in protecting children, she still felt that she was playing more of a policing role than the caring one that had attracted her into nursing in the first place.

Unfortunately, the critique of normalization has been taken too far by some postmodernists who regard all social norms as inherently oppressive (for example, Deleuze and Guattari, 1983, 1984). None the less, the concept of normalization remains an important one in explaining aspects of social control and warning against the dangers of oppression inherent in uncritical 'normalizing' approaches to practice.

A strength of postmodernism discussed by Fox (1993) relates to White's (1991) notion of 'grieving delight' and the Nietzschean concept of the 'eternal return' (Bogue, 1989). Both of these concepts relate to 'difference', an important concept in postmodernism, and to 'finitude', the recognition of the finite nature of human existence.

Fox (1993) explains grieving delight in the following terms:

> Grief sensitizes us to *injustice* – to the added burden of needless suffering, while the element of delight deepens the concern with *fostering difference*. Difference is no longer something to be normalized or tolerated, but to be celebrated. In turn, a caring for difference affirms our humanity, our finitude ... Grieving delight, while a consequence of the postmodern responsibility to otherness, White suggests, constitutes the conditions for an ethical–political engagement with modernity, and an attitude towards the responsibility to act.
>
> (p. 130)

Grieving delight is therefore an important concept in relation to discrimination and oppression. It can be seen as an ontological concept that incorporates personal issues of grief and loss with sociopolitical issues of injustice and inequality (Thompson, 2002a).

The concept of 'eternal return' refers to the hypothetical question of what would our reaction be if we were to live our lives over and over again in fine detail – would it be one of despair or one of exhilaration? The answer to this question will reveal a great deal about our attitude towards ourselves. As White (1990) puts it: 'The burdensomeness of the eternal return will depend on how you are disposed towards yourself – on how you view your life' (p. 67, cited in Fox, 1993, p. 131).

The 'eternal return' is significant as a means of understanding the extent to which we adopt a positive attitude of change towards ourselves, an attitude of *becoming* rather than an essentialist one of fixity. The eternal return:

> is not a desire for repetition, or for a cyclical return of the same, but the opposite: an affirmation of becoming and difference (Bogue 1989: 28–9). The eternal return needs to be read within Nietzsche's philosophy of a will-to-power, an active principle of becoming other, as opposed to reactivity and passivity.
>
> (Fox, 1993, p. 131)

The eternal return has much in common with the existentialist theme of ontological freedom as a precursor to political freedom and emancipation (Thompson, 1992a). If the individual denies or resists the ability to change and develop, then the potential for collective political change is severely limited, and with it the potential for challenging inequality, discrimination and oppression.

A key aspect of postmodernist thought is the affirmation of difference. However, we need to recognize that this is an ambiguous concept. It refers to two separate but related conceptions that are often used interchangeably:

- *Difference as flux* As the example above of the eternal return demonstrates, difference is often used to refer to movement, change, development – in short, flux. In this respect, difference is seen as being in opposition to essentialism. It is therefore similar to the existentialist concepts of contingency and choice of being.
- *Difference as social diversity* Contemporary society is characterized by a multiplicity of social divisions (Thompson, 2001a), and so social diversity is an important question to address. In this respect, difference is seen as being in opposition to normalization, the tendency to attempt to impose restrictive social norms at the expense of diversity and heterogeneity.

In both these senses, difference is an important concept that can be used to challenge oppression – in the first case, the oppressive nature and consequences of essentialism and, in the second, the range of oppressions that includes sexism, racism, ageism and disablism (see Chapter 3). As such, it can play a valuable role in countering oppression and promoting equality.

Weaknesses

Postmodernist thought has proven to be very influential in some quarters. However, despite this influence, it is marred by a number of flaws that seriously undermine its value as a social theory.

Primary among such weaknesses is its tendency towards internal contradiction. For example, the rejection of metanarratives as a serious theoretical proposition is contradicted by the fact that postmodernism itself can be seen as a metanarrative. As Paul Thompson (1993) argues:

> As has been widely noted (Boyne and Rattansi, 1990: 39–40), postmodernism is itself a metanarrative, and one that is greatly undertheorized. The issue, then, is what *kind* of narrative and generalization, avoiding teleological explanation or forms of totalization that impairs much theorizing. Arguments that it is impossible to grasp the whole of reality within a single analytical framework are well taken. But that does not invalidate social theory that seeks to generalize and make truth claim across more limited territories.
>
> (p. 197)

This passage also refers to another weakness of postmodernist thought – its tendency to overstate the case, to indulge in extremism. A clear example of this would be Baudrillard's (1983a) argument that human beings should abandon subjectivity and adopt the fatalism of being as object-like as possible.

Such fatalism is also linked with another weakness of postmodernist thought, namely its nihilism – the mood of pessimism in relation to possibilities of emancipation and social progress that postmodernism engenders. As Crook (1990) comments:

> When radical social theory loses its accountability, when it can no longer give reasons, something has gone very wrong. But this is precisely what happens to postmodern theory, and it seems appropriate to use the overstretched term 'nihilism' as a label for this degeneration. The nihilism of postmodernism shows itself in two symptoms: an inability to specify possible mechanisms of change, and an inability to state why change is better than no change.
>
> (p. 59)

While the modernist belief in absolute progress fuelled by scientific rationality is one that has rightly been challenged, this does not support the postmodernist rejection of the notion of emancipatory progress. Callinicos (1990) captures this point in the following passage:

It is in part because agents have the ability to choose between different courses of action that historical processes do not follow an inevitable path of progress. Lyotard, rightly recognizing that there are no guarantees of human emancipation of the kind the *philosophes* sought to give, wrongly concludes that we must therefore abandon the goal of emancipation itself, and the conception of human nature which it presupposes.

(p. 115)

The postmodernist rejection of the potential for emancipatory progress is therefore not justified theoretically or politically.

This can also be seen to relate to the postmodernist emphasis on playfulness. Hollinger (1994) sees playfulness as a counterbalance to the disappointments experienced as a result of the failure of the belief in inevitable progress. However, such 'playfulness' can also be seen as a self-indulgent refusal to engage in the genuine struggle for emancipation – a means of avoiding the challenges of promoting equality rather than engaging with them. In this respect, playfulness can be seen as an example of bad faith. Postmodernists who prefer playfulness to emancipatory practice are therefore very much part of the problem rather than part of the solution (Thompson, 2001a), in so far as they contribute to legitimizing the status quo and undermining the emancipatory project.

However, we should note that not all postmodernists fall into this trap of rejecting the possibility of emancipatory progress – that is, progress in promoting equality and valuing diversity. This is captured in the following passage from Pease and Fook (1999):

> we side with those expressions of postmodern thinking that do not totally abandon the values of modernity and the Enlightenment project of human emancipation. Only 'strong' or 'extreme' forms of postmodern theory reject normative criticism and the usefulness of any forms of commonality underlying diversity. We believe that a 'weak' form of postmodernism informed by critical theory can contribute effectively to the construction of an emancipatory politics concerned with political action and social justice.
>
> (p. 12)

This is a point to which we shall return later.

In addition, much postmodernist writing can be accused of 'obscurantism' – a style of language that distances and alienates many readers through its unnecessarily obscure references and constructions. This is ironic for a form of social theory that emphasizes the significance of language in relation to power. It is also significant that

66

such obscurantism acts as a barrier to understanding and thereby further impedes the development of a critical social theory that can play a part in challenging power structures and their inherent inequalities.

A good example of such obscurantism is to be found in a hoax perpetrated by a physicist who objected to what he regarded as the inappropriate use of mathematical and scientific language in the works of certain postmodernist writers. Alan Sokal wrote a paper comprising mathematical and scientific language but with no actual meaning (Sokal, 1996). To the great embarrassment of the editors, it was accepted for publication in the journal, *Social Text*. Sokal claimed that he did this to expose 'the empty verbiage of postmodernist discourse and . . . the spectacle of an intellectual community where everyone repeats sentences that no one understands' (Sokal and Bricmont, 1999, p. 192).

Perhaps the most significant weakness of postmodernist thought, however, is the reductionist conception of selfhood. The early work of Foucault specifically rejected human agency. As Best and Kellner (1991) put it:

> the subject must be 'stripped of its creative role and analysed as a complex and variable function of discourse' (Foucault 1977[a]: p. 138). Hence, Foucault rejects the active subject and welcomes the emerging postmodern era as a positive event where the denuding of agency occurs and new forms of thought can emerge.
>
> (p. 51)

However, in his later work, Foucault was to argue that: 'We have to create ourselves as a work of art' (1982, p. 237). He developed an interest in what he called 'technologies of the self', the means by which autonomous subjects are created and maintained. Clearly, then, the later Foucault has rejected the earlier determinism. None the less, despite Foucault's own movement away from a reductionist determinism, others within the postmodernist school of thought have tended to maintain the earlier focus.

Haber (1994) argues that the denial of self implicit in postmodernism stands in the way of the development of a politics of difference. That is, there is a contradiction between the affirmation of difference and the 'death of the subject': 'So in effect, any notion of a politics of difference which accepts the postmodern/poststructuralist disjunction: *either* difference *or* similarity leaves no locus for politics: no community, no self, no viable political theory' (p. 134).

The question of identity is a complex one. We should therefore not oversimplify matters by seeing identity as either a matter of unity and sameness (the traditional, personality-based approach) or a matter of difference (the poststructuralist/postmodernist approach), but rather as a process involving both unity and difference mediated through language and social interaction (see Thompson, 2003, for a discussion of language and identity).

As the discussions in later chapters will confirm, selfhood can be seen as a crucial concept in the politics of empowerment that I shall present as a fundamental part of the promotion of equality.

Perhaps the most damning criticism of postmodernism comes from O'Neill (1995) when he comments on the destructiveness of postmodernism's tendency to 'throw the baby out with the bathwater':

> Many on earth do not eat at all. But that cannot be the question. There is no justice for them. But that cannot be the question. Nor is there any truth for them. But that cannot be the question. Who, then, owns these questions? Why are they not raised without irritation and scorn, if not impatience and ridicule?
>
> These questions go unasked because those of us who own knowledge, who enjoy literacy, health, self-respect and social status have chosen to rage against our own gifts rather than to fight for their enlargement in the general public. We have chosen to invalidate our science, to psychiatrize our arts, to vulgarize our culture, to make it unusable and undesirable by those who have yet to know it. We honour no legacy. We receive no gifts. We hand on nothing. We poison ourselves rather than live for others. We despise service and are slaves to our own self-degradation.
>
> (p. 2)

This very powerful passage illustrates well the pessimistic, nihilistic tendencies to be found in much postmodernist thought and writing.

Beyond postmodernism

The preceding pages have shown postmodernism to be a 'mixed blessing', in so far as it brings both strengths and weaknesses. However, the situation is not quite so simple. This is because many of the strengths associated with postmodernism are not unique to this particular school of thought. For example, the rejection of essentialism, grieving delight (although not referred to as such) and the politics of difference can all be found in existentialist thought (Sartre, 1958, 1976; Thompson, 1992a, 1992b). Indeed, it is no coincidence that

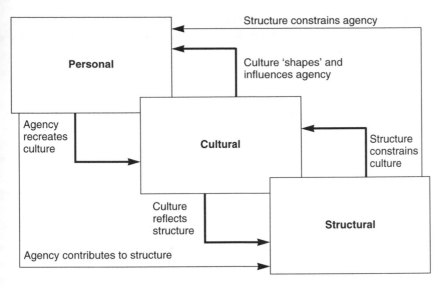

Figure 2.1   The interactions of the personal, cultural and structural levels

both modern existentialism and postmodernism have been strongly influenced by the works of Nietzsche.

Although postmodernist ideas have proven to be very influential and have raised a number of important issues, the overall value of this theoretical perspective can be seen to be quite limited and does little to displace the existentially based critical theory presented in Chapter 1.

The insights of such a dialectical approach relate to the interaction of the individual (the microstructural **P** level) with the wider sociopolitical context (the macrostructural **S** level). However, a dialectical approach need not be seen as a simple two-way process – it can be a set of interacting processes, as Figure 2.1 indicates. What poststructuralism and postmodernism can bring is a greater emphasis on the intermediary role of culture (the **C** level), particularly with regard to the role of language. Consequently, it is to the question of language that we now turn in order to explore the interrelationships between language, discourse and power.

Language, discourse and power

Spender (1990) makes the point that:

> Language helps form the limits of our reality. It is our means of ordering, classifying and manipulating the world. It is through language that we

become members of a human community; that the world becomes comprehensible and meaningful, that we bring into existence the world in which we live.

(p. 3)

This underlines the significance of language as a dimension of human existence, both as a means of making sense of the world and for communicating and interacting with others. Spender (1990) goes on to point out that this involves the workings of power, a point which she illustrates with reference to gender:

> Through my language and socialization I did learn to see as *sensible* many arrangements in my society which an 'outsider' (who did not share my socialization) would find absurd. So at one stage I did learn, for example, that it was sensible to give the least educational experience to those who appeared to take longer to learn. I did learn that it was sensible to classify some forms of skin pigmentation as possessing mystical powers. I did learn that it was sensible that one half of the population should be paid for their work while the other half should not. I did learn that it was sensible to ensure the survival of the species by amassing a vast arsenal that could destroy the planet many times over. And I did learn that it was sensible to see men as superior.
>
> (p. 3)

Language, then, is not only a system of communication but also a vehicle for power (Gergen, 1999).

◄ PRACTICE FOCUS 2.5 ►

As part of his professional training Kevin was required to undertake a project. For this he chose to analyse the significance of language in terms of the interactions between staff and patients. For several days he listened carefully and tried to identify patterns that might be significant. He was simply amazed by the results. He had not realized how significant language was in conveying subtleties of meaning, power relations, hidden agendas (or subtexts) and so on, until he undertook this practical project. This experience helped him to learn the importance of taking language issues very seriously and not dismissing them as trivial.

Language can be seen to be particularly significant in relation to working with people and their problems, and the power dynamics that operate in the interaction between helpers and those we are seeking to help. The following can be seen to be key issues in this regard:

• *Jargon* Although the use of specialized or technical language is necessary at times, there are also times when it is not appropriate. For example, in discussions with service users, jargon can create unnecessary barriers by reinforcing power differences between the two parties. In short, the inappropriate use of jargon can have the effect of alienating the people we are trying to help.

• *Stereotypes* Discrimination can be maintained by a reliance on stereotypical images and assumptions. For example, terms used to refer to older people tend to be unduly negative. Such negative stereotypes have the effect of reinforcing ageist ideology, and thereby bolstering the existing power relations in which older people are relatively disenfranchised (Thompson and Thompson, 2001).

• *Stigma* Some forms of language carry with them a degree of stigmatization. That is to say, certain terms or forms of speech can tarnish a particular individual, group or community. For example, in recent years, attempts have been made to move away from the use of terms such as 'mental handicap' as a result of the stigma associated with them.

• *Exclusion* Language can be 'exclusive', in the sense that some groups are overlooked or marginalized as a result of the use of certain forms of speech. A commonly cited example is that of 'chairman', a term that reinforces the notion that women do not belong in positions of power. Similarly, 'given name' is an inclusive term, whereas 'Christian name' is an exclusive one.

• *Depersonalization* Some terms have a depersonalizing or dehumanizing effect. Terms such as 'the elderly' and 'the disabled' have been criticized for their depersonalizing and derogatory connotations (Fennell *et al.*, 1988; Brisenden, 1986), while 'older *people*' and 'disabled *people*' are seen as far more appropriate. Similarly, the tendency to refer to a child as 'it' can be seen as problematic (Thompson, 1997b).

These are just some of the ways in which language has connections with power and can therefore contribute to the maintenance of inequality, discrimination and oppression. However, what needs to be emphasized is that the question of language is a complex one, and is not resolved by a simple lexicon of taboo words that are to be avoided. As I have argued previously:

> One problem with developing a sensitivity to the discriminatory poten-
> tial of language is that this complex area is often over-simplified and

trivialized. Many people see it as a simple matter of identifying certain 'bad' words (such as 'chairman' or 'blackleg') and trying to avoid them, without necessarily understanding why they should be avoided.

This approach is characterized by the term 'political correctness'. But this in itself is indicative of the deeper problem. The fact that 'political correctness' has become a term of ridicule illustrates the basic point – the power of language to reinforce existing power structures. Because the development of anti-discriminatory practice has cast light on the oppressive potential of language and the need for linguistic sensitivity, a new term has been coined to decry and undermine the focus on the power of language. The term 'political correctness', then, is not the solution – indeed it is a clear example of the problem.

(Thompson, 2002c, p. 94)

The political correctness (or 'PC') issue has had the unfortunate effect of distracting attention from important issues of power and oppression. It has created a lot of confusion and discouraged open debate about the relationship between language and power, inequality, discrimination and oppression. This is a point to which we shall return in Chapter 5.

Wheen (1996) provides a clear example of the distortions introduced to discredit attempts to challenge oppressive aspects of language use:

Anti-PC campaigners complain, with wearisome frequency, about the 'appropriation' by homosexuals of 'that fine old English word "gay"'; did they ever object to the anti-homosexuals' appropriation of the equally fine old English word 'queer'?

(p. 5)

While language has clear links with power, we also need to recognize that the related concept of discourse, as discussed in Chapter 1, is closely intertwined with power relations. As Hugman (1991) confirms, discourse is more than language. Discourse refers to frameworks of thought, meaning and action that have their roots in frameworks of language. As Burr (1995) comments:

A discourse refers to a set of meanings, metaphors, representations, images, stories, statements and so on that in some way together produce a particular version of events. It refers to a particular picture that is painted of an event (or person or class of persons), a particular way of representing it or them in a certain light.

(p. 48)

This can be linked to power in two ways: First, as Burr goes on to say:

> If we accept the view . . . that a multitude of alternative versions of events is potentially available through language, this means that, surrounding any one object, event, person etc., there may be a variety of different discourses, each with a different story to tell about the object in question, a different way of representing it to the world.
>
> (p. 48)

This variety of perspectives or frameworks creates the potential for conflict, for powerful people to present their construction of the world in ways that protect and consolidate their positions of power, at the expense of less powerful people. That is, discourses can be used ideologically.

Second, discourses relate to power in that they shape and constrain the way we see the world. As we noted in relation to social constructionism, there is no underlying absolute reality. Language in general and specific discourses in particular play a primary role in the construction of reality. As Roberts *et al.* (1992) comment:

> Language not only reflects and transmits the values and relationships of a society; it actively creates and maintains them. So all the time we are getting things done with language; we are creating a piece of reality and sanity for ourselves. We are constructing a social reality (Berger and Luckmann 1967), in the sense that we are making relationships and establishing roles and identities in the choices of language we make and our orientation to the world consists, in part, in our language behaviour. We are also acting out the social systems and structures which help us, as a society, to order the world and make sense of it, even if, as with many power structures, we do not benefit from them.
>
> (p. 67)

Gergen (1999) gives a very good example of this. He argues that, if a person believes he or she is depressed and needs to find a cure for that depression, then he or she is reflecting a story (a narrative or form of language) created by the mental health professionals. As he puts it: 'I have swallowed the medical model in which I am the one who requires a cure for my deficiency' (p. 173). Language and discourse, then, can be seen to play an important role in constructing the individual's sense of reality ('I am ill and need medical help to be cured').

Language can also play a part in concealing power. Certain forms of language use can have the effect of 'camouflaging' power relations, thereby reducing the likelihood of such power being resisted or challenged. Montgomery (1995) gives an example of this subtle operation of power through language when he discusses the use of what he calls 'known-answer' questions:

> asking of 'known-answer' questions . . . seems generally to be associated with situations where one participant assumes power and authority over another, a relationship which will often be displayed in the follow-up turn from the questioner, where prior knowledge of the answer will be revealed. Consider, for example, the following interchange between a mother and a teenage daughter:
>
> M: what time did you get in last night?
> D: oh about half eleven
> M: no it wasn't I heard you coming in around twelve-thirty
>
> (p. 199)

A further example of the interlinking of language and power is the actual choice of language used. For example, attitudes towards the Welsh language are a case in point (Morris and Williams, 1994). The choice of language can be just as significant as the choice of words, if not more so (Lynn and Muir, 1996). As Williams (1994) comments:

> The power, influence and significance of words have been acknowledged. For example, a consensus has been reached that some words and phrases are racist or sexist, part of the structure of oppression, and efforts have been made to ban them. Some attention has been paid to the use of interpreters with monoglot clients. It has been argued that words need to be defined so that change can take place. However, the debate about choosing to use one language rather than another, in this case English rather than Welsh, has not been developed to the same degree.
>
> (p. 175)

One problem that is commonly encountered is that speakers of a minority language may be perceived as less intelligent or less able than speakers of the dominant language. Once again, this is a question of power, with minority languages being devalued (Bellin, 1994). Here the potential for speakers of a minority language being discriminated against and oppressed is very great indeed.

◄ PRACTICE FOCUS 2.6 ►

Mair was placed with foster carers on a temporary basis only a few days after her eighth birthday, as a result of her mother's admission to hospital for an emergency operation. Mair was totally fluent in English, although Welsh was her first language, and the language she was used to using at home and at school. The foster carers spoke only English, and, in view of Mair's fluency in English, this was not seen as a problem. However, although Mair appeared to be settling in reasonably well in the circumstances, when it came to bedtime, she became extremely upset and distressed. This caused major problems, and was stressful for all concerned, including the foster carers' own two children. Eventually, after getting to know Mair a bit better, the foster carers began to realize what had caused her distress. The simple fact was that she was used to having her bedtime story in Welsh, and having to make do with a story in English had emphasized very strongly to her that she was not at home, and was not in an environment where she felt secure. From this, the foster carers, and subsequently the social worker, came to realize just how important language and linguistic identity are.

For speakers of some minority languages (Urdu or Punjabi, for example), the potential for linguistic oppression exists alongside the potential for racism. Consequently, there is a danger that the significance of language in its own right becomes submerged in the broader issues of racism (Thompson, 2001a). For speakers of other minority languages (Welsh or Gaelic, for example), there is no direct link with racism, although the danger here is that language issues will be dismissed as insignificant, their importance not recognized due to the ideological dominance of English – English is normalized (in Foucault's sense) as the 'natural' language of the UK. Bellin (1994) gives an example of how this can occur in practice – and how it can be challenged:

> [A] social worker in an area where very few people spoke Welsh was visiting a house and becoming frustrated in an interview with an adolescent. She had relied on English, not realizing that the family spoke Welsh. On getting up to leave, she heard the father say to the young man *'Gwed wrthi 'nawr, cyn iddi fynd'*. (Tell her now before she goes.) She resumed her seat and began again but this time in Welsh. The results were completely different. The reason for the difference was a complete realignment from the use of Welsh. There was a change of 'footing'. She was now aligned with the father's appeal, and much better placed to discuss problems.
>
> (pp. 116–17)

It should be abundantly clear at this stage that language and discourse are very significant with regard to the operations of power. This, in turn, raises a number of significant issues to be addressed in and through practice:

- Language both reflects and reinforces inequality. There is therefore a need to develop a sensitivity to language and the ways in which it can contribute to discrimination and oppression.
- Language can alienate. Some forms of language use bring people together, but others can produce distance and alienation. A lack of awareness of language issues can therefore create barriers to effective practice.
- Language issues are often trivialized. The notion of political correctness has come to be used as a device to distract attention from issues of power, inequality, discrimination and oppression. It is therefore necessary to challenge such trivialization and reassert the significance of language.
- The choice of language is a key issue. For those whose first language is not English, it is important that facilities for communication through their first language are available if required. Without this, there is a very real danger that intervention will be oppressive.
- Emancipatory practice has to take on board issues of language. Forms of practice that are not attuned to the subtleties of language run the risk of (a) missing significant issues and (b) reinforcing or amplifying existing inequalities.

The task of incorporating linguistic sensitivity into day-to-day practice is not always an easy matter. However, the problems arising from approaches that lack an awareness of language issues make the investment of time, effort and energy a worthwhile commitment of personal resources.

Empowerment

Thomas and Pierson (1995) describe empowerment theory as being: 'concerned with how people may gain collective control over their lives, so as to achieve their interests as a group, and a method by which . . . to enhance the power of people who lack it' (p. 134). The term 'empowerment' is therefore a very important one in relation to understanding power and inequality.

However, it is also a term that has developed into a fashionable buzzword, and is often used loosely and uncritically (Gomm, 1993). It is therefore important to be clear about how the term is being used if it is to play a part in the development of emancipatory practice. Empowerment is also a term used by some right-wing commentators to promote a notion of self-reliance as part of a process of discouraging reliance on collective or state measures. As Fawcett and Featherstone (1996) point out, referring to the work of Baistow (1995), empowerment has the potential to regulate as well as liberate. We therefore have to be very clear about the sense in which we are using the notion of empowerment. In view of this, I shall endeavour to clarify empowerment in the context of PCS analysis in order to give it a clear and explicit theoretical basis.

Empowerment can be seen to apply at each of the three levels:

- *Personal* Individuals can be helped to gain greater control over their lives in a variety of ways – for example, through the enhancement of confidence and self-esteem.
- *Cultural* Discriminatory assumptions and stereotypes can be challenged in an attempt to break down an oppressive culture in which the values and interests of dominant groups are presented as normal and natural. Empowerment at this level is therefore concerned with 'consciousness-raising', becoming aware of ideologies premised on inequality.
- *Structural* Power relations are rooted in the structure of society, and so empowerment at this level must involve the eradication, in the long term, of structured inequalities. This involves a collective political response, a concerted programme of action for social change.

Our actions can be very significant at the personal level, particularly in certain circumstances, such as when the individual we are working with is in crisis (Thompson, 1991a). In recent years there has been an increasing recognition of the part staff can play in challenging the cultural level, for example through rejecting discriminatory language and imagery. At a structural level, the extent to which staff and managers can influence the structure of society remains an open question. Two points, however, remain clear:

1. Change at a structural level is a much wider issue than professional practice. The role and influence of social policy are only a part of the much broader backcloth of the politics of radical social change (see the discussion of radicalism in Chapter 5).
2. Although the capacity to have an impact at the structural level is necessarily limited, the greater the degree of empowerment at the **P** and **C** levels, the greater will be the potential for change at the **S** level (see Figure 2.2).

These two points, in turn, identify the need to establish a balance between the two extremes of, on the one hand, a naïve approach that

Low level of empowerment

=

Structures continue
unchallenged

High level of empowerment

=

The potential for structural
change is increased

Figure 2.2   The relationship between personal empowerment and structural
change

assumes professional practice can bring about radical social change in its own right and, on the other, a defeatist approach which abandons any attempt to influence the contemporary social order. Both extremes are highly problematic and bring with them a number of dangers and difficulties, and are therefore significant barriers to empowerment. A naïve approach will tend to alienate potential supporters of empowerment because they reject the uncritical reductionism on which such an approach is based (Sibeon, 1992, 1996). At the other extreme, a defeatist approach will tend to miss opportunities for making a positive contribution towards breaking down the walls of oppression. A positive contribution, however small, is far preferable to defeatism, for, as I argued in Chapter 1, if we are not committed to being part of the solution, we become part of the problem.

Empowerment is a complex process, and one that requires a great deal of further analysis and research if its full potential as a strategy for countering inequality, discrimination and oppression is to be realized. It is a theme to which I shall return at various points in the chapters that follow. As Dalrymple and Burke (1995) recognize, empowerment is a key issue in relation to power and inequality:

> An empowerment perspective which assumes that issues of power and powerlessness are integral to the experience of the service user enables us to move away from pathologizing individuals to increasing personal, interpersonal or political power so that individuals can take action to improve their life situations. Within the existing models of social care practice there is a focus on the individual – problems are individualized (blame the victim syndrome). Interventions often focus on assisting individuals to cope with or accept a difficult situation rather than changing the situation on a structural level.
>
> (p. 52)

A further aspect of empowerment worthy of comment is its relationship to the capacity for social change. Central to the notion of empowerment, as used in the context of emancipatory theory and practice, is the potential for social amelioration, a belief in the possibility and value of people working towards a more just and equal society. Fiske (1996) captures this in the following comment, where he identifies a core element of empowerment:

> The people are neither cultural dupes nor silenced victims, but are vital, resilient, varied, contradictory, and, as a constant source of contestation of dominance, are a vital social resource, the only one that can fuel social change.
>
> (p. 220)

Empowerment, then, involves seeking to use this potential, this fundamental resource, as the basis of emancipation from oppressive practices, assumptions and structures.

◀ **PRACTICE FOCUS 2.7** ▶

Rashid was a relatively inexperienced youth worker. He felt reasonably confident in what he was doing but was well aware that he still had a lot to learn and that he was making too many mistakes. One night, after finishing a groupwork session with a group of boys, he started to take a greater pride in his work. After working with the group for a little while, he was now able to see the changes emerging, to see how the boys were developing and were taking a lot more responsibility for themselves – he was witnessing empowerment in action, and this in turn made him feel more empowered, more positive about making a difference to young people's lives.

Conclusion

This chapter has explored a range of important issues that relate to the distribution of power and its impact on professional practice. In some ways, this is a counterbalance to traditional approaches which have tended to neglect or minimize the significance of power (Hugman, 1991).

By exploring the nature of power and competing theoretical explanations of power issues, I have sought to emphasize both the complexity and the significance of power as a factor in working with people and their problems. In one chapter it has not been possible to address all aspects of power – it is such a major topic that even a whole book would not do full justice to the subject.

The question of power will arise at various points in the ensuing chapters, as it will be a recurring theme in our attempts to understand, and respond to, inequality, discrimination and oppression. In addition, Chapter 6 addresses the organizational context of professional practice, and here again power can be seen as a crucial issue in terms of understanding organizational structures, cultures and dynamics. The close of this chapter, then, is by no means the end of our considerations of the question of power. It is far too important, wide-ranging and fundamental a subject to be restricted to one specific chapter.

'People work' necessarily involves a range of interactions, and it is through such interactions that power so often manifests itself. As Sibeon (1992) comments:

> Power is *emergent*, in the sense of being an *outcome* of social interactions: power, to paraphrase Law's (1986, p. 5) definition, is an *effect* not a *cause* of strategic success achieved by actors during their interactions with other actors in particular situations or in a series of situations. Actors may become more powerful, or less powerful: this is because their capacity to shape events or to obtain their objectives is not a structurally bestowed, predetermined or 'fixed' capacity. Actors contingently grow or reduce in size: they have no structurally predetermined 'size' (Callon and Latour, 1981, p. 280).
>
> (p. 35)

'Actors may become more powerful, or less powerful' is a key issue here, as this is where empowerment comes to the fore. The actions of staff and managers can help people become more powerful (empowerment/emancipation) or can reinforce their sense of powerlessness (disempowerment/oppression). It is for this reason that an understanding of power issues is necessary in order to increase the likelihood of a positive, empowering outcome.

Having explored power at a generalized level, it is now time to consider more specific examples of the use of power as it relates to issues of discrimination and oppression. This is the subject matter of Chapter 3 in which the focus of attention is on processes of discrimination, forms of oppression, and the interrelationships between the two.

3

DISCRIMINATION AND OPPRESSION

Introduction

Promoting equality, as we have seen, involves countering discrimination and oppression. This chapter therefore examines:

- the relationship between discrimination and oppression;
- the various processes by which discrimination occurs;
- the ways in which discrimination can be categorized; and
- the forms of oppression that arise as a result of the various categories of discrimination.

These issues are important in terms of both theory and practice. From a theoretical point of view, the questions addressed in this chapter can help to develop our understanding of some of the complexities surrounding inequality. In relation to practice, the issues discussed here have very significant implications for practitioners seeking to promote equality.

The relationship between discrimination and oppression

Many people use the term 'anti-discriminatory practice' in a broad sense to refer to forms of practice that challenge discrimination and oppression while others take a lead from Phillipson (1992) in drawing a distinction between anti-*discriminatory* practice and anti-*oppressive* practice, reserving the former for a narrow, legalistic approach to inequality. As Thomas and Pierson (1995) comment:

> Some writers have . . . begun to suggest that anti-discriminatory practice might usefully be defined as work designed to address specific, legally defined injustices. Anti-oppressive practice might then be agreed to mean wider social analyses that begin to challenge structures and thereby help people challenge individual aspects of oppression. These

may well be useful distinctions but they are not widely understood in this way and do not have wide currency.

(p. 19)

This is not a distinction I shall be using here, as I do not find it a particularly helpful one. A narrow, legalistic approach is unlikely to challenge discrimination effectively and does not therefore merit the title 'anti-discriminatory'.

Due to the potential confusion over terminology, it is necessary to be clear about how the terms are being used. I shall therefore define discrimination as the process (or set of processes) by which people are allocated to particular social categories with an unequal distribution of rights, resources, opportunities and power. It is a process through which certain groups and individuals are disadvantaged and oppressed. As such, it is a major obstacle to dignity, equality and social justice. As was noted in Chapter 1, processes of discrimination occur at three separate but interrelated levels: personal, cultural and structural. The interactions of these three levels produce a very complex and dynamic matrix which attests to the need to develop an understanding of discrimination at a higher level than a simple focus on personal prejudice or bigotry.

One of the main outcomes of discrimination is oppression. The relationship between discrimination and oppression can therefore be seen as largely a causal one: discrimination gives rise to oppression. Consequently, in order to challenge oppression, it is necessary to tackle discrimination. It is for this reason that I shall now move on to examine some of the main processes that contribute to discrimination (Figure 3.1). I shall concentrate on themes that apply across a range of different forms of discrimination, rather than on particular ones.

Processes of discrimination

In order to develop a clearer and fuller picture of how discrimination occurs I shall present an exposition of eight processes that are closely associated with inequality, discrimination and oppression. This is by no means an exhaustive list, nor are the processes discussed here necessarily mutually exclusive – indeed, there is a very strong tendency for the processes to interact, combine and reinforce one another.

Stereotyping

The processing of information is a complex matter, with an extensive literature base of cognitive psychology. In order to deal with the

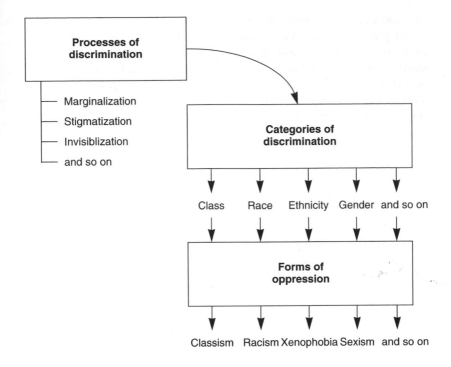

Figure 3.1   Discrimination and oppression

masses of sensory information that we encounter at every moment, it is necessary for the sensory data to be filtered and simplified. One of the ways in which this is achieved is through 'typification'. This involves establishing what is 'typical' of a particular class of things, events, people or phenomena. For example, if we meet, say, a policeman, we will not 'start with a clean sheet' in terms of what we would expect of him – we are likely to start with an idea of what a 'typical' policeman is like. We would then form an impression of how this particular policeman compares with our expectations. A typification is a form of yardstick by which we make sense of some of the complexities of the social world. As such, it is a type of category that allows us to sort our day-to-day experiences in such a way that we feel comfortable with them.

Such typifications are often interlinked – they form a pattern or network. For example, a 'typical' policewoman would share some characteristics with the 'typical' policeman, but would be different in significant ways. Networks of typifications form a major part of our understanding of our world and therefore play an important role in maintaining a coherent thread of meaning and sustaining a sense of ontological security. Typifications are broad categories and do not generally provide the information we need to deal with a specific individual. We therefore have to adjust or even abandon the typification according to how we perceive the individual – typifications are (or should be) the beginning of the process of understanding rather than the end. However, at times, typifications can become fixed and rigid – they can become *stereotypes*. Stereotypes have a number of characteristics:

- They are resistant to change in so far as they tend not to be dissuaded by logic or evidence.
- They are often unduly negative and therefore potentially oppressive.
- They become so ingrained that we tend not to notice that they are there and affecting our perceptions and actions.

Argyle and Colman (1995) offer a useful definition of a stereotype:

> Stereotype from the Greek *stereos*, solid, *tupos*, type, an over-simplified, biased and above all inflexible conception of a social group. The word was originally used in the printing trade for a solid metallic plate which was difficult to alter once cast.
>
> (p. 104)

Stereotypes are frequently closely associated with oppressed groups and actually act as a vehicle for maintaining such oppression. They are an important element of the C level of discrimination. That is, a stereotype is not simply a personal prejudice – it is part of the culture that is 'transmitted' from one generation to the next, thereby proving instrumental in maintaining existing power relations. In this respect, stereotypes are ideological – they encapsulate the power of ideas acting as weapons of social interest.

In order to guard against the oppressive use of stereotypes, it is necessary to become sensitive to stereotypical assumptions, to become aware of how they can subtly shape our interactions. This is an important part of reflective practice (Thompson, 2000a).

◀ PRACTICE FOCUS 3.1 ▶

The training course on anti-discriminatory practice was very well received. In particular, the participants enjoyed, and benefited from, the session on stereotypes. It was a little worrying, but none the less instructive, to realize how easily and quickly people were able to identify stereotypes of various groups of people – and just how deeply ingrained and resistant to change these stereotypical assumptions can be.

Marginalization

This process refers to the ways in which certain groups of people are pushed to the margins of society, and thus excluded from the mainstream. For example, the recognition of disablism as a significant social force entails an understanding of how disabled people tend to be marginalized by:

- social attitudes that patronize, infantilize (see below) and devalue disabled people;
- physical barriers that deny access to certain buildings or areas;
- a lack of positive steps to enable disabled people to participate fully in social, political and economic activities.

Oliver (1996) uses the education system as an example of marginalization:

> The majority of British schools, colleges and universities remain unprepared to accommodate disabled students within a mainstream setting. Thus, many young disabled people have little choice but to accept a particular form of segregated 'special' education which is both educationally and socially divisive, and fails to provide them with the necessary skills for adult living. By producing educationally and socially disabled adults in this way, the special educational system perpetuates the misguided assumption that disabled people are somehow inadequate, and thus legitimates discrimination in all other areas of their lives.
>
> (p. 64)

However, the process does not apply only to disabled people. It refers more broadly to the experience of all oppressed groups, as it is a characteristic of oppression that the people so affected are excluded from decision-making processes and the operations of power in general.

A further example of marginalization arises in relation to language use. As was noted in Chapter 2, where a person's first language is not the dominant one in the society concerned, he or she is likely to experience some degree of linguistic oppression. Speakers of a minority language are therefore likely to encounter marginalization – to have their concerns and issues pushed to one side, ignored or not taken seriously.

Again, emancipatory forms of practice need to be based on a degree of sensitivity, a raised level of awareness of how easy it can be to rein-force patterns of marginalization unwittingly, simply by making 'common-sense' assumptions. It is necessary to develop a critical awareness of how certain groups are systematically discriminated against through this process of marginalization.

Invisiblization

This is a process that has much in common with marginalization but refers specifically to how groups are represented in language and imagery. The basic idea is that powerful, dominant groups are con-stantly presented to us – for example through the media – and are strongly associated with positions of power, status, prestige and influ-ence, while other groups are rarely, if ever, seen in this light – it is as if they have been rendered invisible.

The process is often associated with sexism, particularly in relation to gender-specific terminology which contributes to a masculine-based conception of the world. The clear examples are terms such as chair*man* and *man*power, terms that reinforce the notion that positions of power or places in the public sphere of the world of paid work are not for women. However, there are very many other examples of how this subtle process operates. Spender (1990) discusses the ways in which women's sexuality is constructed as subordinate to men's and thereby invisiblized. She comments on the significance of the term 'penetration' and quotes Susan Brownmillar (1977, p. 334):

> The sex act . . . has as its 'modus operandi' something men call penetra-tion. Penetration however describes what the man does. The feminist Barbara Mehrhof has suggested that if women were in charge of sex and the language, the same act could well be called enclosure – a revolu-tionary concept . . .
>
> (p. 178)

Walter *et al.* (1995) provide another example of invisiblization in rela-tion to the ways in which death is reported in the media. They present a study of the way deaths are reported in newspapers and reveal sig-nificant differences in terms of gender. For example, where murders or other high-profile deaths were reported, men would often be quoted on the front page, while women's comments tended to be paraphrased rather than quoted directly. This reflects the distinction between the private sphere of the home and family and the public sphere of paid work, politics and society, with the front page of newspapers clearly being located in the public sphere and therefore not a domain for women. It is clearly in the public sphere that women are consistently and systematically rendered invisible and thereby excluded.

Gender, of course, is not the only aspect of invisiblization. The process can also be seen to apply to older people, as evidenced by the work of Midwinter (1991) where he demonstrates that older people are seriously underrepresented in the media compared with the actual proportion of society they make up. Similar points have been made in relation to disability (Barnes, 1992).

The process is an example of social construction, a reflection of the complex and intricate network of ways in which social reality is defined in accordance with dominant power relations and the discourses that reinforce and maintain those relations. By 'invisiblizing' relatively powerless people, dominant social groups are able to maintain their hegemony relatively unchallenged.

Infantilization

As we shall see later in this chapter, ageism involves the differential allocation of power, rights, resources and life chances according to age. That is, age is socially significant. In view of this, to ascribe a childlike status to an adult can be seen as a form of disempowerment, a denial of rights and citizenship. The following examples of 'infantilization' are therefore very significant in terms of power, discrimination and oppression:

- Referring to women as 'girls', for example – 'the girls in the office'. Many women find this type of reference offensive and demeaning. However, even where the women concerned do not object, it is still problematic. This is because infantilization reinforces power differentials. It is interesting to note, for example, that a woman in a position of power is far less likely to be referred to as a girl. A female Chief Executive is unlikely to be referred to as 'the girl who runs the organization'.
- Older people are also subject to infantilization. Hockey and James (1993) argue that:

> the 'babytalk' sometimes used by nurses with their sick or geriatric patients and the state legislation which often effectively excludes elderly people from paid work in mainstream economic life are both manifestations of a key logical cognitive structure through which human dependency is created and re-created in Western cultures. Traceable in a series of shared concepts and models, the metaphor of the child provides one important vehicle for and structure within which human dependency of whatever kind is understood.
>
> (p. 13)

- People with physical or learning disabilities or mental health problems also tend to be on the receiving end of this demeaning process. The 'Does s/he take sugar? syndrome', as it is often called, is testimony to the tendency to regard certain groups of people as childlike and dependent, unable to communicate or interact in their own right.

Sometimes infantilizing language can be used as a deliberate 'putdown', but is much more likely to be used in an unthinking, routine way – a pattern of communication that we have learned through socialization. We learn to accept infantilizing language as 'natural' and 'normal'. Infantilization, then, can be seen in line with the distinction I introduced in Chapter 1 – as an unwitting misuse of power, rather than a deliberate abuse of power. It is therefore a process that can be addressed, in part at least, through consciousness-raising and a greater degree of linguistic sensitivity. It is also important to note that it is not only the words used that can have an infantilizing effect, but also other features of communication, such as tone of voice or body language. Unless this important point is taken on board, there is a danger that non-infantilizing words will be used, but the net effect may none the less be one of infantilization.

◀ **PRACTICE FOCUS 3.2** ▶

Mrs Davies attended the day centre for older people for the first time and was initially very pleased with the welcome she received and the nice atmosphere there. However, one thing she did not like, and which made her feel very uncomfortable, was that the staff, many of them very young, referred to her as Margaret, rather than Mrs Davies. She had been brought up in times when the use of first names was regarded as overfamiliar, especially to be referred to as such by someone much younger. As far as Mrs Davies was concerned, it was only children who should be referred to by their first names unless and until there was a close relationship between the people concerned. What really added insult to injury for Mrs Davies was that her friends did not call her Margaret anyway – she had always been referred to as Peggy, but no one had taken the trouble to ask her how she wished to be addressed.

Welfarism

This is a term that refers to the tendency to regard certain groups as being necessarily in need of welfare services by virtue of their membership of such groups. Fennell *et al.* (1988) argue that older people tend to be 'welfarized'. That is, there is a commonly held assumption that being over a certain age brings with it infirmity, incapacity and therefore a need for welfare support through health or social services.

The prevalence of this type of assumption tends to be problematic in a number of ways:

- *It is stereotypical.* It ascribes the characteristics of some members of a group to the whole of that group, despite evidence to the contrary.
- *It is demeaning.* To have someone assume that you are in need of supportive services when you are not can be experienced as demeaning and patronizing.
- *It creates dependency.* Dependency, and the loss of rights and power that go with it, is socially constructed by such assumptions (Phillipson and Thompson, 1996).
- *It reinforces discriminatory discourses.* Welfarism presents older people as a group in need of (expensive) support services, and therefore a social burden and a drain on the economy (Thompson, 1995a).

Older people, however, are not the only group of people to which welfarism can be applied. Disabled people form a further group who have tended to be subject to welfarism. The Disabled People's Movement has, over the years, been very critical of the overemphasis on disabled people's care needs at the expense of their rights.

Medicalization

To ascribe the status of 'ill' to someone is an act imbued with considerable social significance. That is, there are social consequences that derive from the application of such a label. These include:

- *Invalid status* Laing (1965) points out that the tendency to treat sick people as invalids equates with a tendency to treat them as 'invalid' – that is, not valid. To define a person as ill is to remove from him or her some degree of status.
- *Welfarism* The label 'ill' also attracts welfarist responses, as discussed above, with a focus on care rather than rights.
- *Medical discourse and power* Illness places people in the domain of the medical profession. Doctors and associated personnel are given considerable power within a discourse that presents them as experts.

Health and illness are complex issues that require close examination. It is for this reason that Chapter 4 is devoted to the subject of health and its relationship with inequality, discrimination and oppression.

The question of the medicalization of social issues will therefore be an important theme in that chapter. For present purposes, however, it is important to note that:

- Illness is a social as well as physical entity and is therefore significant in terms of power.
- An uncritical use of medical terminology to describe psychological and social factors can have detrimental effects on the people concerned.
- Medicalization is a subtle process that operates at an ideological level. That is, it generally works 'beneath the surface', without our realizing that it is there.

Some of the significant practice implications that arise from these points will be explored in Chapter 4.

Dehumanization

The significance of language as a factor in social relations has already received attention. However, what needs to be emphasized here is the role of language in dehumanization – that is, treating people as things. This can apply in a number of ways, as the following examples illustrate:

- It is not uncommon for certain marginalized groups to be referred to in an impersonal, dehumanized way: 'the elderly', 'the disabled' and so on. Such terms are so well established that they are commonly used without their significance being realized.
- The term 'they' is often used to refer to an individual, particularly someone with learning difficulties. An example of this would be a comment such as the following: 'Tony has got a cold again. He has Down's Syndrome and they catch cold easily.' Tony is presented not as an individual human being but as a member of an amorphous, impersonal group: 'they'.
- In health care settings patients may be referred to by their particular illness or condition. The person with appendicitis becomes simply: 'The appendicitis'. The free human subject becomes a powerless object within a medical discourse.
- Where the specific gender of a child is not known, it is often the case that he or she will be referred to as 'it' (Thompson, 1997b).

What these examples have in common is the theme of powerlessness. In general, it is relatively powerless people who are subjected to dehumanization. Indeed, it can be seen that the process of dehumanization both reflects and constructs such powerlessness. It also reinforces power relations by undermining self-esteem and discouraging acts of personal initiative. As such, it is a form of disempowerment. In view of the destructive effects of this process, it is important that professional practice does not support or contribute to it. A primary feature of this is, as argued earlier, a sensitivity to language. However, although language is clearly the central vehicle for the process of dehumanization, we should also recognize the broader aspects which support and sustain it: images, gestures, actions and interactions – all of which can undermine an individual's or group's humanity, thereby devaluing and alienating the people concerned. As Birt (1997) comments:

> Oppression robs people of their identity as surely as exploitation robs people of the fruits of their labor. Oppression imposes rigid, stultifying identities on its victims. Often it imposes a deformed consciousness on the oppressed which helps to reinforce the very system of oppression which deforms them.
>
> (p. 206)

Trivialization

Promoting equality necessarily involves challenging existing social arrangements and power relations, and so we should not be surprised when attempts are made to counter or undermine such challenges. Trivialization can be seen as one such attempt, as well as a primary form of discrimination in its own right.

An example of trivialization in relation to sexism is the undue attention given to the question of whether it is appropriate for a man to hold a door open for a woman. By concentrating excessively on a relatively minor aspect of gender relations, attention is distracted from the more important aspects of sexist oppression (domestic violence, for example – Mullender, 1996; Taylor-Browne, 2001). At the same time, the whole topic of gender inequality becomes a subject of ridicule, a petty matter not worthy of serious consideration. In this way, trivialization operates as a powerful process that plays an important role in maintaining relations of inequality.

Where attempts to challenge discrimination are made, trivialization can be brought to bear to counter these. An example of this that we have already encountered is that of 'political correctness'. As Wise (1995) puts it: '"political correctness" – a catch-all and derisory term used to discredit all positive action against oppression' (p. 106).

Trivialization is a difficult process to counter in so far as it tends to have the effect of 'upping the stakes'. That is, anyone who challenges trivialization runs the risk of actually being trivialized in response (see Practice Focus 3.3), thereby leading to a situation of potential escalation. Consequently, it is important that such situations are handled sensitively and carefully and, moreover, that people are prepared to support each other in challenging examples of trivialization, so that collusion does not leave an individual feeling isolated and unsupported.

◀ **PRACTICE FOCUS 3.3** ▶

Jenny worked in a staff group that was predominantly male, and which paid little or no attention to issues of gender sensitivity. When she first started to raise such issues, she found that she was being very gently, but none the less firmly, put down, mainly through a process of trivialization. Her comments were seen as 'interesting quirks', rather than serious issues, and the more she spoke about them, the more she was made to feel that she was making a fuss over nothing. Consequently, in order to avoid being labelled as 'awkward' or a 'troublemaker', she sought the support of some of her female colleagues. It was only at this point, when a number of women expressed their concerns together, that the question of gender equality received any attention at all, and it was clear from the response of some of the men that it was not going to be easy to keep the issues on the agenda.

Categories of discrimination

Having considered some of the processes through which discrimination occurs, we can now move on to explore the main categories of discrimination. Such categories are, of course, not absolute or definitive entities – they are intended as a helpful way of breaking down a very complex reality into manageable components in order to aid understanding. In view of this, we need to recognize that such categories are:

- *Contested* There will be competing definitions and conceptualizations, in accordance with different theoretical and/or ideological positions (class is a prime example of this, as we shall see below).
- *Subject to change* Ideas about which forms of categorization are most helpful or appropriate are likely to change over time as they evolve in response to new situations and new understandings.
- *Potentially misleading* Although used as an aid to understanding, categories do not always fit neatly with the complex realities of the social world. We should therefore use them with caution.

I shall discuss in outline six categories or 'social divisions' and explore the discrimination and oppression associated with each of these.

Class and classism

Class is a very complex issue with widely different theoretical conceptualizations. These range from marxist analyses in which class position is determined in relation to ownership of the means of production (factories, machinery and so on) to those of Weber and his followers in which class is related to market position. Marx divided society into two main classes, the bourgeoisie who own the means of production and the proletariat who have to sell their labour (to the bourgeoisie) in order to survive. There have been major changes in society since Marx's time, and so his basic model can no longer be seen to apply in contemporary society. However, there have been many developments of marxist thought that seek to adapt and update his basic tenets (see, for example, Giddens, 1995).

Marxist analyses focus on production as the key element in class allocation. That is, people's class positions are determined by their relationship to the production of material goods. Weber, by contrast, preferred to emphasize market position as the key determinant of class membership (Giddens, 1972). He focused on a person's ability to purchase within the market, rather than the role the person played in producing the goods being purchased. Weber also stressed wider social factors, such as status or honour – life chances or opportunities are governed by social as well as economic factors.

Weberian analyses have strongly influenced modern conceptions of class, such as the Registrar General's classification which is based primarily on occupational group and income. Class is therefore commonly understood as a hierarchy or 'ladder', with an individual's or family's position on that ladder being determined by socioeconomic factors – social in terms of status and education and economic in terms of occupation and income.

A further difference between the perspectives of Marx and Weber arises from their views of social change. From a marxist perspective, class groups are potential instigators of social change, particularly the proletariat in banding together to challenge the dominance of the bourgeoisie. For Weber, by contrast, class and the related concepts of status and party are conservative forces in so far as they have a divisive social effect and thereby prevent the coming together of major class groups to challenge the status quo (Figure 3.2).

Class is a complex sociological, political and economic concept that

Marx	Weber
Class as:	Class as:
a unifying force	a divisive force
based on relationship to the means of production	based on relations of exchange
a source of social change	a source of social stability

Figure 3.2   Marx's and Weber's approaches to class

has significant implications in relation to inequality, as we shall see in later chapters. It has been possible only to scratch the surface here.

The form of oppression that arises from the social division of class is sometimes known as 'classism', although this is not a term that has become as firmly or widely established as the parallel terms of sexism and racism. None the less, whether or not the term classism is used, we can recognize distinct patterns of oppression that are related to socioeconomic position, not least the following:

Economic deprivation   Economic inequalities have been shown to be of major proportions, leaving many people in circumstances of significant poverty. Jones and Novak (1999) make the following important points:

> The poorer people are, the less long they will live, the more disease they will suffer and the more stunted will be their lives than those of the rich. Currently this is reflected in the fact that in Britain infant mortality is four times higher amongst the poorest than it is amongst the richest of the population, while once beyond childhood, life expectancy is cut short by some seven or eight years. Although these consequences have only been reliably measured for the past 100 years, it has always been thus. That this is well known – and there are volumes of research, both official and unofficial, that document the consequences of poverty – does not make any difference.
>
> (p. 108)

Poverty is not simply a matter of a shortage of financial resources. The reality is far more complex, with significant implications in terms of:

- Psychological well-being, particularly in relation to self-esteem;
- Social relations – low income groups can be marginalized or excluded in certain social situations;
- Insecurity – economic deprivation can make it difficult, if not impossible, to plan ahead or develop a 'lifeplan';

- Access to resources and services – for example, health and education (see below).

Poverty is a contested concept, in the sense that different people define it in different ways – and different definitions will, of course, produce different policy responses and different attempted solutions. Novak (1988) points out that: 'To be poor is not just to have less than others; it is also to be without the means of securing the necessary requirements of life' (p. 3). What constitutes the 'necessary requirements of life' is a matter for debate. At one extreme, they are seen in 'subsistence' terms, the bare essentials to avoid death from thirst, hunger or cold. Others, however, see these requirements in broader terms and conceive of poverty as not having the means to participate in mainstream social activities (giving birthday presents, going on holiday and so on – Townsend, 1979). In this latter sense poverty is a form of social exclusion.

Although economic deprivation is clearly an important aspect of class as a social division, it is by no means the only one. Class impinges on a variety of aspects of social life.

Educational disadvantage Educational inequalities have received considerable attention from sociologists over the years (see, for example, Halsey *et al.*, 1980). Although the literature is by no means undisputed, some common features can be discerned:

- Class position can affect educational achievement (Reid, 1992).
- Working-class cultural norms may dissuade many people from investing time and energy in education, due to a 'clash of cultures' (Bourdieu, 1988).
- The material circumstances of a family can affect the age at which a child leaves school and whether or not opportunities for further or higher education are taken up.
- Educational inequalities can then become part of a vicious circle in which educational disadvantage affects life chances more broadly in terms of employment opportunities, prestige or status and access to other resources. The recent emphasis on competition between schools and greater selectivity for parents can be seen as a push in the direction of greater inequality rather than less (Hill, 1993).

Inequalities in health The significant class differences in terms of health and disease have been well documented since the 1980s, the Black Report (Townsend *et al.*, 1988) being a significant milestone in this regard. These issues are a key feature of Chapter 4 and so I shall not comment further at this point.

Classism could also be applied as a relevant concept in a range of other issues, such as the criminal justice system, housing policies and, of course, the judgemental attitudes that assume that working-class people are less intelligent, less motivated and less trustworthy than their middle-class counterparts. Bevan (2002) points out that class is even very relevant in terms of how people are treated when they are dying or bereaved.

Race and racism

The assumption that people can legitimately be divided into biologically based categories or 'races' is a long-standing one. It is none the less a false assumption. As Husband (1987) comments, the very concept of 'race' is a highly problematic one:

> 'As a way of categorising people, race is based upon a delusion because popular ideas about racial classification lack scientific validity and are moulded by political pressures rather than by the evidence from biology' (Banton and Harwood, 1975, p. 8). In identifying the fallacious nature of racial classification Banton and Harwood very appropriately refer to its use as delusionary; for like very many other delusions, racial categorization is remarkably resistant to change and extinction. I would like to propose that one reason for its continuing vitality is that, beneath its apparently simple reduction of complex individuals and societies to self-evidently basic units there lies a highly complex body of emotive ideas. These are ideas which reach out in their reference and significance beyond the immediate forms of racial categorization as such. Rather they invoke a rich matrix of values and images referring to purity–pollution, Christianity–Heathens, national–alien, among others. 'Race', like 'love', is a word often used with innocent spontaneity, and yet it remains highly problematic to determine adequately the boundaries of its denotative and connotative meanings.
>
> (p. iii)

This is a significant passage in so far as it indicates that:

- Racial categories are social constructions rather than biological types.
- Despite the lack of a biological basis to racial categorization, it remains a firmly established concept in everyday thoughts and actions.
- This concept is a very significant and emotive one closely associated with people's values.

• Although widely used in both everyday and academic thinking, race is a highly complex and problematic term.

Race is, then, a social construction, a way of making sense of the world by dividing people into assumed biological categories. However, these categories are not seen as neutral or value-free. What we encounter instead is a hierarchy of racial groups in which white groups are presented as superior to black groups (Ahmad, 1990). And it is this notion that introduces racism, the systematic oppression of certain groups through processes of discrimination that occur at the P, C and S levels.

Although race as a biological category can be seen to be a delusion, racism is certainly not a delusion: 'Whatever racism means in popular thought, it is a social construct that describes a very real human phenomenon and cannot be dismissed as delusion, nor can it always be demonstrated directly and concretely' (Bowser, 1996, p. xi).

While racism has its roots in biologically based ideological assumptions it can also be seen to apply in terms of cultural or ethnic differences. That is, even where biological differences are not assumed to occur, racism can occur by virtue of certain cultural groups none the less being seen as inferior to others. This is what is sometimes referred to as the 'new racism' (Solomos and Back, 1996).

◀ PRACTICE FOCUS 3.4 ▶

Abu was the only black worker in the team but generally felt as reasonably comfortable as he could in a predominantly white environment and atmosphere. He found his colleagues were generally aware of issues of racism and had at least a basic degree of commitment to equality. However, one day, over a cup of coffee, he became involved in a discussion about racism with some of his colleagues. In the course of this informal discussion he became quite perturbed by some of the comments his colleague, Mark, was making. The gist of Mark's views appeared to be that, while the idea of racism was clearly mistaken because it made false assumptions about biological differences between 'races', he had some sympathy for the notion that some cultures are more 'advanced' than others, and were more in tune with what he regarded as a civilized society. Abu found it amazing that Mark, while sensitive to biologically based racism, could not see that this form of cultural superiority argument was equally racist.

Through the assumption of biological or cultural inferiority, racism has a profound effect on the lives of black people or members of minority ethnic groups more broadly. This negative impact can take many forms, including the following:

- Racial violence and harassment (Skellington 1996).
- Inequalities in housing (Mason, 2000); health care (Bayne-Smith, 1996; Ahmad, 1993a); employment (Brown, 1992); education (Gill *et al.*, 1992) and social welfare provision (Burke and Harrison, 2000).
- Derogatory humour and stereotypical representations, for example in the media (McLean, 1996).
- Unfair treatment in the criminal justice system (Skellington, 1996).
- A greater likelihood of being detained in a psychiatric hospital (Watters, 1996).

There is a strong need for these issues to be given adequate attention across the helping professions. Culley and Dyson (2001a) argue that there is considerable evidence to suggest that Britain's health services: 'are not adequately meeting the needs of minority ethnic groups . . . and recent research has been critical of the educational preparation of nurses for professional practice in a multi-ethnic society (Gerrish *et al.* 1996)' (p. 1). And, of course, nurses are by no means the only group of staff yet to get their house in order when it comes to addressing racism.

While some examples of racism are overt and explicit (verbal abuse or physical attacks, for example) others can be more subtle and less noticeable. Carmichael and Hamilton (1969, p. 20) comment on the significance of institutional racism in this regard. They argue that institutional racism:

> is less overt, far more subtle, less identifiable in terms of specific individuals committing the acts . . . [it] originates in the operation of established forces in the society, and thus receives far less public condemnation . . . But it is institutional racism that keeps black people locked in dilapidated slum tenements, subject to the daily prey of exploitative landlords, merchants, loan sharks and discriminatory real estate agents.
>
> (Cited in Ginsburg, 1992, pp. 110–11)

Institutional racism was an important factor identified in the inquiry into the murder of Stephen Lawrence – the Macpherson Report (Macpherson, 1999). For a discussion of the importance of this report, see Marlow and Loveday (2000). This book specifically addresses policing issues, but raises important issues for a wide range of professional groups.

Institutional racism is closely linked to the S level, the structural level of macrosocial and political factors. Racism is therefore part of the way society is organized and reflects Britain's history of imperialism.

Racism, then, needs to be understood as not simply prejudiced beliefs and actions, nor simply a set of discriminatory assumptions, stereotypes and representations (the C level), it is also an important aspect of the social structure – it is a fundamental social division within the contemporary social order. As was argued in Chapter 1, an adequate understanding of racism (and discrimination and oppression more generally) needs to be based on PCS analysis. That is, it needs to incorporate all three levels.

It is on the basis of PCS analysis that we can argue that professional practice should be premised on anti-racism, rather than simply non-racism. For example, if I seek to ensure that my actions and attitudes do not involve elements of racism, but I do not challenge the racist actions or attitudes of others, the cultural representations or structural forces that maintain them, then I am leaving the oppressive framework of racism intact. I remain part of the problem, rather than part of the solution.

Anti-racist practice involves taking a proactive stance against racial oppression in whatever form it manifests itself, rather than merely attempting to salve our own consciences by avoiding committing racist actions or making racist utterances. In effect, to abstain from challenging racism amounts to voting for the status quo of widespread racial oppression.

A further implication of PCS analysis is that racism is a matter of outcome rather than intention. That is, even where our intentions are not racist, if the outcome is that an ethnic minority group are disadvantaged, discriminated against or oppressed, then our actions can legitimately be described as racist, as the following passage indicates:

> Minimisation . . . describes the tendency to play down the issues of discrimination and oppression, for example by arguing that: 'There aren't many black people around here, so racism isn't really an issue.' . . . To argue that ethnically sensitive and anti-racist practice is not relevant in predominantly white areas is to argue that services on offer are tailored primarily to meet the needs of white people – and this clearly has racist implications.
>
> (Thompson *et al.*, 1994a, p. 20)

To ignore the needs of black people is to condone racism, to reinforce existing inequalities and injustices. Anti-racism therefore needs to involve a degree of both self-awareness and awareness of important issues relating to the circumstances of ethnic minorities, including incidences of racism that can have such a profound effect on shaping their experience.

Gender and sexism

A major feature of the social structure is the differential expectations with regard to men and women in terms of:

- social roles (Connell, 2002);
- the sexual division of labour (Elliot, 1996; Harding, 1996);
- emotional responses (Thompson, 1995b, 1997a);
- styles of communication (Tannen, 1992);
- levels of assertiveness (Thompson, 2002c); and
- responses to problems, pressures and stress (Littlewood, 1992).

As with race, such differences are represented ideologically as biological differences, and therefore both necessary and desirable. However, these views confuse sex (biological differences) with gender (socially constructed differences). The latter are subject to variation both historically and geographically. That is, gender expectations change over time and from society to society, culture to culture.

However, it is once again not simply a matter of benign difference, but rather a relationship of domination/subordination. Unequal power relations are reflected in and supported by stereotypical gender expectations. This means that women, the subordinate group within patriarchal societies, experience a number of disadvantages and negative effects, including the following:

- 'Domestic' and sexual violence (Mullender, 1996).
- Sexual harassment (Collier, 1995; Thompson, 2000c).
- Lower pay, worse working conditions, greater obstacles to advancement and so on (Elliot, 1996; Bernard et al., 1995).
- The 'double shift' – an expectation that paid work for women should be in addition to, rather than instead of, unpaid domestic work (McDowell, 1989).
- 'Invisibility' – a tendency for their contributions and achievements to be overlooked or disregarded (as discussed earlier in this chapter).

Sexism is therefore not a frivolous matter to be trivialized and dismissed as a minor consideration – it is a serious social problem that has profound detrimental consequences, primarily for women, although in some ways for men, too (Segal, 1999).

A common misunderstanding is to regard sexism purely as a form of personal prejudice – 'male chauvinism' – without recognizing the significance of broader cultural representations and stereotypes on the one hand, and structural power relations on the other. An adequate understanding must take account of all three levels, **P**, **C** and **S**.

A number of problems arise when PCS is reduced to **P**, not least the following two:

1. Such a narrow focus reintroduces essentialism. That is, it presents sexist actions, attitudes and utterances as if they were reflections of essential qualities of individuals. Complex sociopolitical, cultural and psychological matters are reduced to simple personality traits. This can produce two negative sets of consequences: defeatism (it is assumed that people cannot change their personalities) and defensiveness (people avoiding the subject of equality for fear of being criticized or labelled) – both of these problems are discussed in more detail in Chapter 5.

2. A focus on **P** level issues distracts attention from the part played by cultural patterns, representations and assumptions and the wider context of social structure, social divisions and power relations. In this respect, an overemphasis on the **P** level can be seen as ideological – ideas serving to maintain the status quo and the power relations inherent in it.

It is also important to recognize that many of the problems involved in 'people work' are gender-related and often owe much to sexism. Examples would include:

- *Child sexual abuse* The majority of victims are female, while the majority of perpetrators are male.
- *Domestic violence* Violence in the home follows distinct gender patterns (Mullender, 1996).
- *Depression* Women are affected far more often by some forms of mental distress such as depression (Ussher, 1991).
- *Crime and delinquency* Types and rates of crime also follow gender divisions (see Carlen, 2002, for a discussion of gender and crime).
- *Bereavement and loss* Responses to loss tend to differ along gender lines, often with problematic consequences (Thompson, 1997a; 2001b; Riches, 2002).
- *Health and illness* Gender differences in health can be clearly identified (as we shall see in Chapter 4).

Furthermore, not only are many problems encountered linked to gender, but so too are many of the responses to such problems. For example, there are gender differences in terms of the way offenders are treated within the criminal justice system (Carlen, 2002) and important gender issues to be considered in terms of using techniques such as groupwork (Brown, 1992).

One potentially major obstacle to addressing issues of sexism in professional practice is the deeply ingrained assumptions about gender roles – we are so used to living and working in a patriarchal society that we (women as well as men) take for granted a number of sexist practices and institutional patterns. Sexism becomes like wallpaper, in the sense that we become so accustomed to its processes that we do not notice that they are there – they operate unnoticed in the background for much of the time. One consequence of this is that the problems that arise from sexism are frequently not recognized as such. For example, the considerable pressures many women face as relatively unsupported carers of elderly or disabled relatives may not be recognized as being linked to patriarchal expectations that caring is 'naturally' a female role.

It is for this reason that consciousness-raising – making people more aware of the subtle workings of gender, for example through awareness training – so often features as a basic ingredient of efforts to challenge sexism. In undertaking such consciousness-raising, one of the dangers or potential pitfalls to be encountered is the threat to ontological security. Gender is not simply a social phenomenon, it also applies at an ontological level, an aspect of our experience of, and integration with, the social world (Thompson, 2001b). Consequently, when long-standing taken-for-granted assumptions are challenged, we can feel that our very identity is under threat. Like ethnicity, gender is something that it is deeply rooted in our understanding and experience of the world and therefore needs to be handled sensitively if we are to enable people to move away from oppressive gender relations. If not, there is a danger that the threat to ontological security will lead people to 'dig their heels in' and resist any change of attitude towards gender and sexism.

Age and ageism

An understanding of older people as an oppressed group has been growing steadily in recent years (Hughes and Mtezuka, 1992; Hughes, 1995; Thompson, 1995a; Nolan, 2001). It is increasingly becoming recognized that age, like race and gender, is a social division – a significant factor in the allocation of power, status, life chances, social roles and so on. A person's age will often be a factor that plays a part in shaping his or her social location and the responses of other social actors.

The two groups mainly affected in a negative way by the social division of age are children and older people, although the majority of the literature on ageism relates primarily to the latter. Indeed, the concept of ageism and its wider ramifications have been developed within the emerging tradition of critical gerontology (Minkler and Estes, 1991; Phillipson and Walker, 1986; Thursz *et al.*, 1995).

Ageism often manifests itself as a set of stereotypical assumptions about what, for example, older people cannot or should not do. Such assumptions can place unnecessary restrictions on the people concerned, thereby limiting life chances. As Hughes (1995) comments:

> Ageism then, is a matrix of beliefs and attitudes which legitimates the use of age as a means of identifying a particular social group, which portrays the members of that group in negative, stereotypical terms and which consequently generates and reinforces a fear of the ageing process and a denigration of older people.
>
> (pp. 42–3)

Of course, ageism is more than a set of beliefs and attitudes – it is also a significant aspect of the social structure. Ageism operates not only at the personal and cultural levels, but also at the structural level of sociopolitical and economic relations. In what has proven to be a seminal work in this regard, Phillipson (1982) emphasized the significance of old age in relation to the economy in general and the labour market in particular. He identifies the role of retirement in regulating the labour market as, for example, when early retirement becomes more common at times of high unemployment (when labour supply exceeds demand).

A common ageist assumption is that older people are 'past it', a drain on the economy due to the fact that they no longer contribute to the labour market or the production of wealth. However, this is a problematic assumption in a number of ways:

- It ignores the role of older people as consumers within the economy. Economic success requires consumers as well as producers.
- It fails to recognize the investment in the economy that older people have made over the years through their labours, consumption, savings and so on.

- It relies on a narrow, economistic perspective which ignores the significance of social and political factors in maintaining the economic and social order. It ignores the fact that many older people are active in politics, business and commerce, the judiciary and so on.
- It neglects the role of many older carers who, of course, play an important part in the economy by, for example, looking after grandchildren (or great-grandchildren) (thereby giving the children's parents the opportunity to work) or caring for elderly or disabled relatives (thereby removing the need for public services).

Once again, it is no coincidence that the ideas relating to a particular social group serve to maintain existing power relations and the inequalities they conceal. These relations are maintained, in part at least, by ideology – in this case, *ageist* ideology.

The existence of ageism and its harmful consequences for older people has important implications for professional practice. It requires practitioners, educators and policy-makers to move away from traditional notions of care and dependency towards an ethic of empowerment. As Nusberg (1995) comments:

> Older people are one of the last groups with which the notion of empowerment has become associated. Yet the privileges it represents – the ability to make informed choices, exercise influence, continue to make contributions in a variety of settings, and take advantage of services – are critically important to the well-being of the elders. These are choices often taken for granted by working-age adults, but they have eluded older adults for a variety of reasons, including poverty, poor health, low educational levels, lack of transportation and access to services, negative stereotypes about aging, and overt and subtle age discrimination.
>
> (p. ix)

Developing approaches to practice based on empowerment can be a difficult task in view of the firmly rooted traditions of working with older people in which:

- ageist assumptions are common (Phillipson and Thompson, 1996);
- there is little or no consultation (Thornton and Tozer, 1994);
- services are strongly influenced by the medical model (Thompson, 1995a);
- protection from risks often takes precedence over rights (Thompson and Thompson, 2001); and
- legislation and social policy reinforce notions of dependency (Hughes, 1995).

However, although these are clearly potential obstacles to developing empowerment-based forms of practice, they should not be allowed to become an excuse for defeatism and the abandonment of the anti-ageist project. The challenge of developing anti-ageist practice, although a difficult and demanding one, must none the less remain an essential component of the broader project of emancipatory practice. Bland (1996) echoes this point when she argues that it is important to work towards the elimination of ageist discrimination in much the same way as many people have challenged racism, sexism and disablism. Bland's point can be seen to apply across the helping professions, indeed to all who come into contact with older people, regardless of professional or voluntary role, status or discipline.

◀ **PRACTICE FOCUS 3.5** ▶

Mr Gregory, aged 88, had been suffering from depression for some considerable period of time when his doctor made a referral for specialist help in the form of counselling. When the process of counselling began, Hugh, the counsellor, felt slightly apprehensive as he was not used to working with older people – something he was later to realize was, in itself, a reflection of ageism. As he began to get to know Mr Gregory, Hugh realized to what extent his life was characterized by negativity, by a constant stream of negative images about being old, 'past it', close to death, useless and so on. Hugh had never considered issues of ageism before but his work with Mr Gregory helped him to appreciate the part ageism can play in constructing negative images of old age, images that can become internalized as depression.

As mentioned above, ageism can also be seen to apply to children. The social significance of age applies throughout the life course and not just in old age (Hockey and James, 1993). Children can be identified as a group who are denied rights (Archard, 1993); not consulted, even where the legislative base requires it (Butler and Williamson, 1994; Thomas, 2000, 2001); and excluded from issues relating to death, dying and bereavement (Thompson, 1997b). This is not to say that children should simply be treated as adults. However, it does mean that the social location of children needs to be considered more carefully so that issues of rights and equality can be clarified and taken into account.

Disability and disablism

Traditional approaches to disability focus on medical aspects and the limitations that arise for the individual as a result of his or her physical impairment. Little or no account is taken of wider issues relating to attitudes, cultural expectations and the sociopolitical context. Such approaches have therefore been heavily criticized by a number of writers (Abberley, 1987; Finkelstein, 1980; Lonsdale, 1990; Oliver, 1990, 1996; Oliver and Sapey, 1999) and organizations (UPIAS, 1976). The basis of this critique can be summarized as follows:

- A narrow focus on the individual fails to recognize the significance of disability as the social response to a physical impairment. In addition to any restrictions brought about by the impairment itself, negative, demeaning and patronizing responses to the impairment bring further restrictions. It is the social response to the disabled person that *'dis*-ables' as much as, if not more so than, the impairment itself.
- Traditional approaches serve to 'pathologize' the individual, presenting him or her as a tragic victim to be pitied (or, alternatively, as a brave hero to be respected – in itself an inverted form of pathologizing).
- Care and dependency take precedence over rights, autonomy and independence. Disabled people are presented as 'the deserving poor', people who are in need of care and attention. This can be seen as a form of infantilization, a patronizing approach that overemphasizes the amount of personal care needed and underemphasizes the importance of rights and empowerment.
- Disabled people experience discrimination and a degree of social exclusion. As Oliver (1996) puts it: 'Certainly it is true that disabled people have been systematically excluded from British society; they have been denied inclusion into their society because of the existence of disabling barriers' (p. 158).
- Individualistic approaches to disability fail to address the ways in which disability articulates with other social forces such as race, gender, age and sexual identity to produce a complex matrix of multiple oppressions.

In short, traditional approaches fail to recognize or address disablism. They fail to acknowledge disability as a social division or disablism as a form of social oppression. Consequently, efforts are directed towards making disabled people more comfortable, as if to compensate for their impairment, rather than towards removing the physical, attitudinal and social barriers that have the effect of 'handicapping' disabled people.

It is for this reason that the Disabled People's Movement has strongly promoted the idea of 'rights not charity' and has sought to problematize charity-based attempts to meet disabled people's needs. As the following rather scathing comment from Oliver (1990) indicates, charity is closely linked to begging:

> Perhaps it is a mark of our civilization in the industrialized world that we employ some people to beg on behalf of others; in many so-called less civilized societies, disabled people are at least accorded the dignity of begging on their own behalf.
>
> (p. 93)

It is perhaps no coincidence that the term 'handicap' is associated with the notion of going 'cap in hand' (Barnes, 1991).

◀ PRACTICE FOCUS 3.6 ▶

Morag had always been interested in working with disabled people, and so she was looking forward to the time she was going to be spending at the Disability Information and Advice Centre as part of her training. However, although she did, in the end, enjoy her time there, she found it to be quite a shock at first. She was expecting the focus to be on 'looking after' disabled people, helping them to cope with their own tragic misfortune. She was therefore surprised to find that there was a major focus on rights and campaigning, with a much greater emphasis on the social aspects and contexts of disability than she had assumed would be the case.

Disability provides a clear example of the process of discrimination and its oppressive consequences. Disability acts as a social division, dividing one group of people off from the mainstream, thereby creating a minority. This group is then subjected to discrimination at three distinct but interrelated levels:

- P – personal prejudice which manifests itself as rejection, marginalization, ridicule and so on.
- C – cultural expectations, norms, stereotypes, representations and linguistic forms that devalue and disempower disabled people.
- S – structural relations of power, inequality, discrimination and disadvantage reinforce and underpin oppressive factors at other levels.

After many years of exposure to images of disabled people as needy individuals who require considerable care and protection, it can be difficult to appreciate the significance of the social oppression model of disability. It can be quite a challenge for people who see themselves as members of the 'helping professions' to accept that their good intentions can be experienced as oppressive. However, as we have seen in relation to issues of discrimination and oppression more generally, it is not the good intentions that count, but rather the actual consequences or outcomes for service users. It is the 'lived experience' (*le vécu*) that needs to be addressed, rather than putative intentions. Unintentional oppression is oppression, none the less. In order to move towards forms of practice that address and challenge disablism, it is necessary to ensure that we:

- Do not adopt a medical model. Regarding a disabled person as ill can be profoundly disempowering. We shall return to this point in Chapter 4.
- Work in partnership. Human services workers are not 'experts' who determine a diagnosis and impose a treatment plan. Our expertise lies, rather, in working with people to identify problems to be solved, needs to be met and so on, and possible ways forward. Anti-disablist practice should therefore incorporate full consultation and participation.
- Adopt a broad perspective, taking on board wider cultural and structural factors, in order to avoid overemphasizing individual factors and thereby working on the basis of a distorted picture of the situation. This is not to suggest that the individual should be abandoned in favour of the cultural or structural levels. Rather, it is a plea for an holistic approach that incorporates all three levels.
- Work towards maximizing autonomy and self-determination. No one is fully independent – we all rely on a 'structure of aiding', a network of supports (Thompson, 2001a). Independence, then, is not a question of not needing support; it is more a question of maximizing the control we have over our lives (Adams, 1996). Independence is therefore closely linked to empowerment.
- Do not see disablism in isolation, but recognize the interconnections with sexism, racism, ageism and other forms of oppression. There is little point in tackling oppression in one aspect of people's lives without taking into account other oppressive dimensions of their experience. Anti-disablist practice therefore needs to be seen in the context of the broader project of emancipatory practice.

Sexual identity and heterosexism

For many years homosexuality was regarded as a form of psychiatric disorder, a pathological deviation from the heterosexual norm (Neal and Davies, 1996). It was also, of course, illegal in Britain until relatively recently. Homosexual intercourse remains illegal where one or both partners is under 18, even where such relations are entirely consensual (prior to the implementation of the Criminal Justice Act 1994, the age of 'consent' was 21). In addition, the introduction of the Local Government Act 1990 made it illegal for local authorities to 'promote' homosexuality.

The history of homosexuality in Britain is therefore one of repression and, consequently, oppression. A person's choice of sexual identity can lead to extreme forms of discrimination, resulting in not only a lack of equality of opportunity but also ridicule, rejection, harassment, violence and even murder (Field, 1995). Homosexuality is therefore defined ideologically as a problem (hence the focus on treatment and 'cure'), but relatively little emphasis is placed on social reactions to homosexuality as a source of problems. The degrading and oppressive treatment of one section of the population – gay men, lesbians and bisexuals – can clearly be seen as a social problem and yet the notion of the oppression of homosexuals as a social problem rarely, if ever, receives attention in discussions or the literature base.

Within the helping professions issues of sexual identity have also received relatively little attention. This lack of attention can be a significant stumbling block to good practice. For example, practitioners who fail to address issues of oppression in relation to sexual identity are likely to miss significant aspects of the individual's life experience and the problems he or she faces. Davies (1996a) illustrates this point by reference to (para)suicide:

> Several studies, including a British one (Trenchard and Warren 1984) . . . have found at least 20 per cent of young lesbian, gay and bisexual people have made suicide attempts. Suicide is the second highest cause of death among young people. Verdicts of 'misadventure' and 'accidental death' are sometimes returned by coroners, where it is not entirely clear whether a person killed themselves, to spare the family the shame and guilt still attached to a verdict of suicide. It is impossible to estimate how many young people each year do succeed in killing themselves because of the difficulties they experience and foresee in living their life as lesbian, gay or bisexual, but the figures are probably quite high.
>
> (p. 137)

Similarly, Simon (1996) points out that there may be a reluctance on the part of gay people to seek help: 'Pressures to subscribe to prescriptive, or demanding narratives within their own communities may lead gay couples to fear disclosures of difficulties and fail to find support for working issues through' (p. 115).

These two quotations combine to paint a picture of a situation in which (1) problems experienced by gay people as a result of living in an oppressive society that devalues their sexual identity are likely to go unnoticed and not be addressed by human services workers and (2) gay people are less likely to seek help when needed for fear of what could be called 'heteronormative' responses – responses that assume and reinforce heterosexual norms.

These are examples of 'heterosexism', a form of oppression which Blumenfeld and Raymond (1988) define as 'the system by which heterosexuality is assumed to be the only acceptable and viable life option' (p. 244, cited in Davies, 1996b, p. 42). As with other forms of oppression, it can be seen to operate at three levels:

- *Personal*   Direct prejudice against homosexuality is a commonplace occurrence and often goes unchallenged.
- *Cultural*   Gay men, lesbians and bisexuals are commonly represented in derogatory terms and frequently the butt of humour. Negative stereotypes are widespread.
- *Structural*   Homosexuality is seen as a threat to family values and therefore inconsistent with capitalism and patriarchy (Hocquenghem, 1978).

Ethnically sensitive practice is encouraged by key elements of legislation such as the Children Act 1989 and the NHS and Community Care Act 1990. Similarly, the Disability Discrimination Act 1995 is a relatively recent addition to the anti-discrimination legislation. But, in the case of heterosexism, there has been not only a reluctance to develop anti-discrimination legislation, but also anti-gay legislation in the form of the Criminal Justice Act 1994 and the Local Government Act 1990. In short, homosexuality has not been legitimized in law in the same way as some other forms of social difference, and this can be seen to make the task of anti-discriminatory practice all the harder in the absence of a well-developed legal framework on which to draw. Article 14 of the Human Rights Act 1998 makes discrimination on the grounds of sexual identity illegal, but this relates only to the other articles of the Act and is not a general provision. Therefore even this most significant development in human rights law leaves major forms of discrimination on the grounds of sexual identity untouched. However, the fact that anti-heterosexism is a more difficult form of emancipatory practice to develop should not be seen as a reason for not attempting to achieve it.

One important step towards developing anti-heterosexist practice is the promotion of what has become known as 'gay affirmative therapy'. As Davies (1996c) comments:

> Krajeski (1986: 16) points out the difficulty of finding a name 'which describes accurately a type of therapy which values both homosexuality and heterosexuality equally as natural or normal attributes'. The name with most common usage is gay affirmative. The gay affirmative therapist affirms a lesbian, gay or bisexual identity as an equally positive human experience and expression to heterosexual identity.
>
> (p. 25)

He goes on to argue that:

> Gay affirmative therapists are those whose beliefs and values appreciate homosexuality – and bisexuality – as valid and rich orientations in their own right and who perceive homophobia, not diverse sexualities, as pathological. Such therapists offer clients respect for their sexuality, personal integrity, culture and lifestyle.
>
> (p. 40)

Davies is concerned primarily with counselling and psychotherapy. However, it should be clear that the same arguments can be applied to working with people and their problems more broadly, and indeed to social interactions generally. Gay affirmative forms of practice are therefore an essential part of challenging and undermining the oppression of heterosexism.

◀ PRACTICE FOCUS 3.7 ▶

Tina had worked with a variety of clients across the mental health spectrum. She was in the process of helping Colin, a young man who had been abusing alcohol to quite a serious extent. At one point, he said to Tina: 'I suppose you think my drinking is all part of me being gay.' Up to that point Tina had not even known Colin was gay and, anyway, would not have connected his drinking to his sexual identity. When she asked Colin why he had made that remark, he went on to explain how so many people in the past had seen the fact that he is gay as a sign of weakness or inadequacy, another problem to be solved. This made it clear to her that Colin had been on the receiving end of a lot of heterosexist discrimination and had not encountered, or even expected, anything resembling gay affirmative practice.

Closely related to this is the notion of a 'politics of respect'. A. Wilson (1993) argues that efforts to achieve equality must be accompanied by a focus on respect, specifically a respect for differences. She presents sexuality as an important part of a person's identity and sense of well-being and therefore argues that it is important that each individual's sexual orientation is respected. To fail to do this is to engage in heterosexist discrimination and thereby cause, reinforce or exacerbate oppression.

The question of identity is also very relevant in terms of developmental psychology. As we noted in Chapter 1, identity is not a fixed 'essence', but rather a continuous process of self-definition. One important aspect of such processes of identity that is often overlooked is that of coming to terms with one's sexual identity, particularly where this is a homosexual identity and therefore at odds with dominant ideological expectations (Field, 1995). The processes by which a gay person either conceals their sexual identity or 'comes out' are therefore very significant both psychologically and socially. And yet this is a topic that rarely features in the literature relating to the life course and identity formation, thereby revealing the heteronormative nature of the established knowledge base and the need to address it critically rather than take it at face value.

Conclusion

One of the dangers of discussing specific processes of discrimination and specific forms of oppression is that it can give the misleading impression that they exist in isolation, separate from one another, rather than as parts of a complex matrix of multiple and interacting oppressions. It should be remembered, then, that the presentation of separate sets of issues is a tool to aid understanding, a strategy for presenting highly complex ideas in a more 'digestible' form. However, once the component parts have been understood, this is not the end of the learning process. The next step is to seek to integrate the component parts, to weave them together into a coherent whole. Or, to put it another way, the process of *analysis* (breaking a complex whole down into its component parts) needs to be followed by the process of *synthesis* (combining them into a meaningful pattern) – in short, a dialectical approach (Thompson, 1992a, 2000a).

In order to facilitate this process Chapter 4 focuses on a particular field of study that is often of significance for the helping professions – that is, the ways in which inequality, discrimination and oppression relate to health (and ill-health). We shall have the opportunity to explore many of the disparate themes that have emerged in this chapter, but this time in the context of a concrete field of study and practice in which many of these issues combine, interact and influence one another. It is therefore to the topic of health that we now turn.

4

HEALTH

Introduction

The concept of health is one that is usually taken for granted not only in health care settings but also across the helping professions generally. It acts as a unifying theme for many forms of intervention by practitioners. Indeed, Aggleton (1990) points out that health is one of those terms that are commonly used but prove to be very difficult when it comes to defining or explaining them. This chapter does not seek to provide a definitive account or explanation, as it is recognized that health is a fluid concept open to a wide variety of interpretations.

A central theme will be the status of health and related concepts such as illness and sickness as social constructions. My aim here, then, is to look beneath the surface of the everyday understandings of health and reveal some of the complex social and political processes that can be seen to operate. I therefore subject the notion of health to critical scrutiny and show it to be a very problematic term with regard to issues of discrimination, oppression and equality. The discussion introduces concepts from the sociology of health and the critique of the medical model, as well as drawing on existentialism as a theory base that helps us understand health as an ontological concept, rather than purely a biological one.

I shall attempt to demonstrate that health issues, and their links with power and oppression, are of relevance to all involved in working with people and their problems, and not simply those who work specifically within the health care field. Notions of what is healthy and what is sick or pathological are not restricted to health care settings. They also have a profound influence in social welfare, education and related professional activities, and can be seen to shape policies and practices in a wide variety of disciplines. As we shall see, what counts as 'healthy' is a crucial concern across the helping professions, a fundamental theme that needs to be addressed if our understanding of equality issues is to be developed.

A key aspect of this field of study is the role of metaphor. Often oppressed groups are seen either directly or metaphorically as 'ill'. In particular, older people, disabled people or gays, lesbians and bisexuals are often presented ideologically as ill or sick. One crucial consequence of this is that the metaphor so easily becomes translated into a literal meaning, creating a discourse which thereby adds further to the oppression experienced. For example, ageist ideology draws such close links between old age and ill-health that old age is often presented as if it were an illness in its own right (Scrutton, 1992).

My focus in this chapter, then, will be on 'unpacking' health and revealing it as a profoundly ideological concept that has wide-ranging ramifications with regard to inequality, discrimination and oppression. I begin, therefore, with a consideration of health as a social construct.

The social construction of health

Jones (1994) points out that health is 'a physiological and a psychological state but it is also fundamentally a social state' (p. 1). That is, health clearly has a social dimension. Referring back to the discussion of social construction in Chapter 1, we can see that health has no fixed and definitive meaning. It is used in a fluid way to the extent that it means different things in different contexts. As Jones goes on to explain, health is understood in different ways by different people according to differences in age – younger people emphasizing energy and vitality, older people focusing more on coping, managing to get around and so on.

Of course, age is not the only factor involved in the differentiation of health. As we shall see in greater detail below, health is closely related to a range of social factors, not least class, race and gender. It is therefore necessary to conceive of health as socially constructed. That is, it is defined in relation to the social context in which it occurs.

Sedgwick (1973) notes that the very notions of health and disease are socially constructed, rather than naturally given. For example, he presents potato blight as a competition between two organisms (the potato and the 'blight'). It is only the value that we place on potatoes as a food source that leads us to describe what happens as a 'disease process'. To describe someone or something as 'healthy' is therefore to exercise a value judgement that involves relating the person or thing to an underlying social norm of what constitutes a desirable state.

It is this that allows us to use 'healthy' (or 'sick') in a metaphorical sense, as the following examples illustrate:

- A 'healthy' organization is one that does not infringe socially acceptable mores and is consistent with social expectations as to how organizations should play a part in social life.
- A 'sick' society, by contrast, is one in which law and order and moral values are deemed to be under threat.
- A 'healthy' interest in, for example, the opposite sex is one which is neither too little (reflecting a heterosexist assumption that an absence of heterosexual desire is pathological) nor too great (excessive desire also being seen as pathological).
- A 'sick' joke is one that offends moral values and/or standards of acceptable humour.
- A 'healthy' bank balance is one that is adequate for our needs, one that does not lead to marginalization through poverty and deprivation.

All these examples reflect the fact that health implies more than a biological state of well-being, and incorporates a judgement as to whether the state referred to is socially desirable. It is in this respect that we can see health as not only a social construction, but also an ideological one – a concept or construction that both reflects and reinforces existing social relations and thereby legitimizes the status quo and the discourses on which it is based.

Health, then is not a neutral concept, nor is it something that can be accepted uncritically as a social good to be promoted. One person's 'health' is another person's oppression (heterosexism, for example). It is a complex social phenomenon that needs to be analysed and questioned. To use it as a blanket term to describe states and processes that are socially valued and therefore to be encouraged is to conceal the ideological processes that operate beneath the surface. Indeed, ideology can be seen to operate through a process of 'camouflage'. By presenting the interests of dominant groups as if they were the interests of all, inequalities are concealed and thereby protected. As Foucault (1981) puts it: 'Power is tolerable only on condition that it mask a substantial part of itself. Its success is proportional to its ability to hide its own mechanisms' (p. 86).

Health needs to be understood in terms of not only its social context (the social factors that influence and constrain biological well-being) but also its social nature. That is, health is intrinsically social due to the fact that it is socially defined or constructed. Health is not only a concept that relates to the social world, it is one that is defined and created by it – it is constituted in the social order.

The complexities of health as a sociological, as well as biological and psychological concept, mean that we must treat the notions of health, sickness and disease with some degree of caution. This is not to say that these notions should be avoided altogether, but rather that they should be used carefully and sensitively in order to avoid reductionism and oversimplification.

Miles (1991) refers to the tripartite distinction commonly made in medical sociology:

> Sociologists usually make a distinction between disease and illness. The term disease, in sociological literature, refers to a biological or clinically identified abnormality which is considered 'pathological' by medical practitioners; illness refers to a person's experience of being unwell. In such sense disease is an 'objective' disorder, that is, assessed by someone other than the patient and illness is a 'subjective' feeling of symptoms, self-assessed by the individual (Helman, 1981; Armstrong, 1989). There is a third dimension of ill-health, i.e. the social and functional consequences which may follow disease or illness, and this is usually distinguished by the term sickness.
>
> (p. 3)

While this can be seen to be a helpful distinction in some ways, it is also problematic. An example of its strengths would be that a person can have a disease (heart disease, for example) without necessarily experiencing illness. However, one of the problems associated with this approach is that it overemphasizes the biological dimension at the expense of the broader social and political dimensions. It therefore neglects the ideological role of health. Indeed, in this respect it reflects a common tendency where ideology is concerned – for the biological dimension of a complex, multifaceted situation to be overemphasized to the point where it comes to be seen as the primary or only dimension (as in sexism, racism and so on). This is a process of legitimation in which the stability and consistency associated with biology are used to justify and maintain existing power relations. It may be no coincidence, then, that this tripartite distinction reflects a professional hierarchy or division of labour: 'the physician is professionally trained to cure disease, the clinical psychiatrist to deal with illness and practitioners of clinical sociology are directed towards sickness' (Turner, 1995, p. 3).

Health, then, may begin with biology, but does not end there. It also involves psychological, social, economic, political and, as we shall see below, ontological dimensions (Figure 4.1).

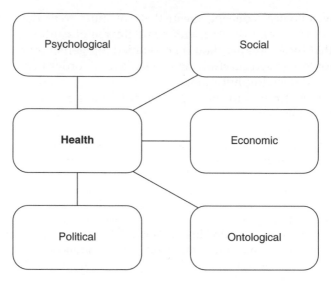

Figure 4.1   The dimensions of health

Health discourses

Health can be construed and talked about in a variety of ways. That is, it is subject to a variety of discourses. Perhaps the most dominant discourse in relation to health is that of the medical model in which health is presented primarily as an absence of disease. The major focus of the medical model is on the human 'organism' and his or her condition in terms of the presence or absence of pathology. Although this is a commonly accepted view of health and ill-health, the model is none the less problematic, as Turner (1995) points out:

> The medical model is reductionist in the sense that all disease and illness behaviours would be reduced causally to a number of specific biochemical mechanisms. Furthermore, the medical model is exclusionary in that alternative perspectives would be removed as invalid. Finally, the medical model presupposes a clear mind/body distinction where ultimately the causal agent of illness would be located in the human body (Engel, 1981).
>
> (pp. 9–10)

As a discourse, the medical model is not only a set of ideas and assumptions, it is also a set of:

- linguistic forms that both encapsulate and sustain the discourse;
- social practices – actions presented within the discourse as normal, natural and reasonable; and
- power relations.

These are not separate features of the discourse but, rather, intertwine to produce a complex social formation. The language forms used both reflect and reinforce power relations and present certain actions as normal and legitimate – they 'belong' with the discourse, in the sense that they are compatible with the social reality encapsulated in the discourse (Barker and Galasiński, 2001).

As Burr (1995) argues, a discourse presents a particular version of events; it paints a particular picture. The picture painted by the medical model is one in which:

1. Considerable power is vested in the medical profession.
2. Individuals ('patients') become passive objects of the 'scientific' process of medical diagnosis and treatment.
3. Wider aspects of health are seen as secondary to individual pathology.

Each of these is worthy of closer attention:

1. The allocation of power to the medical profession inherent in medical discourse has significant implications in terms of:

(i)   jurisdiction over matters relating to physical health being extended to matters of mental and emotional distress (see the discussion of mental health below);
(ii) doctors (especially psychiatrists) being seen as 'experts' on social problems, current affairs and so on – for example, as contributors to television or radio documentaries and newspaper columns;
(iii) patriarchal ideology – the medical profession is male-dominated and reflects a patriarchal power base.

As we shall see below, this power can be used to reinforce discrimination and oppression, thereby standing in the way of equality.

◀ Practice focus 4.1 ▶

Following a childhood relatively free of illness, Peter had taken little interest in his own health. Consequently, he took little notice of issues like diet, exercise, smoking and drinking. He was therefore very shocked when he experienced his first heart attack at the age of

41. At first, he was just pleased to have survived and was grateful to the medical and nursing staff for helping him through. However, as he gradually recovered and became stronger, he became very angry towards his own doctor: 'Why had nobody warned me?' 'Why was this allowed to happen?' It was not long before he realized how irrational and unfair these thoughts of his were, but he was now beginning to appreciate how passive he had been towards his own health, seeing such matters as primarily the concern of doctors and nurses.

2. The degree of expertise associated with doctors is such that patients frequently adopt a passive approach to their own health and/or medical condition. This can lead to a failure or unwillingness to take responsibility for those aspects of our health that are within our control, for example, diet, exercise and preventative measures. In some cases, this can have a disastrous effect, as in the case of cancer or heart disease where our own (in)actions contribute to the problem.

3. The medical model is primarily individualistic in its focus and therefore pays little or no attention to wider social, political or economic concerns. This means that issues such as poverty, racism or ageism are not given full recognition as factors that contribute to ill-health, while a great deal of money is invested in 'hi-tech' equipment (Thunhurst, 1982; Nolan *et al.*, 2001a).

The dominance of the medical model is so strong that it is generally taken for granted as the way of conceptualizing health and illness. Critics of the medical model can therefore expect to be regarded with some degree of suspicion or even contempt. However, such critics may have an important contribution to make to our understanding of discrimination and oppression in the context of health. Ivan Illich, for example, makes many relevant points.

An important concept introduced by Illich (1977) is that of 'social iatrogenesis'. This refers to the ways in which the social organization of health care becomes a causal factor in the experience of ill-health:

> Social iatrogenesis designates a category of aetiology that encompasses many forms. It obtains when medical bureaucracy creates ill-health by increasing stress, by multiplying disabling dependence, by generating new painful needs, by lowering the levels of tolerance for discomfort or pain, by reducing the leeway that people are wont to concede to an individual when he suffers, and by abolishing even the right to self-care.
> Social iatrogenesis is at work when health care is turned into a standardized item, a staple; when all suffering is hospitalized and homes

become inhospitable to birth, sickness, and death; when the language in which people could experience their bodies is turned into bureaucratic gobbledygook; or when suffering, mourning, and healing outside the patient role are labelled a form of deviance.

(p. 49)

An iatrogenic illness is one caused by medical intervention, whether as an expected side-effect or as a result of error or incompetence. In such cases, the focus is on the specific actions of the medical practitioner concerned. Social iatrogenesis, by contrast, relates not to the micro-level actions of individuals, but rather to the macro-level of the social organization of medical and health care services – the institutionalized structures in which individual medical practice occurs. The ideas, language and social practices that structure medical interventions – in short, medical discourse – serve to undermine the very health gains the interventions are intended to achieve. As was noted in Chapter 1, oppression often arises as a result of structural arrangements, despite the good intentions of those concerned.

In recent years, the medical model has come to be challenged by a range of 'alternative therapies' which seek to reduce the reliance on drugs and technology and reintroduce more 'natural' forms of treatment and prevention. Such approaches run counter to dominant forms of medical practice and therefore pose a challenge to the medical model and its repertoire of treatment interventions. However, we can also see that they retain many elements of medical discourse. While there is a stronger emphasis on the whole person in terms of lifestyle, psychological well-being and so on, such 'holistic' approaches none the less remain within an individualistic framework and therefore neglect wider issues. As Coward (1993) comments:

> The alternative health movement has become a place where the individual can play out, in a highly personal way, a sense of the corruptions of modernity and the struggle against these corruptions. Now the corruptions are no longer the religious sins of greed, sex and envy, nor the economic sins of capitalism but rather bad parenting, bad diet, bad posture, the abuse of food and nature. The solutions to these are rarely political. They are individual. It is up to individuals to transform themselves, to deal with the pain and suffering imposed by modern life.
>
> (p. 99)

This is an example of 'blaming the victim', focusing on the individual who experiences the problem, rather than the wider circumstances that lead to the problem (Beattie et al., 1993).

This is not to say that the emerging discourse of holistic medicine has little or nothing to offer, but rather to recognize that such approaches tend to make the same mistake as the medical model – to fail to devote sufficient attention to the sociopolitical context of health in general and of health inequalities in particular.

In parallel fashion, a broader conception of health in terms of social well-being reflects both a movement away from the medical model and an affinity with it. This view of health is associated with the World Health Organization, as Aggleton (1990) explains:

> In 1946 the World Health Organization (WHO) defined health in a way very different from any of the definitions so far considered. It defined it as 'a state of complete physical, mental and social well-being and not merely the absence of disease or infirmity' (WHO 1946). While this kind of definition sets high targets to be achieved, it has been criticized for its idealism, for specifying a state of being which it is impossible to attain. It also puts forward a rather absolute view of health by suggesting that we are all unhealthy unless we have attained complete mental, physical and social well-being.
>
> (p. 8)

This perspective moves away from the narrow, biologically based confines of the medical model but, in so doing, has the effect of reinforcing medical power. The discourse of health as social well-being has not reduced the power of the medical profession, but rather extended it into fields beyond the domain of physical ill-health. Illich (1977) once again links this to iatrogenesis:

> Iatrogenic medicine reinforces a morbid society in which social control of the population by the medical system turns into a principal economic activity. It serves to legitimize social arrangements into which many people do not fit. It labels the handicapped [sic] as unfit and breeds ever new categories of patients. People who are angered, sickened and impaired by their industrial labour and leisure can escape only into a life under medical supervision and are thereby seduced or disqualified from political struggle for a healthier world.
>
> (p. 51)

This is an example of what Illich calls 'the medicalization of life'. Such a process not only transfers considerable power to one particular professional group, but also has the effect of depoliticizing issues of social discord, distress and deviance (Pearson, 1975). In this respect the discourse plays a clear ideological role, in so far as it bolsters existing power relations by distracting attention from the sociopolitical aspects of human distress.

Health inequalities

A major feature of medical discourse, as we have seen, is its individualistic focus. It rarely succeeds in rising above the level of the individual. One consequence of this is that broader patterns of health and ill-health are not given the attention they deserve. In particular, the question of inequality in health and health-care provision can be overlooked within the narrow parameters of the medical model. It is my intention, then, to rectify this imbalance to some extent by exploring the significance of inequalities in health. I shall focus on issues of class, race and gender before moving on to address particular points in relation to age and disability.

Class
The Black Report of 1980 (Townsend and Davidson, 1988) revealed considerable inequalities in health across the class spectrum. Using the Registrar General's classification of income groups as a frame of reference, differences in health were measured. From this study the following points emerged:

- Significantly higher infant mortality rates among 'unskilled manual' parents. At birth or during the first month of life, the rate is double that for the highest class group (professional).
- Differences in the use of health service facilities, for example: 'the evidence suggests that working-class people make more use of GP services for themselves (though not for their children) than do middle-class people, but they may receive less good care' (Townsend and Davidson, 1988, p. 198).
- The incidence of accidents is strongly class-linked (the higher the class grouping, the lower the accident rate).
- Chronic sickness rates are closely parallel to infant mortality rates. That is, they are far lower in the higher class groups.

A later report (Whitehead, 1988) confirmed that social inequalities in health continued to exist and, in some cases, there had actually been a widening of the gap (death rates, for example). In view of the continuing problems of deprivation that have persisted into the 1990s, and no doubt beyond, it seems likely that class inequalities will remain a feature of UK society for quite some time to come.

While space does not permit a detailed analysis of the possible causes of class inequalities in health, we can at least begin to sketch out possible links in terms of:

- poor-quality housing, overcrowding and so on;
- poor diet linked to low income;
- higher rates of smoking in working-class groups;
- industrial injuries and diseases more prevalent within working-class groups; and
- the stress associated with discrimination and oppression.

Although not intended as a comprehensive list, these points should be sufficient to begin to develop the links between the individual's experience of health and the social context in which it occurs.

Race

In view of the close association between black communities and working-class status (Solomos and Back, 1996), we can readily recognize that very many ethnic minority groups will be disadvantaged in terms of health as a result of their class position. However, it is also important to recognize the additional layer of inequality that arises as a result of racial factors.

One significant factor to consider is the need for health-related services to be ethnically sensitive. As Jones (1994) comments:

> If staff (whatever their cultural background) make assumptions based on their own cultural norms and values, without taking into account that their patients may not share these values, it will be difficult to deliver good health care. A 'colour-blind' or 'culture-blind' health service, suggest Mares et al. (1985), 'is likely to be less effective, and may even prove negligent of the health care needs of minority ethnic patients'.
>
> (p. 313)

An example of culture-blindness is the failure of the NHS to address conditions such as sickle cell disorders and thalassaemia which 'mainly (but not exclusively) affect black and minority ethnic groups' (Anionwu, 1993, p. 76). Anionwu argues that the NHS needed to be forced by the pressure of black communities to put these conditions on the agenda, and would not have done so without this pressure.

One contribution to such pressure is the report of the Independent Inquiry into Inequalities in Health (Acheson, 1998) which:

> makes it patently clear that there is a need to train health workers in 'cul-

tural competence'. The report also recommends that further developments of services which are sensitive to the needs of minority ethnic people and which promote greater awareness of their health risks should be implemented.

(Papadopoulos, 2001, p. 47)

However, as was argued in Chapter 1, ethnically sensitive practice is not enough on its own. It needs to be seen as a step towards antiracist practice, rather than a replacement for it. To address cultural issues without taking account of racism is to omit a large and significant element of the life experience of members of ethnic minorities. This applies as much to health as it does to other aspects of the helping professions (Stubbs, 1993).

◀ PRACTICE FOCUS 4.2 ▶

When Mrs Begum was admitted to hospital she was pleased to note that the menu included a variety of foods, reflecting a recognition of the preferences of different cultures. However, her pleasure over the menu's suitability proved short-lived. When she received her first meal, the patient in the next bed commented very loudly on her dislike of 'that foreign stuff' and her disapproval that it should be served in a British hospital. When Mrs Begum complained to one of the nursing staff about the other patient's racist comments, she was dismayed to find the response she received was one to the effect that she should not 'let a little thing like that bother her'.

Ahmad (1993b) links racial inequalities in health to wider inequalities in citizenship. He argues that there are considerable inequalities in health between black and white groups and that these are largely a result of racial oppression, a point that is echoed in much of the literature on race and mental health. Indeed, there is a growing literature that points to racial discrimination in relation to health, as summarized by Skellington (1996). Such discrimination takes many forms, including the following:

* higher rates of admission to psychiatric care for black people;
* a greater likelihood of being admitted to hospital on a compulsory basis (under the Mental Health Act 1983);
* significantly higher rates of being diagnosed as schizophrenic (the significance of such a diagnosis will be discussed below);
* a tendency for black people to receive harsher forms of medication, together with a higher level of usage of electro-convulsive therapy; and

- a greater likelihood of being admitted to psychiatric care from court or prison.

It is therefore necessary to recognize the significant role of racism in the way mental health is conceptualized, experienced and dealt with, as indeed with health issues more broadly, including health promotion (Douglas, 1996). When we consider racial inequalities in health in the context of the widening of the concept of 'health' to incorporate moral and sociopolitical factors, we can see that the relationship between race and health is a complex one that operates at cultural and structural levels, and is not simply a matter of personal prejudice or individual pathology.

Gender

While women generally have a longer life-span than men, the situation with regard to health is far less favourable (Miles, 1991). Although, as Whitehead (1988) acknowledges, the relationship between gender and health is complex and in need of further research, inequalities are none the less discernible. Jones (1994) summarizes some of the gender differences in health in the following passage:

> Patterns of gender socialization produce systematic differences in the behaviour of the sexes which link to health status. For example, men indulge in risk taking behaviour to a greater extent than women: faster driving, rates of smoking and drinking and the greater use of dangerous drugs are some key examples of this. This helps to explain their higher rates of accidents, cirrhosis of the liver, lung cancer and coronary heart disease. Women with 'problems' tend to turn instead to (or to be prescribed) tranquillizers, although the rate of smoking (and lung cancer and heart disease) among women has been rising in recent years. Men also make less use of dentistry and other preventive services than women.
>
> (p. 253)

Although, in some respects, men's rates of illness are higher than women's, the consistent pattern that emerges is one in which men report fewer illnesses than women. However, we cannot deduce from this that women experience more illness than men, as there are gender differences in the willingness to seek help, men generally being more reluctant to approach professionals for assistance (O'Brien, 1990).

A further complication arises in terms of the relationship between gender and class. As Arber (1990) points out, class differences are usually measured on a family or household basis, rather than individually, thereby masking gender differences. She argues that a woman in a male-dominated occupation such as management is likely to experience more stress than her male counterpart (and, by implication, a higher exposure to illness). This leads Arber to argue that:

> Relationships between class and health for women should be considered in their own right rather than always held up to and compared with the male standard . . . if the primary concern is to understand how material circumstances influence women's health it may be more appropriate to leave the strait-jacket of class, and more directly measure women's material circumstances.
>
> (p. 39)

The situation with regard to gender inequalities in physical health is therefore far from simple and is closely intertwined with factors such as class. Similarly, inequalities in mental health can be identified, but the situation here is also complex.

Miles (1991) points out that epidemiological studies show a preponderance of women among people deemed to be in need of psychiatric care. These can be seen to feature in two main areas:

1. *'Neurotic' disorders* Miles refers to a number of authors who have argued the case for a link between the experience of stress, hardship and frustration and mental health problems (Chesler, 1972; Oakley, 1981; Busfield, 1983; Rosenberg, 1984; Pride, 2001). The basic argument is that women's position in a patriarchal society generates higher levels of anxiety.
2. *Depression* In what has become something of a classic text, Brown and Harris (1978) drew links between women's experience of depression and inequality, particularly the sense of hopelessness 'consequent upon the loss of important sources of reward or positive value' (p. 270). In other words, the lowering of self-esteem associated with women's subordinate position is identified as a key factor in the onset of depression. Busfield (1996) also notes that reported incidences of depression for women are more than double those for men.

Ussher (1991) argues that men and women are 'regulated' differently. For example, she points out that the figures relating to women's psychiatric admissions and experiences of depression are fairly evenly balanced with the figures relating to men's imprisonment, violence and criminality. That is, mental health problems are, for women, a socially structured pathway for responding to distress and frustration.

This discussion of health inequalities has been an exploratory one and only begins to develop an analysis of the intricacies of the subject. However, the need to appreciate the significance of inequality in relation to health has been firmly established – a further example of the central theme of health as a social construct.

Health, disability and age

The concept of illness is an important one in terms of both disablism and ageism. For disabled people, the assumption that disability is a form of illness can have profoundly oppressive and disempowering consequences (Oliver, 1990). Similarly, for older people, the assumption that old age inevitably brings health problems (or is even an illness in its own right) is also very problematic in its consequences (Thompson, 1995a).

We are once again in the realms of the medical model. Older people and people with disabilities, regardless of their age, so easily come under the purview of the medical profession, such is the dominance and pervasiveness of medical discourse. Lonsdale (1990) argues that the responsibility for disabled people has, during this century, shifted from the family to professionals, particularly the medical profession. This creates a power relationship, to the favour of the doctor and the detriment of the disabled person.

Oliver (1990) argues that doctors do have a role in dealing with physical impairments but that this is often overstepped:

> Some of these involvements are, of course, entirely appropriate, as in the diagnosis of impairment, the stabilisation of medical condition after trauma, the treatment of illness occurring independent of disability and the provision of physical rehabilitation. But doctors are also involved in assessing driving ability, prescribing wheelchairs, determining the allocation of financial benefits, selecting educational provision and measuring work capabilities and potential; in none of these cases is it immediately obvious that medical training and qualifications make doctors the most appropriate persons to be so involved.
>
> (p. 48)

The question of going beyond the medical role is an important one to which I shall return below. The expansion of medical control represents not simply the ambitions of individual doctors, but rather a more complex development in which medical discourse has come to play an important role in maintaining existing power relations. That is, this is a phenomenon that operates at the C and S levels as well as the P.

The development of the Disabled People's Movement (Campbell and Oliver, 1996) can be seen as a response to the medical model, a resistance against professional power, particularly the power of doctors. The social model of disability therefore focuses on rights as well as needs, and empowerment as well as care. To treat a disabled person as if he or she were ill simply because of a physical impairment is to infringe that person's rights, to construct an impression of the person that does not reflect the reality.

There are strong parallels here with the way older people are often treated as if they were ill, simply because they are old. Scrutton (1989) is critical of this tendency to conceive of old age in medical terms:

> The medicalization of ageing is consistent with an image of old age as a process of inevitable physiological and biological decline. It suggests that the process can be temporarily halted only by skilled intervention by professional medical staff. These claims and the fatalism of dominant attitudes towards elderly health need to be seriously examined.
>
> (p. 21)

In a later work, Scrutton uses the term 'medical ageism' to refer to the ways in which negative images of ageing are propounded through the strong association between old age and ill-health, an association reinforced by medical discourse (Scrutton, 1992). O'Neill (1996) takes this a step further when he argues that ageism, both within society generally and the health care system specifically, is a contributory factor in undermining older people's health.

Sidell (1995) discusses Antonovsky's (1984) model of 'salutogenic' health. This involves seeing health as a continuum, rather than simply a dichotomy of healthy versus ill. As people move through their lives, their position on this continuum will continue to change – it is not a fixed entity. As Sidell points out, this reverses the stereotype that older people are a high risk group – no one is entirely free from risk. According to this model, health is not an absence of disease, but rather our ability to cope with our location along this continuum: 'The questions change from what stops people becoming sick to what helps them to become healthy in spite of disease' (1995, p. 16).

A theme that applies across both age and disability is the social construction of dependency. This refers to the ways in which dependency becomes a self-fulfilling prophecy – that is, because health and social welfare services tend to assume a higher level of dependency than is actually the case (Finkelstein, 1991), and because the ethos is primarily one of care rather than empowerment. As Fox (1993) argues: 'Care is power, and the possibility of resisting that power entails a refusal of care qua care, and of the very meanings which are associated with professional carers' (p. 71).

This strongly parallels the Disabled People's Movement's emphasis on the tendency for professionals to patronize disabled people, albeit unintentionally perhaps. Indeed, it is ironic that the good intentions of caring staff are often a source of problems for the people concerned – problems that arise as a result of efforts to provide care standing in the way of people taking greater control over their lives (a point to which I shall return below).

◀ **PRACTICE FOCUS 4.3** ▶

When Megan took over as officer-in-charge of *The Elms* residential home for older people she was keen to move away from a medical-ized ethos of caring and focus more on rights and choice. Consequently, one of the first things she did was to set up a resi-dents' committee to make decisions about certain aspects of how the home was run, choice of food, choice of entertainment and so on. At first it proved very difficult to make this work. Megan met with considerable apathy and even hostility from some people. However, she persevered and eventually managed to achieve her aim. She was then delighted to see people playing a much more active role in decision-making, and noted a clear difference in the atmosphere in the home. She was pleased to see important steps being made away from an ethos of passively receiving care to a much more active approach to residential life.

This is not to say that older or disabled people do not ever require care. That would clearly not be the case. However, it does identify a need to adopt a more critical perspective on caring, to understand when caring is appropriate and when it is more appropriate to con-centrate on rights and empowerment. Adopting a 'caring' approach means much more than simply providing care in an unthinking, uncritical way. In this respect providing care is not a morally neutral activity. At times it can be highly beneficial and greatly appreciated by the people concerned. At other times, however, it can do more harm than good by being intrusive, sapping confidence and creating dependency (Sapey *et al.*, 2001).

Of course, there are times in the lives of older or disabled people when they do fall ill, when medical attention and care may well be appropriate. However, this is a far cry from regarding old age and dis-ability as factors which, by their very nature, require medical inter-vention. The former is an example of a humane society, the latter an example of a potentially very oppressive form of social control based on stereotyping and marginalization.

Mental health

The subject of mental health is one that has been surrounded by controversy for a considerable number of years. A central debate within this controversy is whether it is appropriate to use the term 'mental illness' – can mental health problems legitimately be seen as a form of illness? Lake (1987) would respond in the affirmative, at least as far as depression is concerned: 'If we define illness as a condition which incapacitates, debilitates, and destroys the quality of life of an individual, then there can be no alternative but to describe depression as an illness' (p. 13). However, if we were to adopt this definition, then poverty and divorce could both be seen as illnesses!

A related misconception is that, because mental health problems 'respond' to drug-based or other physical treatments (electro-convulsive therapy or ECT, for example), then this 'proves' that they have a physical basis. However, there is, once again, a fundamental flaw in this logic, as Pilgrim and Rogers (1993) very effectively demonstrate:

> It may be argued that biological treatments that bring about symptom relief themselves point to biological aetiology (such as the lifting of depression by ECT or the diminution of auditory hallucinations by major tranquillizers). However, this may not follow. For instance, thieving can be cured quite effectively by chopping-off the hands of perpetrators; but hands do not cause theft. Likewise, a person shocked following a car crash may feel better by taking a minor tranquilliser, but their state is clearly environmentally induced. The thief's hands and the car crash victim's brain are merely biological mediators in a wider set of personal, economic and social relationships. Thus effective biological treatments cannot be evoked as necessary proof of biological causation.
>
> (p. 5)

Banton et al. (1985) take the argument a step further when they claim that to locate personal and social distress at a biological level is to distract attention from the wider sociopolitical forces operating, and to focus on individual treatment and cure rather than social action or other forms of collective response. Writers from both black and feminist perspectives have put forward a similar line of argument, noting that an individualistic focus has the ideological effect of camouflaging racist and patriarchal processes that lie beneath the service of a medical model of mental health problems (Watters, 1996; Busfield, 1996).

From a social constructionist perspective, mental health problems can be seen in terms of social relationships and discourses, rather than simply a personal state. As Gergen (1999) explains:

> From the present standpoint depression is not an individual disorder; an individual 'does depression' as a culturally intelligible action within a context of relationship. Therapeutic attention thus moves outward from the individual mind ('what is wrong with him?') to the relational scenarios in which the person is engaged. In what kinds of relationship is the depression invited, with whom, and under what conditions? Are other moves in these relationships possible?
>
> (p. 137)

Mental health problems are clearly far more complex than a simple reliance on the medical model would have us believe.

With regard to issues of race and racism, the examples given earlier in this chapter illustrate the dangers of adopting a narrow perspective that pays little or no attention to the significance of racism in black people's lives. With regard to gender and mental health problems, the title of Ussher's (1991) book on this subject captures a fundamental question: *Women's Madness: Misogyny or Mental Illness?* She explores in considerable detail the ways in which women's experiences of distress and oppression become constructed as mental disorder:

> Women are not mad merely because of our hormones, our genes, our faulty learning, our cognition or our unconscious desires. Our madness is not an illness; it is disguised as such by the legalistically worded classifications meted out to women. And why is it women who are mad? why is it that it has always been women? Is this madness actually the result of misogyny, as many feminists would claim, and are the symptoms not madness at all, but anger or outrage?
>
> (p. 6)

◀ PRACTICE FOCUS 4.4 ▶

Anne was diagnosed as suffering from depression and was referred to Social Services for 'support'. The social worker soon discovered that Anne felt hemmed in by other people's expectations of her as a woman – other people seemed to be deciding what she should do and who she should be. She felt trapped and had therefore gone 'inside herself', into a depression. Consequently, a major focus of the subsequent work with her was the significance of women's position in society and how this had in part contributed to her sense of powerlessness. This was to prove to be a major step forward in helping her regain control of her life. (Based on Thompson, 1991b)

An uncritical acceptance of mental health problems as forms of illness can therefore be seen as highly problematic in terms of the potential for discrimination and oppression. Other problems associated with the medical model of mental distress include the following:

- To be diagnosed as mentally ill involves a great deal of stigma, often resulting in considerable disadvantage and a loss of life chances (Bailey, 2000; Miles, 1987).
- Such labels, when applied, tend to become permanent and can have the effect of 'invalidating' the person's whole identity or sense of self (Rogers *et al.*, 1993).
- To be seen as ill, especially as mentally ill, involves the removal of a degree of responsibility for one's own actions or circumstances (Turner, 1995). In matters of mental distress, this denial of responsibility may stand as a barrier to progress through bad faith (Thompson, 1992a).
- Responses to mental health problems tend to be physically based and therefore have the effect of, at best, 'dampening' or controlling the problems, but do not address such problems at the root – hence the claims that psychiatry relates more to social control than to the alleviation of personal distress (Ingleby, 1981; Pride, 2001).
- Similarly, physically based treatments can do a great deal of harm – for example, through the side-effects of medication. Many of the characteristics associated with mental disorder derive not from the 'illness' but from the drugs used to control it – for example, the 'shuffle' walk caused by some forms of psychotropic medication or the dry mouth (and consequent restless tongue movements) brought about by drug treatments – a further example of iatrogenesis.
- Doctors are given considerable power over non-medical matters, thereby placing political matters (that should otherwise be addressed through democratic processes) in the hands of professional decision-makers. Existing power relations, and the discrimination and oppression inherent within them, are therefore maintained by this model (Navarro, 1986).

Perhaps the biggest debate in terms of mental illness is that which surrounds schizophrenia. While firmly established within psychiatry as an illness, the concept of schizophrenia has had many critics. A well-known critique is that of Laing (Boyers and Orrill, 1972) who presented a range of alternative views of schizophrenia. A central theme of Laing's writings is the rejection of the notion that the thoughts and communications of people with schizophrenia are unintelligible.

Laing's thinking changed and developed over time, and so a full analysis of his theories is beyond the scope of this book. However, it is worth noting that, despite considerable variability in the quality and coherence of his theoretical work, he remained consistent in his view that schizophrenia was not an illness, but rather an existential response to an impossible situation – an attempt to 'live the unlivable'. A concept used by Laing is that of the 'double-bind', an idea first introduced by Bateson in the 1950s – see Bateson (1980). Basically, 'double-bind' refers to a situation where a person cannot win:

> If I say something like: 'Don't do what I say', I am placing my listener in an impossible position as my message is self-contradictory. In some families this form of communication is commonplace. This is often accompanied by a degree of scapegoating. A particular member of the family bears the brunt of the family's problems and the 'sick role' becomes an attractive escape route. Hence a disturbed family pattern 'produces' a disturbed individual with bizarre patterns of communication.
>
> (Thompson, 1991b, p. 55)

The concept of schizophrenia as an illness has also come under attack from more conventional scientific quarters. Boyle (1990) presents a long and detailed argument to the effect that the concept has no validity as a scientific construct. She argues that research has yet to demonstrate the links between 'schizophrenic' behaviour and brain dysfunction. Medicine involves studying patterns of bodily functioning, she explains, whereas psychiatry involves studying behaviour and assuming that such behaviour represents bodily functions and that there are consistent patterns to be found. She disputes that there is sufficient empirical evidence to support either of these assumptions.

At some points, Boyle's arguments overlap with Szasz's (1961) point that mental illness is metaphorical – that is, the disturbed thoughts and behaviours associated with mental health problems appear as if they were signs of an illness. Boyle shares this view of psychiatry as an enterprise rooted in metaphor, an enterprise that struggles to provide sufficient hard evidence to legitimate the assumptions that mental health problems are necessarily biological in their origin.

A clear implication of the critique of mental illness as a valid concept is that the inappropriate application of a stigmatizing label of mental illness can have profoundly oppressive effects, not only in the short term but throughout a person's life. Mental health is therefore a subject that needs to be handled very carefully and sensitively if we are to avoid such oppressive consequences.

◀ **PRACTICE FOCUS 4.5** ▶

Len was discharged from the army after he had a 'nervous break-down'. After several months of active combat he had become very tense and anxious. He lost his confidence and became very with-drawn, and was ultimately no longer able to fulfil his duties in the army. After leaving the army he underwent a course of counselling that helped him regain his confidence and helped equip him to meet the challenges of everyday life. However, although the coun-selling had been very successful indeed, the fact that the label 'mental illness' had been applied to Len meant that he had great dif-ficulty obtaining employment suited to his skills and experience. Prejudice relating to the label of 'mental illness' looked as though it would prevent him from achieving his potential.

Before leaving the subject of mental health and the critique of the medical model, it is worth considering some of the misunderstandings that are commonly associated with this critique. I shall address three in particular:

1. *Mental distress does not exist.* To argue that mental health prob-lems do not amount to an illness or disease in the biological sense is *not* to argue that people with mental health problems do not experience considerable distress and suffering. The immense pain, grief and suffering are not in any doubt – it is their status as an illness in need of physical treatment that is being questioned.
2. *Mental health problems have no connection with biology.* The funda-mental argument is that there is insufficient evidence to assume that mental health problems such as depression or schizophrenia are 'caused' by biological pathology. However, this is not to say that there is no link between mental distress and biology. Some mental problems are closely associated with biological dysfunc-tion, dementia being a prime example (although see Kitwood, 1993, for an alternative view of this). Psychiatry, according to its critics, often sees links that are not there. This is no reason, however, to fail to see the links that are there. We must distin-guish between those situations where there is evidence of a bio-logical basis and those where the evidence is unconvincing or non-existent. However, even where a biological link is accepted, there is still a need to go beyond the model and to recognize the significance of psychological and social factors.
3. *Psychiatrists are evil people who oppress vulnerable people.* The cri-tique, it should be noted, is of psychiatry, rather than psychia-trists. This can also be applied to doctors more generally – it is not

necessarily the individual actions of doctors that are being taken to task, but rather the medical discourse that operates ideologically to perpetuate dominant assumptions about (mental) health and illness. This is not to say that doctors, including psychiatrists, do not act in good faith (Busfield, 1996). Rather, the argument is that the ideological foundations on which current practice is based are seriously flawed and do a considerable disservice to vulnerable people whose distress and problems are often not addressed because of the narrow blinkers of medical hegemony.

Health and social welfare

In addressing issues of mental health we are already operating on the terrain of social welfare and the social policy areas of personal social services. However, there are also other ways in which health and social welfare overlap and interweave. It is to an exploration of some of these areas that we now turn.

As we have seen, health is not simply a biological matter – it also has psychological and social dimensions. It is not surprising, then, that health matters should overlap with social welfare concerns in a number of ways, including the following:

- Illness can have psychological consequences – for example, by producing a range of emotions, affecting motivation, memory and patterns of thought.
- Illness can also have social consequences in terms of income, employment, social relations and lifestyle.
- Psychological factors can contribute to ill-health – for example, through stress (Thompson, 1999).
- Social factors can contribute to ill-health – for example, through poverty, poor housing, unemployment.

In the day-to-day reality of working with people and their problems, it is therefore necessary for staff and managers from different disciplines to work together, to collaborate in a multidisciplinary endeavour. Where such collaboration occurs, there is, therefore, scope for medical discourse to shape social welfare outcomes, policies and practices. One clear example of this is the medicalized response to child abuse. The language commonly used in child protection reveals a great deal about the influence of the medical model. For example, practitioners speak of 'diagnosing' child abuse without questioning whether it is possible to diagnose abuse. Child abuse is not simply a specific injury – it is a complex matrix of physical, psychological, social and legal factors that goes far beyond the parameters of a medical diagnosis. In addition, the textbooks continue to refer to post-abuse interventions as 'treatment'. Some may argue that this simply represents a metaphorical use of language. However, as Parton (1985) has demonstrated, dominant views of child abuse are premised on a 'disease' model in which the 'pathology' resides in the parents and becomes apparent through their relationship with the child(ren). Although this model does not stand up to critical scrutiny, due to its inability to explain many aspects of child abuse, it none the less remains a persuasive and pervasive way of conceptualizing the problem of child maltreatment. Here again we are in the domain of ideology – powerful ideas representing power interests, even though the logic underpinning those ideas is easily shown to be seriously flawed.

Parton (1985) argues that the disease model focuses on a narrow set of issues, such as parenting abilities, and thereby perpetuates an individualized conception of abuse. In so doing, it does what ideology so often succeeds in doing – it distracts attention from wider social, political and economic issues and the power relations that are associated with them. In this respect, the individualized disease model 'lets off the hook' the structural factors that contribute to child abuse. Parton's recognition of this leads him to argue for a more preventative approach that takes account of wider social issues:

> Rather than being primarily concerned with trying to identify abusive families and provide individualized treatment we need to concentrate our energies on primary prevention strategies and wider social reforms. Child abuse must not be seen in isolation from the social stresses and insecurity experienced by many children and families and cannot be separated from the range of children's policy issues and the attack on social deprivation. In attempting to meet the needs of all children and families, and not just the selected few, we can be more assured that we will be tackling the problem at hand.
>
> (p. 187)

In a later work (Parton, 1988), he argues that it is partly because of a medicalized approach to child abuse that child protection practitioners, especially social workers, are often blamed when things go wrong. This is because, he argues, there is an expectation that professionals should be trained to recognize the 'symptoms' of child abuse. When they fail to do so (or wrongly assume that abuse has taken place), this is assumed to be because either (i) they have received inadequate training in the recognition of 'symptoms' or (ii) they are incompetent. The reality, of course, is that investigating child abuse is a complex psychological, social and political matter that cannot be reduced to identifying 'symptoms'.

The symptoms or 'indications' that are associated with abuse can be present in families where no abuse appears to be taking place, yet absent in some families where abuse has been clearly identified. A simple medical model therefore sets practitioners up to fail – it places them in a 'no-win' situation by failing to recognize the complexities they face, thereby adding extra pressures to what is already a pressurized undertaking.

One ironic aspect of this situation is that a medical model, which tends to pathologize parents by oversimplifying the circumstances that lead to abuse, also then tends to pathologize child protection workers by oversimplifying the highly complex set of factors involved in such work. However, although this is ironic, it is not beyond explanation. We are once again dealing with ideology – the individualization of child abuse distracts attention from wider issues and the power relations they support, as Figure 4.2 illustrates.

Child abuse is only one example of a broader process of the medicalization and individualization of social problems. Other examples would include:

- *Crime and delinquency* Offenders are often presented as 'sick', particularly if their offences involve an element of cruelty.
- *Drug and alcohol abuse* Although there is clearly a physiological aspect to drug and alcohol abuse, it is not unusual for the social and behavioural aspects to be construed in medical terms.

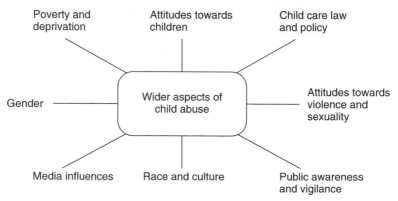

Figure 4.2   Wider aspects of child abuse

As part of her professional training Tanya spent a short period of time on a drug rehabilitation unit at the regional psychiatric hospital. She understood the biological aspects of drug abuse and the damage that could be done to the body. However, what she found really surprising was the extent to which other aspects of the patients' lives were also conceived in biomedical terms, the extent to which their behaviour and attitudes were seen as part of an illness. She found this quite unsettling and spent a great deal of time considering the issues surrounding illness and behaviour.

Medicine and social control

Related to the medicalization of social problems is the role of medical power in social control. Writers such as Illich (1977) and Zola (1972) have put forward what has become known as the 'medicalization of life' thesis. Building on Illich's notion of 'iatrogenesis' we can see that modern society has reached a stage of what Illich would call 'structural iatrogenesis', which Jones (1994) describes as:

> the stripping away from human culture of ways of coping with birth, pain and death and their replacement by a sanitised, technological medical intervention against which individuals and societies are unable to fight back. People stop relying on and trusting each other and depend only on medical intervention.
>
> (p. 456)

It would be a mistake, however, to see such developments as a conspiracy or the result of deliberate attempts by doctors to establish themselves in positions of authority and control. Rather, as Zola (1972) argues, such developments are better understood as responses to an increasingly bureaucratic and technological form of social organization, and one that relies heavily on the role of 'experts', thereby placing considerable power in their hands. Or, to put the argument in PCS terms, the situation has arisen as a result of structural factors (industrialization, increased reliance on technology and so on) which relate closely to cultural factors (medical discourse, shared assumptions about doctors as experts and faith in medical science). The **P** level actions of individual doctors can then be seen as a reflection of the broader **C** and **S** factors (and part of the process of maintaining and reproducing them), rather than, in any simple sense, the cause of the situation.

One very clear example of the medicalization of life is, ironically, the medicalization of death, the move away from traditional ways of dealing with death towards approaches firmly rooted in medical discourse. Seale (1995a) discusses the relationship between medicine and death and comments on what can be seen as the over-reliance on medical expertise:

> Because, ultimately, medicine cannot save us, death is segregated, removed from social life in institutions in an attempt to banish what is beyond control. In avoiding open discussion of death with those who are dying, and often placing dying patients in a side-room off the main ward, hospital staff contribute to this segregation. Funeral rituals are increasingly taken over by professionals and lack personal content. Through these means death is made hygienic, and nature is held at bay.
> (pp. 189–90)

Walter (1994) takes the argument a step further by arguing that death has been medicalized in two senses:

1. The place of death is predominantly a medical setting, with two-thirds of the people who die in Britain doing so in hospital.
2. Bereavement is regarded by many as a form of illness. See, for examples, the articles by Lindemann (1944) and Engel (1961), both very influential in their time, and a 'standard text' on bereavement, namely Parkes (1980).

Seale (1995b) presents the hospice movement as a reaction against medicalization, an attempt to reintroduce a more human approach to issues of death and dying. Howarth (1996) also argues that there are now many such attempts to move away from a medical model: 'a manifest rejection of modern scientific and medical rationale' (p. xiv). In addition, Howarth makes the important point that: 'the cultural mechanisms surrounding death and dying reveal much about the state of social life and the living' (1996, p. xiii). That is, the fact that death is characterized by medical discourse and hegemony reflects the fact social life is also so characterized.

The medicalization of life can be seen as a form of social control. Because important moral and political decisions (about the allocation of resources, for example) are redesignated as matters of professional decision-making, the power to influence, or even control, moral and political issues is given to doctors. As we saw earlier in this chapter, the notion of health has distinct ideological connotations, in so far as it helps to police the boundaries between what is (socially) normal and abnormal.

There are also a number of other ways in which medical and health matters can be seen as questions of social control, as the following examples indicate:

- mental health, as discussed earlier;
- decisions about fitness for work, eligibility for benefits and so on;
- the use of medical and psychiatric reports to aid decision-making in courts;
- the regulation of pregnancy, childbirth and women's sexuality (Turner, 1995); and
- access to social housing.

These are, of course, in addition to the issues of child abuse and other social problems already discussed in this chapter.

The 'Body-without-Organs' – the ontology of health

The 'Body-without-Organs' (BwO) is a concept first introduced by Deleuze and Guattari (1984). It refers not to the physical or anatomical body, but to a 'political surface' upon which discourses are 'inscribed'. That is, Foucault's notion of the body as a site of power can be used to explain medical hegemony and the significance of health. The BwO is a symbolic entity – it represents the interplay of discourses and resistance to such discourses. As such, it is an important concept for understanding how power operates in and through notions of health and illness.

A related, and equally important concept is that of 'territorialization'. Medical and other discourses are said to 'territorialize' the BwO, to establish the parameters in which it is able to operate. That is, power relations construct limits as to what it is possible, desirable or acceptable for the individual to do. This territorialization therefore brings forth the need for 'de-territorialization' or resistance – the need to challenge received ideas that are unnecessarily constraining.

Fox (1993) describes the BwO in the following terms:

> The BwO is the outcome of material production, and material production (as well as the production of desire) is a consequence of the political BwO. So it is the location at which biology and the social collide. On the BwO are inscribed . . . the discourses of the social, alongside the sensations of the body-pleasurable and painful – and the positive desire of other BwOs. On its surface, intensities vie and intermingle: from the patterning of the BwO emerges the fabricated, political, ephemerality of identity – the human subject.
>
> (p. 143)

This is both reminiscent of, and compatible with, existentialism. For example, Sartre (1958) draws a distinction between *being* a body (our basic, biological reality – facticity) and *having* a body (our sense of self that is much more than our biological starting point – contingency). It is by understanding that 'biology is not destiny' that we are able to begin to break free from the disempowering discourses that construct human reality as a limited and unnecessarily constrained form of existence, rather than one that is open, creative and capable of multiple interpretations and therefore multiple choices of being. Medical discourse therefore confuses essence (fixity) with existence (becoming). It is in this regard that dominant discourses about health are conservative – they support the status quo and the existing power relations that are part and parcel of it (Figure 4.3).

We are here touching on one of the recurring themes of the book – the need to recognize that the biological dimension of human existence is only one aspect of a complex multifaceted reality. The psychological, social, political and economic dimensions also have a significant role to play, as does the ontological dimension which to some extent acts as unifier of the other aspects, in so far as it focuses directly on lived experience (*le vécu*).

Another ontological concept that is relevant to health is that of ontological security. As we noted in Chapter 1, we rely on a sense of security to help us cope with the demands of everyday life and to maintain a coherent thread of identity. From this we can posit an interactive or

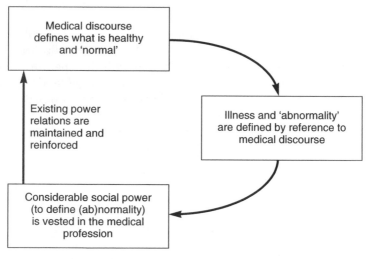

Figure 4.3   Medical discourse and the status quo

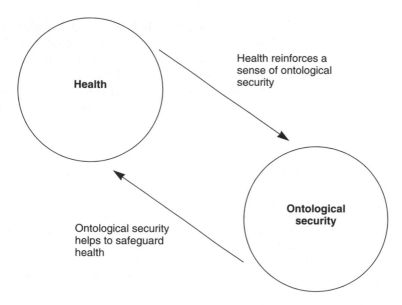

Health reinforces a
sense of ontological
security

Health

**Ontological
security**

Ontological security
helps to safeguard
health

Figure 4.4   The health–ontological security dialectic

dialectical relationship between the two – between ontological security and health (Figure 4.4).

Health problems can have the effect of undermining ontological security, as exemplified by comments such as: 'I don't feel myself today'. Conversely, where ontological security is threatened in other ways – by major life changes, for example – this can have a detrimental effect on health as a result of the stress involved (Totman, 1990; Thompson *et al.* 1994a).

◀ PRACTICE FOCUS 4.7 ▶

Gerry had not had a day's sickness absence from work in over seventeen years. He prided himself on his fitness regime and his sensible diet. However, the situation changed quite drastically when his wife, Diane, died in a car accident. Following this, Gerry found himself beset by a series of minor ailments. Whatever 'bug' was doing the rounds, it was almost certain that Gerry would be among the first to get it. He no longer felt 'on top' of his life, and this seemed to have affected his resilience to illness. It was quite some time before Gerry was able to shake off this period of one illness after another.

There are parallels between this relationship and Antonovsky's

(1979) notion of the role of a 'sense of coherence'. Antonovsky proposed what he called a 'salutogenic paradigm', a view of human existence as being characterized by disorder and constant challenges to our well-being. A basic focus of Antonovsky's theory is the degree of success we have in coping with the demands and threats that we face each day. A key factor in this coping is our orientation towards our life and the challenges it presents. Antonovsky refers to this orientation as a 'sense of coherence' (SOC):

> The sense of coherence is a global orientation that expresses the extent to which one has a pervasive, enduring though dynamic feeling of confidence that (1) the stimuli deriving from one's internal and external environments in the course of living are structured, predictable and explicable; (2) the resources are available to one to meet the demands posed by these stimuli; and (3) these demands are challenges, worthy of investment and engagement.
>
> (1987, p. 19, cited in Antonovsky, 1993)

Although by no means identical, the concept of SOC would seem to have much in common with ontological security and the interplay between phenomenological questions of perception, meaning and purpose (the subjective dimension) and broader issues of social relations, political and environmental factors (the objective dimension).

One apparent weakness in the SOC concept is its reliance on a psychological perspective that is not sufficiently counterbalanced by a sociological perspective. Whereas ontological security is located at the intersection of psychological and sociological factors in both existentialism and structuration theory, sense of coherence is presented primarily as a psychological concern. This is not to say, however, that the concept cannot be developed to a more sophisticated level of analysis and thereby rendered more productive as a means of explaining the complex interactions between individuals and the social world.

Indeed, this is the strength of the concept of the BwO – its location at the point of intersection of the biological (being a body) and the social (having a body in a social world largely shaped and constrained by dominant discourses). The concept of the BwO, although abstract and perhaps quite difficult to assimilate at first, enables us to understand some of the ways in which broader power relations are reflected in, and reinforced by, the way the notions of body, health, disease and so on are used to construct particular understandings of what is 'normal', 'healthy' and therefore desirable. The power structures of society are mirrored in the ways in which the human body is socially constructed in terms of health and illness, normality and abnormality.

Or, to put it another way, dominant discourses are inscribed on the BwO. Turner (1995) gives an example of this when he discusses the significance of women's health and sexuality in relation to dominant power interests:

> Medical ideology constitutes women as psychologically and socially vulnerable and therefore in need of close medical (that is male) surveillance, advice and guidance (Ehrenreich and English, 1978). Since in the medical literature both menstruation and pregnancy are regarded as 'medical problems', there is a basic logic to the medical view that women are, as it were, natural patients. This view of women as sick is one dimension of the contradictory medical view of women's sexuality. Women have to be simultaneously 'damned whores' and 'God's police' (Summers, 1975). From the male medical point of view, women both reproduce men within the moral confines of the family and function as a moral police force, but their very sexuality means they are equally prone to whoredom. Sexual deviance . . . in women was particularly threatening to the social fabric; it was for this reason that an endless debate has surrounded the whole problem of illegitimate births and the social standing of women (Gill, 1977).
>
> (pp. 102–3)

This passage provides a clear illustration of the interrelationship between dominant discourses (in this case, a patriarchal model of gender relations) and the human body (specifically women's bodies in this example). Health can therefore be seen as an important ontological concept, in so far as it is an aspect of human existence that operates at the intersection of the individual's experience of the world and the broader social, political and economic structures and cultural formations that shape and constrain that world.

Conclusion

This has been a wide-ranging chapter, covering the social construction of health; health discourses; medicine and social control; health inequalities; health disability and age; mental health; health and social welfare; and the ontology of health. The underlying themes of the discussion have been those of:

- the recognition that health and illness are much more than biological entities;
- the important relationships between health and wider sociopolitical factors, particularly power relations;

- the significance of the concept of health in terms of discrimination, oppression and inequality; and
- the recognition that health is a key issue (or set of issues) for all staff and managers involved in 'people work' and not simply those who work specifically in a health care setting.

Overall, health can be seen as part of the process of structuration. That is, it is partly through the way health-related issues are constructed and dealt with that the social structure at a macro-level is reproduced over time in and through the actions of individuals and groups at the micro-level. That is to say, health is one of a range of factors that mediate between structure and agency.

Drawing out the implications of this for practice is, of course, a complex task. However, an important starting point for this task is the need to approach issues of health and illness critically, and not to take them at face value. The discussions here therefore support the argument that professional practice work needs to be based on critically reflective practice – a form of practice that does not simply skate over the surface of dominant discourses, but rather looks beneath that surface to take account of, and respond constructively to, the discrimination, oppression and inequalities that are to be found there.

5

LEARNING FROM THE PAST

Introduction

Attempts to challenge discrimination and oppression are, of course, not new. Very many efforts have been made to promote equality, some of which have brought some degree of success, while others have not. My aim in this chapter is not to chart the historical development of such efforts, but rather, more modestly, to identify a range of approaches that have been adopted and experimented with, focusing in particular on the problems and difficulties associated with them. My intention, then, is to present a summary of various strategies and tactics that have been utilized in an attempt to promote equality so that our current and future efforts do not have to 'reinvent the wheel' or repeat the mistakes of the past.

In providing this overview, I am, of course, not attempting to 'play God' and decide ultimately what is good or bad in terms of challenging discrimination and oppression. Such issues are political matters and are therefore, by their very nature, contested and open to multiple interpretations and evaluations. I am therefore not trying to dismiss previous efforts wholesale in order to clear the way for providing the definitive answer to the problem of inequality. It should be clear from the theoretical framework presented in Chapter 1 that such an absolutist approach is neither possible nor desirable: 'one of the implications of existentialism is that there can be no panacea, no easy answers, as human existence is characterized by struggle and challenge' (Thompson, 2000b, pp. 82–3).

By reviewing a range of equality strategies I am hoping to achieve the following:

• To alert practitioners, managers and educators to some of the dangers associated with some forms of equality practice so that we are not doomed to repeat the mistakes of the past.

- To provide, in summary form, a broad picture of some of the important steps that have been taken in seeking to counter discrimination and oppression.
- To provide the basis for further debate and analysis of what needs to be done to make positive progress in this complex and demanding area of theory, policy and practice.

The chapter is based on my own experiences as a practitioner and manager; teaching about equality and diversity issues on a wide range of courses and training workshops; undertaking and supervising research on these and related issues; many years of seeking to influence organizations from within (as an employee) and from without (as a consultant); as well as reading widely on the subject. None the less, this chapter remains a personal view of inequality and the success or otherwise of attempts to reduce or eradicate it. I would not want the arguments presented here to be seen as an example of the dogmatism that I shall be criticizing below.

The chapter is divided into two main sections. The first presents a range of overarching themes that can be seen to characterize a number of efforts to tackle inequalities, themes that I see as fatal flaws that seriously weaken, or even undermine completely those efforts. The second section presents a much longer list of more specific issues in relation to 'learning from the past', presenting a brief but broad overview of a range of equality strategies.

Overarching themes

In total I shall present seven overarching themes, seven factors that are commonly found across a range of initiatives. The discussion of the themes builds on some of the theoretical discussions already presented in earlier chapters.

Essentialism

As noted in Chapter 1, essentialism refers to the tendency to confuse the creativity, openness and variability of human existence with fixity, an underlying 'essence' or essential quality that cannot be changed. Essentialism is highly problematic in relation to inequality in at least three main ways:

1. It presents individuals as fixed and immutable and therefore having little or no scope for change. Essentialism is characterized by comments such as: 'I can't help it, that's the way I am.'

Strategies that reinforce essentialism are therefore self-defeating in so far as they reinforce the myth that people cannot change their behaviour or attitudes. In existentialist terms, essentialism encourages and condones bad faith and therefore stands in the way of authentic practice.

2. This can also be seen to apply at a societal level. Essentialist beliefs include the idea that inequality is 'natural' (and by implication desirable) and the notion that progress is inevitable as society develops (and does not therefore require any investment of time or energy on our part). In this respect, essentialism clearly operates ideologically. That is, essentialist ideas serve to legitimate existing social arrangements and the power relations which sustain them. Essentialism is therefore part of the problem rather than part of the solution.

3. An acceptance of essentialism involves focusing primarily or exclusively on the **P** level without taking into account wider concerns at the **C** and **S** levels. It therefore presents too narrow a picture and distorts the complex realities of social life. This is a common problem in tackling discrimination. For example, to say that someone 'is a racist' is to imply that this is part of them, a component of their identity. While this may well be the case with some people (members of far right organizations, for example) it is misleading to see this as being the case. It is not only misleading, but also very unhelpful in the following three ways:

   (i) It ignores the fact that people who would not identify themselves as racists may well perpetuate racism unwittingly, whether by acts of omission or commission (Thompson, 2001a)

   (ii) It can create unnecessary (and counterproductive) feelings of guilt that can stand in the way of progress (see the discussion below of 'Defensiveness').

   (iii) It can reinforce bad faith, as discussed in point 1 above.

An example of essentialism from an equality practice point of view can be found in relation to challenging heterosexism. Davies (1996a), in a paper that seeks to promote anti-heterosexist forms of therapeutic practice, displays a strong element of essentialism in making the following comment:

> Since sexual orientation seems to be beyond our active control, like our eye colour, it is a sad indictment of our society that people are driven to kill themselves because they cannot see a future as lesbian, gay and bisexual.
>
> (pp. 137–8)

While the stigma associated with a gay, lesbian or bisexual identity is something to be rejected as discriminatory, to support the argument with the essentialist notion that sexual orientation is 'beyond our active control, like our eye colour' is a dangerous tactic. Giving credence to essentialism can be seen as counterproductive, in so far as it indirectly adds weight to the line of argument so often used to justify inequality – that it is 'natural' and beyond our control.

Reductionism

This refers to the process of reducing a complex, multifaceted reality to a simple, single-level explanation. A common form of this process that relates to inequality is that of biological reductionism. That is, complex sociopolitical factors are presented as if they are simply matters of biology. This can be seen to apply to a number of forms of oppression, as outlined in Chapter 1.

This tendency to rely on biological reductionism is, of course, not a matter of coincidence. Biology is commonly used as the basis of ideological legitimation. Biological matters are seen as relatively fixed and stable, and are therefore useful as arguments to support the status quo and thereby legitimate the social arrangements that maintain powerful groups and individuals in their positions of power.

Segal (1999) points out the weakness of relying on biological arguments to explain social, psychological and cultural matters:

> The irony is that human beings are never simply at the mercy of their biology, even were there consistent evidence for significant sex differences which could be mapped on to the human genome . . . [A]ny form of genetic reductionism flies in the face of all serious genetic theory since the 1970s, which rejects earlier assumptions that genes determine human action in any stable or straightforward way. A behavioural trait can be said to be genetic only if genes alone provide the best explanation for its origin, and this is simply not the case for *any* complex human trait. A multiplicity of other mechanisms always interact with the compound genetic codings bearing upon any single human event.
>
> (p. 154)

Biological reductionism therefore operates ideologically in much the same way as essentialism.

An example of a reductionist approach to inequality is that of race awareness training, a now discredited approach that involved a confrontational form of training in which white participants were put under pressure to 'own up' to their racism. As Gurnah (1984) points out, this process proved to be very ineffective, and indeed counterproductive to a certain extent. Such training was located primarily if not exclusively at the **P** level, as if anti-racism were simply a matter of changing the attitudes and behaviours of individuals without due consideration of the cultural and structural levels and their impact on those attitudes and behaviours. This is an example of psychological reductionism – PCS is reduced to 'P', and so the complex multifaceted reality of racism and anti-racism is distorted to fit into a predominantly psychological model. As we shall see later in this chapter, there are also other forms of reductionism that can be seen to apply.

◀ PRACTICE FOCUS 5.1 ▶

When, as part of an in-service training course, Pat was told that she was racist because 'all white people are racist', she objected strongly to this. The trainer tried to interpret her response as a sign of both 'guilt' and 'denial'. However, when Pat tried to point out that the trainer's views were based on reductionism and were, moreover, oppressive in their own right, the trainer was at a loss as to how to respond. Pat therefore took the opportunity to make the point that racism operates at a number of levels and simply to brand individuals as racist because they are white is a gross oversimplification. Other participants on the course were pleased that Pat had the confidence (and the necessary understanding of the sociology of racism) to challenge what they saw as quite an offensive overgeneralization.

The discussion of structuration theory in Chapter 1 emphasized the significance of the interplay of structure and agency, of macro and micro. To focus on one and neglect the other is therefore to distort the reality of the social world and our part within it. Reductionism is therefore out of step with structuration theory and other approaches that seek to do justice to the intricacies of social life.

Dogmatism

The difficulties arising from adopting a dogmatic approach were discussed briefly in Chapter 3. However, this is a topic of sufficient importance to warrant being revisited here in more detail.

A dogmatic approach is one that involves adopting a closed mind in relation to a particular issue or set of issues and not being willing to take on board alternative points of view or perspectives. This may, for some, be a deliberate strategy, a conscious decision not to be influenced by other people's views in order to maintain a particular ideological 'territory'. For many, however, it is more likely to arise from a lack of understanding of the complexity of the issues involved, insecurity about their own position, pressure from others, or a combination of the three.

A number of factors can be identified that are likely to contribute to dogmatism, not least the following:

- *Essentialism* Dogmatism often rests on the assumption that there is an absolute truth, a 'right answer' that can be uncovered. And, of course, the person who adopts a dogmatic approach believes that he or she has 'uncovered' that definitive answer, and is therefore going to be reluctant to be dissuaded from it.
- *Reductionism* Simple, straightforward answers can be very appealing and so, in some circumstances, people may wish to hold on to such answers, even though they are oversimplified, because they bring with them a degree of (apparent) certainty and security.
- *Emotional responses* Issues of discrimination and oppression can prove to be an emotive subject-matter. This is partly because people may feel threatened when they are challenged about something they have taken for granted for a very long period of time. In such circumstances, it is not surprising that some people may 'dig their heels in' about particular issues (see the discussion below of 'defensiveness').
- *Collective responses* Because inequality is a political issue, responses to it are often of a collective nature. That is, people band together to tackle the problem by challenging the ideologies and social practices that sustain it. While such collective responses are generally an advantage (as I shall argue in Chapter 7), one potential disadvantage is that people may feel the need to 'toe the party line'. That is, a reluctance to undermine a collective response may lead to an unwillingness to think critically about the arguments that apply (a form of 'groupthink' – see Janis, 1972; Burgoon *et al.*, 1994).
- *Academic and political fashions* Certain approaches can, at times, achieve the status of a fad or fashion. For example, Gomm (1993) comments on how the notion of 'empowerment' has become a 'buzzword'. As we shall see in Chapter 6, the development of the diversity approach is in danger of falling into this trap. Where this occurs there is a danger that particular arguments or courses of action are adopted uncritically. In addition, fundamentally sound ideas can be distorted to the point where they become dangerous as a result of an uncritical zeal (partnership is also a good example here).

Papadopoulos (2001) makes apt comment when she argues that:

Not only has antiracism evolved as a dictatorial form particularly in the context of local government, but it has also served to trivialise and isolate the struggles against other political antagonisms such as the contradictions of social and economic inequalities, the struggles of women and other marginalised groups. Yet, in Britain today, 'race' cannot be understood or grasped if it is falsely divorced from all these other political processes and power struggles.

(p. 53)

She also speaks of the 'moralistic excesses practised in the name of anti-racism'. My concern is that it is genuine attempts to challenge racism and to establish race equality that are so often dismissed because they have been tarred with the same brush as dogmatic actions and attitudes of certain individuals and factions who appear to have little understanding of the complexities of race and racism and of discrimination and oppression more broadly. In other words, dogmatism discredits and undermines genuine efforts to promote equality and value diversity.

Although there are clearly a number of reasons why dogmatism should come to be relied upon, the costs of such an attitude should also be borne in mind. Dogmatism can not only distort the situation, and thereby stand in the way of an appropriate course of action being decided upon or implemented, it can also discourage and demotivate people who may otherwise be committed to challenging inequality. That is, dogmatism on the part of one or more people can lead to demoralization and defeatism on the part of others.

◀ **PRACTICE FOCUS 5.2** ▶

In a class discussion on racism, Mike, one of the most enthusiastic students in the group, made a comment to the effect that he thought that racism shown towards Irish people in Britain was also an important issue to address. However, the tutor leading the discussion told him that racism related primarily to skin colour and, because Irish people were white, they were not to be included in a discussion of racism. Mike did not agree with this and felt that the tutor was oversimplifying some complex issues. However, discouraged by what seemed to be a dogmatic attitude to racism on the part of the tutor, Mike did not challenge this and resolved not to contribute to discussions about racism again for fear of 'putting his foot in it'.

Determinism

In Chapter 1 the point was made that people often indulge in what existentialists call 'bad faith'. This refers to the tendency to seek explanations for our behaviour outside ourselves, as if we have little or no control over it. This is an example of essentialism, the idea that there is an underlying fixed reality, an immutable 'essence'. However, it is also an example of determinism, the belief that our actions are largely determined by factors beyond our control – in effect denying or minimizing a role for agency.

An example of determinism in attempts to challenge discrimination and oppression would be the crude forms of radical social work that emerged in the late 1960s and early 1970s. As Pearson (1975) put it: 'The client in "radical social work" has become a wooden, dehumanised figure at the bargain basement of a welfare-rights stall. The cult of activism in "radical social work" rules at the expense of its humanising object' (p. 135).

Pearson's comments are indicative of a wider critique of approaches that were loosely based on marxism, or at least the economic reductionism that came to be associated with marxism (Thompson, 1992a). The workings of class and other macro-level social forces can so easily become the focus of concern, with the effect that actual individual human beings become lost in the analysis of structural factors (see the discussion of the 'Polo mint' effect below).

Giddens' theory of structuration is helpful in clarifying the problems that can arise. As we have seen, structuration refers to the process whereby human actions reproduce the social structure and its system of social relations, while also being influenced and constrained by those relations. That is, the social structure is both the outcome and the context of human actions. However, this should not be seen as a deterministic theory, one in which one layer of analysis (structure or agency) is seen to 'cause' or determine the other. The interaction between the two is dialectical and so the outcome cannot be determined in advance. As Giddens (1995) comments: 'The concept of social reproduction ... is not in and of itself an explanatory one: all reproduction is contingent and historical' (p. 27). This is an important comment from Giddens, as it emphasizes that structuration is:

- *Contingent* It is not determined in advance. What happens owes much to the actions of the people concerned (agency) and the context in which it occurs (structure). Or, to put it in Sartrean terms, we are what we make of what is made of us (Thompson, 1992a).
- *Historical* What occurs now will owe much to what has happened in the past – the structures and influences that have built up over a significant period of time. The past is therefore the context for the present and the future that we are in the process of constructing

through our actions. To paraphrase Marx, people make history (agency) but not in circumstances of their own choosing (structure).

In order to understand the social world and people's place within it, it is therefore necessary to take account of both structure and agency (and the interactions between the two). To adopt a deterministic approach is therefore to neglect the agency dimension and thereby fail to do justice to the complexities of human existence in a social context.

As we noted in Chapter 2, deterministic tendencies can also be discerned in postmodernist writings particularly in relation to the notion of 'subjectless history'. We should therefore be wary of being complacent in assuming that the deterministic versions of radical practice are no longer in the ascendancy. The danger of falling into the trap of determinism is therefore an ever-present one.

Defensiveness

It is very understandable that people should not want a label such as 'racist' or 'sexist' attached to them. Consequently, it is not surprising that many people approach issues of discrimination and oppression in an extremely cautious way, very wary of giving others ammunition with which to attack them. It is therefore very unfortunate and regrettable that so many efforts to tackle inequality can be seen to have the effect of raising such anxieties further, rather than allaying them or using them constructively as a step in the direction of positive change. An example of such an approach that has already been mentioned is that of Race Awareness Training (RAT), in which participants were required to recognize and admit to their own racism.

Such a tactic is both essentialist (racism is 'inside' the individual) and reductionist (cultural and structural factors are given only minimal attention and are not adequately integrated into the analysis). However, such approaches to education and training are also highly suspect in terms of the rationale for their effectiveness. In particular, they can be seen to run counter to the 'Yerkes–Dodson law of adult learning' (Cropley, 1977). This 'law' is based on the idea that we can understand learning in terms of a continuum between high and low levels of anxiety (see Figure 5.1). Where there is little or no anxiety, the result is likely to be complacency and a relative absence of learning. At the opposite extreme, where anxiety is at a high level, the likely outcome is one of defensiveness in which those involved feel under threat. They therefore tend to concentrate on surviving the situation with their self-esteem intact, rather than taking the opportunity to learn. It is at the optimal level of anxiety that learning is maximized –

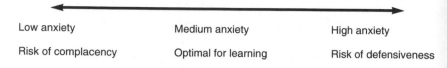

| Low anxiety | Medium anxiety | High anxiety |
| Risk of complacency | Optimal for learning | Risk of defensiveness |

Figure 5.1   The Yerkes–Dodson law of adult learning

at the middle range, neither too low nor too high, where anxiety is manageable and can be experienced as stimulation and motivation (this is also an important element of stress theory – see Thompson *et al.*, 1996a; Thompson, 1999).

Attempts to deal with inequality that are based on threat and fear are therefore highly problematic (as are those based on dogma, see Practice Focus 5.2), partly because they are based on a lack of understanding of learning processes and the obstacles to learning that can be generated, and partly because such methods can be seen as a form of oppression in their own right, involving as they do, an abuse of the power education and training staff have over course participants in a formal setting.

But it is not only in a training context that defensiveness can be generated by an insensitive and ill-informed approach to challenging discrimination and oppression. As Practice Focus 5.3 (below) illustrates, defensiveness can arise in other ways. In fact, wherever inequality is recognized as a target for change, the potential for creating defensive responses is sure to exist.

In view of this, efforts made to develop an open and trusting work environment (and indeed learning environment) can be seen as very worthwhile and important. Just as an 'ethos of permission' (Thompson *et al.*, 1996a) is recognized as an important element in staff care, so too can it be seen as necessary for creating and sustaining an atmosphere in which:

- People do not feel threatened. They may well be challenged about particular aspects of their behaviour, language or attitudes, but this should be a constructive process that encourages change, rather than an atmosphere of fear in which people are too wary and defensive to risk entering into any form of change process.
- People who experience discrimination can feel able to discuss their concerns and experiences, if they so wish, without worrying about 'fanning the flames' or creating a very unpleasant situation that achieves nothing and may ultimately be destructive.
- Newcomers to the situation very quickly learn that discrimination

and oppression are taken very seriously but are dealt with sensitively and constructively. This can help to ensure that a staff group's commitment to promoting equality does not fade away over time.

- People feel able to discuss issues openly so that the scope for developing collaborative alliances is increased.

◀ **PRACTICE FOCUS 5.3** ▶

Jan was delighted to be appointed as coordinator of the newly-established multidisciplinary team. The team were keen to support her and make the whole venture a success. Things started to go very well until Jan made it clear that she wanted to make equality issues a priority in the team. She met a lot of resistance to this (for example, one female member of the team saying it was not fair to discuss gender issues in the team as it would make the men feel uncomfortable). What struck Jan particularly, though, was the way such issues were always 'derailed' when raised at meetings. It took next to no time for the subject to be changed whenever equality issues came to the fore. Jan began to worry a great deal about this, concerned that defensiveness about 'getting it wrong' was leading some team members at least to avoid the subject whenever possible.

Of course, the idea that a sensitive, constructive approach is likely to be far more effective than one based on threat and fear does not mean that it is never appropriate to adopt a more confrontational approach. There may well be times when someone's unacceptable behaviour – sexual harassment, for example – does not respond to a constructive approach and calls for disciplinary procedures (or is of such a serious nature that formal procedures become immediately applicable – Thompson, 2000c). My argument is that such responses should be used in the specific circumstances where they are warranted, rather than applied in a blanket fashion as a matter of course.

In my view, Brechin *et al.* (2000) capture the point superbly when they comment that: 'Not defensive but defensible practice is the order of the day' (p. xv).

Non-dialectical approaches

Dialectical reason can be characterized by three main elements as follows:

1. *It is dynamic* It involves, by definition, a flow of time, a movement through history. It is not a static, once-and-for-all analysis, but rather a recognition of the dynamic nature of social reality

and human existence. It is therefore a tool used to help understand the processes of change that constantly go on all around us – it is not an attempt to capture a timeless essence or ultimate truth.

2. *It is interactive* The changes with which it is concerned can be mapped in terms of the interaction of conflicting forces – for example, class in marxism; structure and agency in structuration theory; subjectivity and objectivity in existentialism.

3. *It 'totalizes'* This does not mean that it seeks to uncover a definitive 'totality', an overall truth – that would be profoundly undialectical. Rather, it seeks to understand phenomena in terms of processes of totalization, to adopt a 'helicopter vision' that provides an overview of the factors involved without focusing too closely on one or other aspect of the situation.

Attempts to promote equality have at times proved to be non-dialectical in each of these three respects. A failure to recognize the dynamic nature of social reality can be detected in some approaches. For example, some forms of radical feminism have been criticized for seeing male dominance as an historical constant and therefore neglecting to analyse the specific historical circumstances that have provided fertile soil for patriarchy to flourish (Lovell, 2000; Segal, 1999). A weakness of this approach is that the non-dialectical nature of the analysis seriously undermines the capacity of the theory to identify the historical processes which could potentially be reversed in order to challenge patriarchy.

Another form of feminism provides an example of the neglect of the interactive dimension of dialectical reason. Liberal feminism has been criticized for focusing too narrowly on the individual and thereby failing to take sufficient account of the social forces that are likely to resist and counteract the efforts of individuals. That is, it neglects an analysis of the wider social context in which the actions of individuals are located. Instead of recognizing the dialectical interplay of the liberal forces for change and the contrary forces geared towards protecting the status quo, liberal feminism concentrates almost exclusively on the former at the expense of the latter. Such a non-dialectical approach therefore leads to a failure to address significant aspects of the social field, the important role of ideology, for example.

In terms of 'totalizing', the following passage from Laing and Cooper (1964) is helpful:

Sartre sees the various theories of sociology, anthropology and psycho-analysis as more or less partial realizations of some moment or moments in the dialectic. Since they are not grasped by dialectical reason they are blown up into total theories, and inevitably run into contradictions which their authors try to deal with by ad hoc hypotheses, or simply ignore.

(p. 15)

What this refers to is the tendency to take one aspect of the situation (the psychological or the sociological, for example) and present it as if it were the only or primary aspect – one part is mistaken for the whole. Legalistic approaches, to be discussed below, can be seen as an example of this type of non-dialectical perspective on inequality – the legal dimension is given too much prominence and is not recognized as one factor among many within a complex matrix that is constantly changing.

Some postmodernists reject the dialectic as part of their critique of what they call 'dichotomous thinking'. They point out that: 'Dichotomous thinking implies that most phenomena fit into "binary" and "oppositional" categories, in which one item of the binary is devalued in relation to the other, and mutually exclusive as well (e.g. you must either be a "victim" or a "perpetrator")' (Fook, 2002, p. 73).' However, this is not so much a rejection of the dialectic as a tool of understanding complex social issues as a critique of an essentialist and reductionist use of the dialectic which fails to appreciate its dynamic nature. The 'poles' of the dialectic are not fixed categories, but rather, fluid elements which change through the interplay of con-tradictions on which the dialectic is based.

Drift

One of the dangers involved in many types of work, but particularly in 'people work', is that of drift. By this I mean the tendency to lose sight of what we are doing and why we are doing it. I have previously linked this to a failure to adopt what I would call 'systematic practice':

A systematic approach to practice is one that is clear and focused with little or no tendency to vagueness or drift. That is, systematic practice involves having clear objectives and a firm focus on the actions being taken and their effects.

This is an important approach to all aspects of people work and seeks to avoid traditional forms of practice that are characterised by drift and uncertainty.

(Thompson, 2002c, p. 174)

When people are busy and under pressure, perhaps with conflicting demands on their time and energy, it is not surprising that they may lose track of the process they are going through in terms of what they are trying to achieve and how they are intending to achieve it. In short, they lose their strategic focus.

This can be a general characteristic of busy practitioners who start to focus so closely on the details of what they are doing that they lose 'the big picture' of how what they are doing on a day-to-day basis fits into the overall plan of action. Where this occurs the actual steps taken can prove counterproductive – they may go against the purpose of the work being undertaken. For example, a worker may become so involved in helping someone to sort out their day-to-day problems that they may not realize that, in doing so, they might be undermining the overall aim of making that person more independent and less reliant on professional help.

In relation to matters of inequality, discrimination and oppression, this tendency to drift away from the purpose of the work being done may be even greater due to the additional pressures that can be involved (see, for example, the discussion above of 'defensiveness'). Consequently, many basically sound attempts to promote equality can be undermined, or even sabotaged completely, by 'drift'.

The process of drift can be encouraged by equality policies that are brought into being but are not monitored or evaluated. This can lead to policies that exist on paper but have little or no purchase on actual practice within the organization concerned. Where this occurs, such policies become devalued or even the object of ridicule. This can also have the effect of devaluing equality policies in general, contributing to the view that such policies represent only a tokenistic response with no genuine basis of commitment to challenging discrimination. They can therefore encourage cynicism and defeatism.

In order to guard against the dangers of drift, it is necessary to make sure that:

- The objectives of equality strategies are clearly identified and recorded. A vague and generalized aim of 'promoting equality' without specific objectives may actually increase the likelihood of drift and the lack of a strategic focus.
- Such objectives need to be reviewed on a regular basis and progress towards them considered and evaluated. As circumstances change it may become necessary to revise the objectives, or modify the steps considered necessary for achieving them.
- Pressures of work are not allowed to become so great that equality

issues become sidelined. Work overload can be a significant source of drift, and so it needs to be recognized, particularly by managerial staff, that a failure to control workloads can seriously undermine equality initiatives.

- A destructive atmosphere based on fear and threat is not allowed to develop. As noted above, the absence of an 'ethos of permission' can be highly problematic, leaving people reluctant to discuss the issues for fear of being criticized. If people work in a destructive, tense atmosphere, then drift can become an attractive and convenient way of avoiding difficult issues.

Once again we can see that a collective response in which people support each other can be of considerable value in meeting the challenge of resisting the tendency towards drift.

Specific issues

The overarching themes outlined above often feature in specific approaches to promoting equality or, if not in the approaches themselves, in the arguments (inappropriately) used to support them. That is, an approach that is not inherently reductionist may be represented in a reductionist way by someone who is unaware of (or does not care about) the problems associated with reductionism. Such themes will therefore reappear at times within the discussion of specific issues. The specific issues and overarching themes are not entirely separate. Indeed, the dividing line between what is a specific issue and what is an overarching theme is not a hard and fast one. That is to say, the material in this chapter is organized in a way that I hope will be helpful – but, in organizing it in this way, I am not claiming that this is a definitive framework to adopt.

I shall outline a number of issues that I have become aware of through my own research and practice, and no doubt readers will be able to add their own examples and insights. My comments are not intended to be unduly critical or dismissive of the efforts of others, but rather to use the opportunity to learn from the past so that previous efforts will not have been wasted. My aim, then, is primarily a constructive one.

Treating everybody the same

Although not as popular a belief as it used to be, the idea that equality is best served by 'treating everybody the same' remains a strong influence. For example, it is a comment frequently made when issues of equality arise on the agenda, or on training courses when equality practice is the topic to be addressed.

Of course it is a notion that is fundamentally flawed. This is because it fails to recognize existing inequalities at the **P**, **C** and **S** levels. To propose treating everybody the same is therefore to propose maintaining existing inequalities intact. 'Treating everybody the same' therefore involves, among other things:

- maintaining a physical environment where many disabled people are denied access, participation and their rights to be treated as full citizens;
- sustaining the structures and cultural expectations that make a major contribution to the under-representation of women, ethnic minorities and so on from positions of power;
- marginalizing and stigmatizing the needs of people who do not fit into the conventional mainstream (the 'white malestream', as it is often called).

At times the 'treating everybody the same' notion may be used cynically by those who wish to maintain inequality – a tactic for distracting attention from the issues in an attempt to sabotage progress. However, in many instances, it is the basis of a genuine belief in how best to promote equality, albeit a belief that does not hold water when subjected to closer scrutiny.

As we noted in Chapter 1, equality is not a matter of sameness. Indeed, equality can be closely linked to the idea of difference and the valuing of diversity. This is a point that we shall explore in more detail in Chapter 6.

The politics of tolerance

A plea often made by people wishing to promote equality is one for 'more tolerance'. While this is, in some ways, a positive notion and one to be supported, it is also one that is quite problematic. What makes it problematic is the 'subtext', or underlying message, that accompanies it. The argument that something should be 'tolerated' carries with it the strong connotation that there is something 'wrong with' or 'negative about' the particular behaviour topic or issue. For example, to suggest that we should 'tolerate' homosexuality strongly implies that homosexuality is basically wrong or undesirable but, for reasons of fairness, we should allow it. If we reverse the situation, the hidden message of tolerance becomes clearer. That is, if we were to suggest that heterosexuality should be tolerated, this would strike people as a very strange thing to say.

In view of this, it is necessary to be wary of the notion of tolerance and to recognize that it has connotations we would not necessarily endorse. Indeed, we could take this a step further and argue that 'tolerance' has the effect of maintaining existing power relations. This is a subtle but important argument: where a regime of power seeks to eliminate all examples of deviance from its desired norms, a risk of a backlash reaction is created. However, where a manageable degree of deviance from those norms is allowed ('tolerated'), this more liberal approach runs less of a risk of a backlash reaction and is therefore a more effective form of social control. What is therefore more helpful than 'tolerating' certain behaviours or issues, is to affirm them, to support their right to exist in a free society. This is consistent with the idea of valuing diversity – seeing differences as positives, rather than as problems to be solved or difficulties to be eradicated.

Inversion

Carniol (1990) argues that:

> our purpose is not to do a flip-flop, that is, not to 'put us in power' so that we can then boss others around. Rather, it calls for a reconstruction of social relations themselves, so that no one gender, class, race or sexual orientation will be able to dominate others.
>
> (p. 141)

This is an important point to make, as such a flip-flop 'inversion' could be seen to be problematic in at least two ways:

1. It is often the basis of misunderstanding on the part of people who feel reluctant and unsure about embracing a philosophy of equality. For example, it is often wrongly assumed that the aim of feminism is to create a society in which women dominate men, rather than one in which equality is the norm. I once encountered an example of this in a student essay. The student presented some good arguments as to the need to challenge gender-based oppression and promote equality. However, she then went on to berate feminism by citing it as an example of a threat to gender equality.
2. In line with my comments above about the dangers of losing a strategic focus, it can be argued that some efforts made in the name of promoting equality have been geared more towards a 'flip-flop' inversion than to genuine equality. I would argue that this is often due to people not thinking through the consequences

of their actions – in short, failing to adopt systematic practice – but may also at times be a reflection of the non-egalitarian aims of some activists. An example of this danger of inversion would be the early days of Malcolm X's campaign for black power where some of the steps taken implied a goal of black supremacy rather than racial equality.

There is a parallel here with Marx's argument that the 'dictatorship of the proletariat' is a step towards an egalitarian society. Of course, this begs the question of whether the proletariat would be willing to give up this dictatorship in due course after having become accustomed to its privileges.

Unrealistic expectations

'Idealism' is an ambiguous term. Aside from its more technical philosophical uses, it can be used in a positive sense (having a vision of the ideal can be a source of inspiration, providing motivation, energy and commitment) or in a negative sense (unrealistic, out of touch with reality). It is in this latter sense that idealism can be problematic.

Although working with people and their problems generally operates at the fulcrum of the personal and the political (private and public issues, to use Mills' phrase – Mills, 1970), and is therefore deeply immersed in issues of discrimination and oppression and the power relations that sustain them, this is not to say that such work is the 'answer' to these problems.

In view of its pivotal location between the personal experience of oppressed groups (and others in need) and the sociopolitical context, professional practice is necessarily a part of the complex matrix of inequality and strategies for challenging and undermining it. Staff and managers therefore have an important part to play in promoting equality. The key word here, though, is *part* – it is not the whole story. Inequality operates at structural and cultural levels and so it would be naïve to assume professional practice could have enough influence at these levels to eliminate discrimination and oppression (see Figure 5.2).

◀ PRACTICE FOCUS 5.4 ▶

After some months of failing to establish equality issues as an explicit feature of the team's work, Jan decided to tackle the issue head-on by expressing her concerns fully and forcefully at a team meeting. It became a very fraught meeting, with people clearly very uncomfortable, but Jan was determined not to allow the situation to

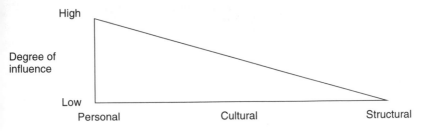

Figure 5.2   Degrees of influence
Source: Thompson (2001a)

continue. In trying to identify what the barriers to progress were, Jan was interested to note that one apparent problem was that at least three members of the team had a defeatist attitude: 'These things are so ingrained in society that there's nothing we can do about them.' This gave Jan a 'lifeline'. She was now able to challenge that view and set about trying to clarify the ways in which equality practice could be part and parcel of everyday practice – how the team could make a contribution to greater equality (or at least avoid exacerbating inequality) without necessarily setting itself the unrealistic aim of eradicating inequality in society generally.

Legalism

Both Braye and Preston-Shoot (1997) and Dalrymple and Burke (1995) argue that, although the law is part of the framework of dominance and subordination that maintains the social order, it also contains within it the potential for challenging discrimination and oppression. A number of pieces of legislation can be utilized to highlight inequalities and to take steps towards reducing or eliminating them (see Figure 5.3).

However, while this is clearly a very useful avenue to explore and use to the full, the danger lies in relying too heavily on legal remedies. This is not an argument for taking action outside of the law! Rather, it is a proposal that we should go beyond narrow, legalistic approaches. There are very many situations where the direct application of the law may not be possible or helpful, but where other measures may well be – through direct practice, training, theory development, policy review and so on. We should therefore be wary of limiting our actions to the narrow legal framework.

The development of the diversity approach owes much to a dissatisfaction with such a narrow, legalistic approach , in so far as it seeks to address unfair discrimination in all its forms, and not simply those that are illegal. And, indeed, in relation to those which are illegal, it

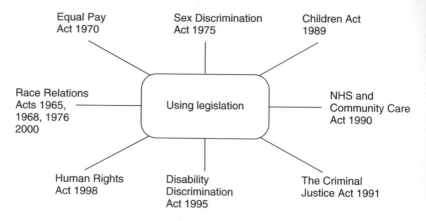

Figure 5.3   Using legislation

seeks to go beyond simply ensuring compliance with the law and to develop a more proactive approach which integrates the value of diversity into the overall strategy of the organization (see Chapter 6).

Naïve politicization

Helping people understand the sociopolitical basis of some aspects of the problems they face can be a helpful strategy for empowerment (as I shall argue in Chapter 7). However, this process of politicization is not to be confused with a naïve and crude reductionism that presents progress as a simple matter of waging a political battle against the powers that be. A much more subtle and sophisticated approach is called for.

In an earlier paper (Thompson, 1991b) I argued that challenging medical hegemony in mental health services must amount to more than 'declaring war' on psychiatrists. If effective progress is to be made, a much more tactical approach must be adopted, one that recognizes the complexities and intricacies of inequality and seeks to develop responses that are carefully tailored to the specific situation being addressed.

Flax (1992) argues that it is not a straightforward matter of replacing oppression with emancipation – this is far too simple an understanding of a complex field of study. Fawcett and Featherstone (2000) point out that, here, Flax is drawing in part on the work of Foucault who argued that: 'oppositional discourses often extend the very relations of domination that they are resisting' (p. 13). That is, if we adopt a naïve politicization approach, we run the risk of being counterproductive in replacing one form of injustice with another (see the discussion of inversion above).

◀ PRACTICE FOCUS 5.5 ▶

Jacquie was a student on placement at a health centre in a very socially deprived area. She was quite happy and settled until she reached a point where she started to appreciate the significance of poverty for people's health and general well-being. She took this issue very seriously and read widely on the subject, something her supervisor was keen to encourage her to do. However, the supervisor was less than keen on Jacquie's response to her reading. In her work with patients at the centre, Jacquie began to emphasize the importance of poverty and deprivation in their lives, but she did so in an extremely crude and oversimplified manner. She seemed to think that simply pointing out to people that poverty was significant would somehow make their situations better. She had not thought through the consequences of her actions or considered a strategy (particularly a collective strategy) for tackling such issues. What actually happened was that she became a laughing stock, dismissed as a naïve 'politico', interested not in people but only in political principles.

Healy (2000), writing from a postmodernist perspective, also warns of the dangers of adopting a politically naïve view when she argues that: 'Postmodernists reject visions of massive social transition as a chimera and demand, instead, greater caution and constraint in the formation of critical practice objectives and processes' (p. 2). These are complex issues and need to be handled carefully and sensitively, rather than left to a crude, political dogmatism based on naïveté and oversimplification.

Political correctness

As we have seen, political correctness is currently a widely used term. It refers to a reaction against equality practice, rather than being a genuine approach to promoting equality in its own right. It is a reified, reductionist concept used ideologically to demean, ridicule and therefore undermine equality strategies. It is therefore not a term to be embraced, as it serves more to sabotage equality initiatives than to support them.

However, it is surprising how many people do not understand or appreciate this and use political correctness as a goal to be aimed for. For example, in reviewing a student's progress on a work-based placement, the supervisor told me that: 'He [the student] has learned a lot about discrimination. He's much better now at political correctness than he was at the beginning of the placement.' The subsequent discussion indicated that she equated political correctness with emancipatory practice, and she was not aware at all of the reductionist, essentialist and dogmatic properties of the notion of PC – although she very quickly appreciated their significance after we briefly explored them together.

The idea that there are definitive right answers (or 'right on' answers, as Divine, 1990, calls them) simply waiting for us to discover them is a dangerous one. The notion of political correctness is one example of this danger. It stands as an obstacle to the development of critically reflective practice.

What is particularly worrying about political correctness is that it has led to an oversimplification of the situation in relation to language usage. The idea of political correctness has become closely associated with a dogmatic approach to which forms of language should and should not be used if we are to avoid reinforcing discrimination (Thompson, 2003). This has had the unfortunate effect of distracting attention away from genuine issues relating to the potentially oppressive use of language, contributing to the process of trivialization discussed earlier.

Following fashion

Although perhaps not as fickle or ephemeral as fashions in clothing, academic and professional fashions none the less exist. There are a number of problems associated with this, not least the following:

- It detracts from systematic practice. By concentrating on what is the 'in' thing to do we can lose track of what is the best thing to do in the circumstances, in view of the objectives being pursued.
- It encourages the use of uncritical thinking, especially through the use of 'buzzwords'. For example, words like partnership, empowerment and participation have been liberally used without the people using them necessarily having a clear understanding of what they mean or what their implications are. The importance of these concepts is therefore watered down.
- Important measures can fall into disuse because they are seen as 'old hat' – that is, unfashionable. For example, crisis intervention is an approach that has suffered from the vagaries of fashion (Thompson, 1991a), and so its value in providing an effective response to some of the problems oppressed groups experience has been lost in many cases.

One example of following fashion came to light when I used the term 'anti-discriminatory practice' at a meeting. A training officer present at the meeting interrupted and said 'It's anti-*oppressive* practice now'. When asked what she saw as the difference between the two, she was unable to articulate this, but she clearly 'knew' that the latter was a more fashionable term than the former. As we noted earlier in this chapter, following fashion for the sake of it is a form of dogmatism – it discourages critically reflective practice rather than promoting it.

Displaced anger

It is very understandable that people who experience oppression should feel very angry about it, and that others who have a sense of injustice about inequality should share some degree of that anger. And indeed, there are times when an angry response is an appropriate and effective one. My argument, then, is not that anger is never an appropriate or helpful response. Clearly that would not be borne out by the history of the struggles against oppression. The point I wish to make is that an angry, aggressive response is not helpful as a 'blanket' approach that can be applied to all situations. As the literature on assertiveness has shown us, there are often times when a calmer approach can be more effective in achieving the desired results.

Similarly, such anger may be displaced in the sense that it becomes directed at inappropriate targets. For example, Elizabeth Wilson (1993) expresses regret at some of the ways in which anger has previously been misdirected:

> Feminists did, of course, rightly target men as oppressors, but the men who ended up as the immediate objects of attack were men within the Left, trades unionists, who in the general order of things were not the main oppressors, on a collective scale at least – however unpleasant their behaviour as individuals might be. While feminists attacked 'left men', the white, male ruling class went unscathed.
>
> Similarly, when racism came onto the agenda, who were the main objects of attack? Not the National Front, not white men, not the Tory Party or even the Labour Party: it was white feminists or white working-class people who bore the brunt, which was nevertheless misdirected at those (in the case of feminists, at least) who were most easily guilt-tripped, again leaving the most racist practices and institutions unscathed.
>
> (pp. 111–12)

It can, of course, be difficult at times to contain anger or to channel it constructively, but I would none the less argue that it is important to try to do so wherever possible. The strength of feeling generated by oppression can be a positive force for change or, if we are not careful, it can be used ideologically against us to pathologize and to stigmatize.

Underestimating stress

Working with people and their problems brings with it a range of pressures that can easily spill over into harmful stress (Thompson *et al.*, 1996b). For many people, some of those pressures can arise from having to deal with the consequences of discrimination and oppression: poverty and deprivation; racism; 'domestic' violence; elder abuse and so on. However, the challenge of promoting equality in a profoundly inequitable world can also bring what at times can be immense pressures. In addition, the pressures of challenging discrimination and oppression can also be of significant proportions. Such pressures include:

- 'unlearning' previous patterns of socialization;
- challenging individuals, groups and organizations and, potentially at least, entering into conflict with them;
- anxiety about 'getting it wrong' and, at times, fear of being labelled racist, sexist and so on.

When we add these to what is already likely to be a highly pressurized job, we can see that there is a very real danger of staff and managers becoming stressed. It is therefore necessary to ensure that:

- stressors are kept within manageable proportions;
- coping resources are identified and utilized;
- support systems are available, accessible and effective.

One of the ironic features of stress in this context is that it is often at times of stress (when perhaps ontological security is threatened) that we can revert to old habits, return to our 'comfort zones'. Consequently, if stress is not handled appropriately (by individuals and by organizations), the result can be the abandonment of progress already made as old assumptions and old ways of working reassert themselves as part of a process of protecting oneself from the pressures that have become too great to manage.

Burnout instead of time out

Closely related to the concept of stress is that of 'burnout'. This relates to the process whereby a worker uses up his or her emotional resources to the point where a fairly mechanical, dehumanized form of practice is the result. Research has shown that this problem is particularly applicable to the helping professions due to the emotional component of the tasks involved (Maslach and Jackson, 1981). The emotional demands of tackling inequality can therefore be seen as increasing the possibility of burnout occurring.

One factor associated with burnout is the process whereby initial enthusiasm and commitment subside, to be replaced by more and more disillusionment. This can also apply in relation to emancipatory practice. Initial zeal can lead to disillusionment and eventually to burnout – and a member of staff experiencing burnout is likely to be much less sensitive to important issues and is more likely to adopt a cynical approach.

In order to avoid burnout it is therefore necessary to ensure that preventative steps are taken, particularly the following two:

1. Initial enthusiasm to be maintained and nurtured, rather than allowed to produce a pendulum swing towards burnout. It may be necessary to temper initial zeal so that it is less intense but longer lasting.
2. People to take 'time out' from the efforts and emotional demands from time to time so that there is no gradual build up of pressures to the point where burnout becomes the escape route. It is important that workers are able to practise 'self-care' so that their own needs are met.

Some people may argue that the problems of oppression are so vast and so urgent that it is a form of self-indulgence not to channel all available energies into the struggle. However, I would argue that this is an unrealistic view, in so far as it fails to recognize the importance of time out and the dangers of people burning out because their own needs are not being met. There is therefore an important skill in finding the optimal balance between 'effort in' and 'time out'.

Tokenism

Tokenistic approaches to inequality are those which 'go through the motions', often without any underlying commitment, and without any real change being effected. This can be seen to fall into two categories:

1. Deliberate tokenism whereby there is an intentional aim of giving an appearance of a commitment to equality without making any changes to power relations and so on. This is where we have 'rhetoric rather than reality'.
2. Tokenism by default where there is a genuine wish for change, but where a lack of understanding of the issues, or a lack of appreciation of their complexity, fails to produce any effective change.

Tokenism can take many forms. For example, it may be a case of using the 'right' words (chair or chairperson instead of chairman) but without any change in the way women are treated or the opportunities they may have for occupying positions of power. Another example would be that of 'non-permeation' on a training course or educational programme. This occurs when issues of discrimination and oppression are addressed in one specific session, sequence or module but without being integrated into other aspects of the curriculum. Consequently, a student may attend a class on inequality in the morning and yet, on the afternoon of the same day, attend a class on human development where issues of gender and sexism, ethnicity and racism are not covered because the tutor adopts a 'white malestream' approach to psychological and social development. Similarly, there may be teaching on ageism running alongside sessions on old age that take no account whatsoever of older people as a marginalized and disadvantaged social group.

Tokenism therefore occurs where an apparent or superficial commitment to equality can disguise the lack of any substantive work to make positive progress.

◀ PRACTICE FOCUS 5.6 ▶

After attending a course on discrimination and oppression, Andrew was keen to make sure that equality issues were high on his team's agenda. Consequently, he implemented one of the ideas that had been raised on the course – he established equality practice as a standing item on the team meeting agenda. However, this proved not to be helpful. Reviewing the situation some six months later, Andrew, with hindsight, was able to see that he had imposed the idea on the team without first generating their commitment to the issues. Consequently, the team had indulged in 'tokenism', with the issues being discussed only superficially or not at all. ('Nothing to report on equality issues, so we'll move on to the next item on the agenda.') On the surface, it looked as though this was a team committed to promoting equality, but the reality was very different.

A hierarchy of oppressions

The dangers of instituting a hierarchy of oppressions have already been commented on. Setting up one form of oppression as more important than others is likely to have a 'divide and conquer' effect and thereby provide ammunition for those who oppose equality. This is not to say that people should not have particular interests or commitments – it would be naïve to assume that all people could attend to all forms of oppression in equal measure.

The point being made, rather, is that each element of oppression being addressed should be:

- dealt with in its own right, rather than as something that is more or less important than another form of oppression;
- seen in the context of multiple oppressions – the different forms of oppression are not separate and isolated, but rather operate as dimensions of experience interacting with and upon each other;
- tackled in accordance with its impact on the person(s) concerned, rather than the interests of the worker.

A further aspect of the hierarchy of oppressions problem is when a worker adopts a favourite 'ism', perhaps at the expense of the overall picture. For example, there may be some good work undertaken in respect of the significance of racism on a black woman's life but with little or no attention paid to the role of gender and so on.

An important 'antidote' to these problems is an emphasis on the dialectic. If we remember that oppressions are not fixed, static entities, but rather are interactive forces within a dynamic dialectical process, we are less likely to see each aspect on its own. A dialectical approach helps us to see each aspect as part of a broader whole – a changing, developing whole.

Separatism as an end rather than a means

Given the tendency of dominant groups to reproduce those patterns of domination in and through social interactions, it is not surprising that some marginalized groups have at times adopted a strategy of separatism. That is, through seeking to work together in a context where a dominant group is not present, greater progress can be made.

An example of this would be the women's movement in which some groups of women choose to meet together to develop anti-sexist policy and practice without men being included. Similarly, some black groups have been formed with a deliberate policy of excluding white people. The intention is one of creating a secure environment in which people can speak openly about their experience and their proposals without fear of causing offence and/or attracting a backlash reaction.

I have known of many people who object to this strategy on the basis that it is divisive and actually perpetuates discrimination. While appreciating the rationale behind this argument, it can be a problematic point of view if separatism is seen an end in itself, rather than as a means to an end. That is, where women's groups, for example, have the opportunity of meeting on a women-only basis in order to develop confidence and build a mutually supportive collective spirit, this can be a positive and helpful strategy in promoting equality. However, if separatism is seen as an end in itself, then clearly this raises implications about, and problems for, the development of an open and egalitarian society where life chances are not restricted by relatively arbitrary socially constructed categories.

◀ PRACTICE FOCUS 5.7 ▶

There were only two black students on the course, out of a total of forty students. The teaching staff realized that this might cause difficulties for the two black students who could feel isolated and unsupported, particularly as racism would be a topic to be discussed from time to time. Consequently, it was arranged for the black students to be allocated a black 'mentor' to meet with them from time to time and run a small-scale support group. This was favourably received by the two black students and the majority of white students also felt it was a good move. However, there was a small minority of white students who objected, stating that they saw it as divisive or even as 'racist'. Their antagonism to any form of apparent 'separatism' was quite strong and there were many arguments about these issues. Everyone agreed that separatism was not an appropriate end to aim for, but there were differences of opinion as to whether it could be a useful and appropriate means to an end.

Inelegant challenging

The notion of 'elegant' challenging is one that derives from the teachings of neurolinguistic programming, a theoretical approach to interpersonal and therapeutic interventions (Alder, 1994). It refers to the type of challenging that succeeds in getting the point across without alienating or antagonizing the person being challenged (based on the premise that alienation and antagonism will not produce positive change). Elegant challenging is proposed as a more effective method of bringing about change in attitudes and behaviours than a more aggressive approach. In short, it amounts to confronting the issues without being confrontational.

Inelegant challenging, by contrast, can do much more harm than good. An overzealous and tactless approach can be very problematic in terms of:

- producing a hostile response and a tense atmosphere in which change is far less likely to be accomplished;
- producing a defensive response, with the result that equality issues become a difficult subject and one to be avoided;
- providing ammunition for detractors from emancipatory practice to dismiss the person concerned as a 'hothead' or an 'extremist';
- mirroring oppressive relationships in which a powerful person seeks to 'bully' the other party into submission.

Inelegant challenging is therefore not only likely to be less effective, it may also be counterproductive or even an oppressive action in its own right.

It has to be recognized that elegant challenging is a highly skilled undertaking and could take some time to be developed fully. This supports my earlier point that emancipatory forms of practice involve a number of pressures and demands – there are no simple answers or straightforward, formula solutions. However, a point that should not be lost is that professional workers are often quite skilled at effective challenging (as a necessary part of many professional tasks, such as problem-solving, conflict resolution, negotiation and so on), and so it becomes a question of transferring those general skills to the specific scenario where a discriminatory or oppressive remark or action is to be challenged.

Watering down the vocabulary

In some settings at least, an awareness of discrimination and oppression has increased significantly in recent years. For example, the professional journals now carry a number of equality-related papers, especially in social work but also across the helping professions more generally – for example, the nursing literature is increasingly paying attention to issues of equality and diversity. As part of a strategy of promoting equality this is clearly something to be welcomed. However, it also brings with it at least one problem.

A raised level of awareness has resulted in certain terms being used more than ever before. The danger here is that their usage can become overgeneralized, sometimes to the point that their meaning and impact become seriously watered down. If we overuse words such as 'discriminatory' and 'oppressive', and particularly if we use them inaccurately or inappropriately, their currency becomes devalued and the very real pain, suffering, deprivation, indignity and inhumanity of oppression can be trivialized and not given their due attention.

Some examples of this problem that I have encountered include the following:

- A student complains that he is being 'oppressed' because his (extremely poor-quality) essay is deemed to fail.
- A member of staff in a residential home describes the need to work shifts as 'discriminatory'.
- A lecturer refers to being allocated an additional task to do as 'oppressive'.
- A team leader of a multidisciplinary team describes a bereaved man as 'sexist' because he requests a male counsellor.
- A student is criticized for employing 'racist' language because she uses the term 'black coffee'.
- A worker describes having to return to work after a period on leave as 'oppressive'.

Clearly, then, an uncritical use of key terminology has the effect of devaluing the whole enterprise and distracting attention from the seriousness of genuine oppression.

Taylor and White (2000) make a similar point when they bemoan the tendency to oversimplify terms such as 'oppression':

> there is a tendency for anti-oppressive practice to become a rather empty exercise in which practitioners assert their knowledge about various forms of 'oppression' or 'disadvantage', or simply gloss people into categories as 'oppressors' and 'oppressed' without understanding or interrogating how 'oppression' is brought about by practitioners in their encounters.
>
> (p. vi)

Rejecting theory

Some proponents of emancipatory practice have at times shown a tendency to reject theory as 'bourgeois' (Thompson, 1992a). While it is certainly true that much of the traditional literature base takes little or no account of discrimination and oppression (see, for example, Robinson, 1995, where psychological theory is criticized for failing to address issues of ethnicity and racism), this does not justify the rejection of theory *per se*.

The tendency to reject theory can therefore be seen as problematic in terms of:

- *Dogmatism* Theoretical frameworks give us the tools with which to analyse patterns of thought and behaviour and to provide constructive challenges to competing explanatory frameworks. Without this we are left with dogma that is asserted in such a way that the voices of those who shout loudest are the ones that are heard.
- *Reductionism* Without a well-developed theory base, we will be ill equipped to deal with the complexities of inequality and will therefore be much more prone to reductionism and oversimplification.
- *Essentialism* The rejection of theory implies that there is one 'true' approach or one right answer. Indeed, this is often the rationale provided to justify abandoning theory: 'We know what the problem is, we know what the answer is, why bother with fancy theories?'

In view of this we can see that the rejection of theory is not only unhelpful but can also, at times, be positively dangerous.

Defeatism

Defeatism is not so much a way of promoting equality as an excuse for not doing so. The argument tends to run along the following lines: 'I know that inequality is unjust and should not be allowed to continue, but the problem is so vast and so deeply ingrained that there is nothing we can do about it.' The premises of this argument are probably valid but the conclusion drawn from them is not.

While it is necessary to recognize the limitations of emancipatory practice (as argued in the discussion above of 'unrealistic expectations'), this is not to say that no progress is possible. Indeed, a point often made in relation to the environment is that it is dangerous to assume that, because the problems of pollution and so on are so great, there is little or nothing an individual can do. The argument put forward in Chapter 1 that, if we are not part of the solution, we must be part of the problem, is applicable to both the environment and inequality. Because each of us is part of the complex matrix of discrimination and oppression, we cannot stand in a neutral position in relation to such issues. Our actions can improve, exacerbate or condone the situation. To adopt an attitude of defeatism is, at best, to condone the status quo and the inequalities on which it rests, and at worst, to exacerbate them by failing to take the necessary steps to address particular concerns.

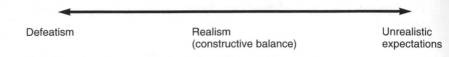

Defeatism   Realism   Unrealistic
                                    (constructive balance)   expectations

Figure 5.4   The balance between defeatism and unrealistic expectations

An example of defeatism would be a situation in which ageist attitudes are not challenged because 'it's too ingrained for me to do anything about it'. This failure to challenge on the worker's part could then be interpreted by the people concerned as an indication that he or she is in agreement with such attitudes, thereby reinforcing their legitimacy and, in so doing, making it more difficult for others to challenge (hence becoming part of the problem).

Defeatism stands at the opposite end of the spectrum from unrealistic expectations, with both extremes being highly problematic while the middle ground represents a more realistic, constructive and positive balance (Figure 5.4).

The 'Polo mint' approach

A facetious title belies a serious point about the tendency to focus on one level of discrimination at the expense of the others. The most common form of such reductionism, as we noted earlier in this chapter, is that whereby the **P** level is the centre of attention, with little or no reference to the **C** or **S** levels. However, the example I am presenting is in some ways the reverse – an emphasis on the **C** and/or **S** levels, but with little or no attention paid to the **P** level. The person is omitted from the picture, thereby reflecting a form of determinism in which the broader levels are deemed to 'cause' (rather than influence or constrain) behaviour and attitudes at the **P** level – structure features in the equation but agency does not (Figure 5.5).

This approach can sometimes be partly the result of the overzealousness referred to above in relation to burnout. Someone who discovers for the first time the significance of the cultural and structural levels may embrace issues at these levels with gusto, perhaps neglecting the **P** dimension in the process. There is a parallel here with Sartre's (1976) critique of marxism in which he takes issue with the tendency to reduce Marx's dialectic of praxis and sociopolitical context to a crude economic determinism in which the person and his or her actions ('praxis') are more or less totally absent.

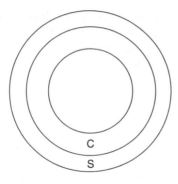

Figure 5.5   The 'Polo mint' approach

Ewan had done quite well on his professional training course and was keen to complete his final assignment successfully. His task in the assignment was to describe an example of his practice and link this to one or more theoretical perspectives he had learned about on the course. He chose to focus on emancipatory practice and set about the task with gusto. However, he was horrified, after having the assignment marked, to find that he had failed. The marker had commented: 'You seem to have a good understanding of cultural and structural factors relating to oppression but you omit totally any reference to the person – it is as if you are describing the client as just a pawn in the hands of wider forces, rather than a person who can, and perhaps, does resist such forces. Your analysis is far too deterministic and has the effect of dehumanizing the client – a form of oppression in its own right.' Once Ewan got over the initial shock of failure, he was able to look back over the assignment and recognize that he had indeed neglected a key dimension of the situation – the person.

The good is the enemy of the best

This notion, deriving from Freudian psychoanalysis, is one that is much more broadly applicable. It refers to the process by which some degree of progress in addressing a problem or resolving an issue can, by releasing tension and instilling confidence, lead the person concerned to settle for this situation rather than to continue to tackle the issue – the good (an improvement in the situation) therefore stands in the way of the best (resolving the situation altogether).

Freud was using this idea in the context of a therapeutic process but it can also be used to account for a range of situations, including those that involve seeking to promote equality. It is sometimes the case that, in a situation where the motivation to bring about change is quite high, the motivation can actually dissipate once a degree of progress is made, as the problem becomes less extreme and therefore less urgent or pressing.

An example of this process would be a group of staff who work together to produce an equal opportunities statement. Once this has been achieved they feel better about the situation, pleased that they have made progress. At this point other priorities may take over, other demands require attention, and the equality issues take a back seat. Consequently, the equal opportunities statement may never be fully implemented because:

- no code of practice was drawn up;
- no implementation plan, with clear targets and timescales, was set;
- the statement was not monitored or evaluated.

In order to avoid the problem of 'the good is the enemy of the best', it is therefore necessary to ensure that the process of promoting equality is followed through, that it becomes an ongoing concern, rather than a matter that can be dealt with through a particular measure or policy and then forgotten about.

Conclusion

It should be more than apparent by now that there can be no simple, formula solutions to the problems of inequality. Each approach will have advantages and disadvantages, strengths and weaknesses. What I have attempted to do in this chapter is to focus specifically on the weaknesses and disadvantages, not to 'score points' against others or their efforts, but rather to provide opportunities for learning from what has gone before (and is still continuing in many instances).

I recognize that some readers may find this a depressing chapter, comprising as it does a catalogue of errors and pitfalls. In presenting the ideas in this way I realize that I run the risk of demotivating some people, of pushing them towards the defeatism of which I have complained. However, I feel that this is a risk worth taking in view of the benefits to be gained from learning lessons from the past so that future energies are not wasted revisiting old mistakes, dead-ends and unnecessary detours. As the saying goes, forewarned is forearmed.

In Chapter 7 I present what could be seen as a counterbalance to what has been presented here. In that chapter I shall present a number of positive strategies for promoting equality, some of which can be seen as overarching themes, and others which are geared more towards specific issues. It perhaps goes without saying that these will not be simple solutions. Rather, they are presented as strategies that can be used as an aid to critically reflective practice, rather than as a substitute for it.

However, before discussing such strategies it is necessary to explore a further aspect of the context in which both inequality and emancipatory practice operate. The organizational context is a significant part of the complex matrix of inequality and so a consideration of its implications for the development of forms of emancipatory practice forms the basis of Chapter 6.

6

THE ORGANIZATIONAL CONTEXT

Introduction

Mullins (1996) makes the important point that:

> We live in an organizational world. Organizations of one form or another are a necessary part of our society and serve many important needs . . . Organizations play a major and continuing role in the lives of us all, especially with the growth of large-scale business organizations and the divorce of ownership from management. It is important, therefore, to understand how organizations function and the pervasive influences which they exercise over the behaviour of people.
>
> (p. 4)

Understanding the organizational context of professional practice can therefore be seen as an important matter, such is the influence of organizational structures, cultures and practices. This is particularly the case in relation to inequality, as the organization in which we work can be an asset in tackling discrimination through supportive policies and practices, or it can be a major source of such discrimination and can exacerbate existing inequalities.

Organizations are dangerous places. They are major sites of power and conflicts of interest, and so considerable harm can result from the complex and potentially destructive processes that go on between individuals, between groups, and between organizations and their employees. This chapter cannot realistically address all the subtle intricacies and various combinations. However, what we can do in the space available is to explore a number of important issues relating to the organizational context of professional practice.

I shall begin by considering power relations within organizations. Such relations operate at both formal and informal levels, each with a major role to play in shaping organizational life. This sets the scene for an examination of inequality within organizations, spanning a range of spheres of discrimination.

Organizational culture forms the basis of the next section, with a consideration of how shared norms, values and assumptions within an organization can have a significant bearing on the actions and attitudes of staff employed within it. Understanding how organizations work is also an important concern of 'human resource management' (HRM), a development of traditional personnel management. Some of the key elements of HRM are explored with a view to showing their relevance to discrimination and inequality.

Our attention then turns to the 'management of diversity', an approach to inequality that is concerned with presenting diversity and differences as positive factors. Following this, stress is the topic to be addressed. Occupational stress is a significant feature of organizational life and is also significant in relation to inequality. This leads to a discussion of the 'organizational operator'. This involves outlining the knowledge and skills required to work effectively within an organization in order to maximize opportunities for promoting equality by challenging discrimination and oppression.

Power relations – formal and informal

Salaman (1979) makes the point that: 'power within organizations is related to the distribution of power outside the organization' (p. 112, cited in Hugman, 1991, pp. 64–5). In this respect, organizations can be seen as microcosms of the wider society, with structural relations of class, race, gender and so on replicated between individuals and groups within the dynamics of the organization. The workings of power within organizations will therefore follow recognizable patterns to a certain extent at least. However, there are also more specific issues relating to organizational power relations that merit our attention.

Organizations, by their very nature, involve power relations in so far as the goals of the various individuals and groups are not necessarily compatible (Dawson, 1996). Indeed, organizations can be, and often are, sites of major conflict, both overt and covert. As Fox (1993) comments: 'All organizations are mythologies constituted discursively to serve particular interests of power, and contested by other interests of power' (p. 49). Overt conflict manifests itself in industrial relations problems and other visible signs of a conflict of interest. However, covert conflicts are much more commonplace and are frequently 'camouflaged' by everyday working practices, hidden within the minutiae of interpersonal interactions and organizational norms, and often referred to by the euphemism of 'office politics'. As Deetz (1994) comments:

Organizational life could be an explicit site of political struggle as different groups try to realise their own interests but the conflicts there are often routinized, evoke standard mechanisms for resolution and reproduce presumed natural tensions (e.g. between workers and management). The essential politics in everyday interaction thus become invisible.

(pp. 185–6)

Signs of conflict within an organization are not, therefore, indications that the organization is 'failing' or 'in difficulties' – they are part and parcel of organizational life. Such conflicts and tensions generally lie beneath the surface but tend to emerge from time to time. It is therefore a mistake to see organizations in consensual terms. Although much consensus is likely to exist in any organization, this will be underpinned by a range of relations based on conflict of interest – in short, power relations.

Power relations in organizations can be divided into two types, formal and informal. I shall discuss each of these in turn.

Formal power relations

Formal power relations are those which are officially constituted as part of the organizational structure. That is, they arise from the hierarchy on which an organization is based, the 'reporting structures', as they are often known. One group of staff 'report' to one or more supervisors/line managers who, in turn, 'report' to the next level, and so on. Within this hierarchy each 'layer' has a degree of control over those below. Such control can be in the form of sanctions, ultimately that of dismissal. However, such examples of power are the 'tip of the iceberg' in terms of the subtle operations of power. Less overt, but equally effective, forms of power operate beneath the surface. These are discursive forms of power, bound within subtle discourses, as discussed in Chapter 2. That is, power is 'inscribed' on the day-to-day interactions through taken-for-granted assumptions, norms, patterns and practices. In this respect, power is closely linked to organizational culture (see below). Discursive power is closely associated with two (sets of) factors:

- *Knowledge* The role of knowledge and the control of information plays a significant part in decision-making and other power-related processes.
- *Language* The terminology and styles of language we use contribute to the 'shaping' of our experiences. Language is a fundamental part of the construction and maintenance of discourses.

Organizational discourses, then, are frameworks of understanding that help us make sense of organizational life – they are part of the process of 'meaning-making'.

Understanding how discourses operate is therefore important in helping us understand the workings of power in organizations. However, we should be wary of relying too heavily on the concept of discursive power. The primary reason for this is, as Knights and Vurdubakis (1994) point out, that the theoretical work of Foucault, from which the notion of discursive power arises, neglects the significance of agency – it is unnecessarily deterministic.

Discursive power, then, has to be seen as part of our understanding, rather than a key to it. It is a concept that can be used in addition to structure and agency, rather than as a substitute for them (see the discussion of 'structuration and beyond' in Chapter 1).

Informal power relations

While power clearly operates at a formal, hierarchical level, through structures and sanctions, supported and reinforced by discourses, this is not the only set of power relations. Power in organizations also operates through informal channels. Behind the organizational tree-diagrams that chart the formal managerial hierarchy and reporting structures lies a network of informal power relations that can be just as powerful. These include:

- the 'charisma' of particular individuals – that is, their ability to influence others by virtue of their personality;
- rule-bending – some people are able to achieve their ends and/or block the progress of others by 'bending the rules' or manipulating situations to their advantage;
- knowledge and experience – more experienced members of staff can often have more of an influence than less experienced people who are officially in more powerful positions;
- informal networks – people can work together to avoid, subvert or counter more formal channels of authority.

◀ PRACTICE FOCUS 6.1 ▶

When Helen took up her new post she was keen to get to know everyone and to become familiar with the relevant policies and procedures. She was introduced to all the staff and the members of the senior management team. However, as she started to settle in, it was not long before she realized that the 'official' management hierarchy was quite different from the way power actually worked in practice. For example, it was quite clear that the deputy manager was far more powerful and influential in reality than the manager, despite the fact that the manager in principle had far more power due to his position. The deputy was very clearly the 'power behind the throne'.

The ability to recognize, and work constructively with, informal power relations is a basic building block of what I shall discuss below under the heading of 'the organizational operator'. Understanding power relations, formal and informal, is a fundamental part of tackling inequality, in so far as it sets the scene for developing strategies.

Inequality in organizations

The hierarchical nature of organizations introduces a degree of formal inequality. Although some organizations attempt to operate along more democratic lines, unequal power relations are a general characteristic of organizational life. In addition, as noted earlier, the social divisions of the wider society also manifest themselves in organizations. Indeed, organizations can exacerbate such inequalities. I shall therefore outline each of the major forms of inequality as they apply to organizations.

Class

Class is a contested term in sociology, with differing definitions and conceptualizations. However, a recurring theme across such perspectives on class is that of socioeconomic position, the economic power that comes with a particular occupation or status. Clearly, then, organizations and class are closely interlinked in so far as organizations play an important role in the allocation of economic rewards, and thus, partly at least, of class position.

At a very basic level, employing organizations can have a major impact on employees' socioeconomic position through such processes as promotion/demotion and redundancy ('delayering', 'downsizing'). In addition, of course, the power to implement such processes provides a range of potential threats that can serve to 'discipline' the workforce, to discourage them from challenging the status quo and the actions of management.

However, if we conceive of class in broader than economic terms, other important factors come to light. For example, issues of class values and lifestyle may be significant at certain times, with resulting clashes or conflicts of interest. This may be particularly noticeable in the helping professions where class issues may be very much to the fore (for example, the links between poverty and poor health). Practitioners are therefore likely to find themselves frequently at the intersection of competing class interests – for example, between the needs of their clientele and the competing priorities of managers wishing to respect political mandates to reduce public spending and encourage private provision (Clarke, 1996).

Race and ethnicity

The existence of racial discrimination in employment practices is long established and well documented (see, for example, Brown, 1992; Phizacklea and Miles, 1992; and Skellington, 1996). It is therefore recognized that employing organizations frequently contribute to existing patterns of racism in relation to their employees. This includes unfair treatment in terms of:

- allocation of workload;
- access to training;
- promotion opportunities; and
- working conditions.

Dominelli (1989) also points out that black workers are often expected to act as race relations experts, and therefore to take more than their fair share of the responsibility for challenging racism.

However, racial inequality in organizations relates not only to employees, but also to users of services. Indeed, there are many examples on record of organizations wittingly or unwittingly acting in ways that can clearly be seen as racist. Anti-racist practice in organizations therefore needs to operate at the levels of both personnel/ human resources and service provision.

Gender

Hearn and Parkin (1993) make the point that organization theory has tended to neglect the gender dimension of organizational life. Indeed, they see the gender-blindness of 'malestream' theory as a significant weakness in understanding the complex dynamics that operate in organizations. Morgan (1986) captures the position in the following passage:

> Many organizations are dominated by gender-related values that bias organizational life in favour of one sex over another. Thus . . . organizations often segment opportunity structures and job markers in ways that enable men to achieve positions of prestige and power more easily than

women, and often operate in ways that produce gender-related biases in the way organizational reality is created and sustained on a day-to-day basis. This is most obvious in situations of open discrimination and various forms of sexual harassment, but often pervades the culture of an organization in a way that is much less visible.

(p. 178)

The situation is particularly salient in the helping professions where the predominant pattern is that of a largely female workforce at the grassroots level, but with a male-dominated management. This gives rise to a situation often described as the 'glass ceiling' (Grimwood and Popplestone, 1993), an invisible barrier that restricts the number of women who achieve management status. Women are therefore under-represented in positions of power.

◀ PRACTICE FOCUS 6.2 ▶

Jenny had not long taken up her first post on the managerial ladder when she was asked to attend a conference on 'Management for the New Millennium'. She travelled down to the conference not really knowing what to expect but looking forward to learning more about management. Over the three days of the conference she did indeed learn a lot. However, what struck her most forcibly was the number of men there. She was used to working in settings where women were in the majority but she started to realize now that the world of management power is predominantly a man's world. She was not naïve enough to expect a gender balance at a management conference, but the sheer weight of male numbers did bring home to her quite forcibly just how male dominated the world of management is.

Newman (1994) argues that traditional conceptions of management have arisen from male-oriented organizations such as the military, factories and the civil service. She goes on to argue that the 'new managerialism' that has become influential in recent years also has a strong masculine orientation.

The difficulties that women face in seeking to achieve positions of power within organizations are clearly of significant proportions and are subtly woven into the fabric of organizational life. Even at a very basic level, women can have difficulty finding a voice, as the following example from Grimwood and Popplestone (1993) illustrates: 'A woman makes a point at a meeting, it is either ignored, talked over, put down or interrupted. The same point is later made by a man as if it is his idea; it is listened to and discussed' (p. 98).

This is just one example of the many ways in which the gender inequalities in the wider society manifest themselves in and through organizational arrangements and practices. Perhaps the most obvious example of inequality is that of sexual harassment. Where women are subject to unwelcome sexual advances from men in positions of power over them, the outcome is likely to be oppressive, placing the women concerned in an extremely difficult and pressurized situation. Sexual harassment is therefore quite an extreme example of gender inequality in organizations and the harm and distress that it causes.

Sexual identity

The question of sexuality is one that has received a lot of attention in the organizational theory literature (see, for example, Thompson and McHugh, 1995). The focus has tended to be on heterosexuality, with relatively little attention paid to homosexuality, although Hearn and Parkin (1995) is a notable exception. The significance of sexual identity in organizations is therefore relatively under-researched.

Hearn (1987) makes the point that: 'many business and other public organizations have compulsorily heterosexual ideologies, practices and "organization sexualities"' (p. 108). This notion of 'compulsory heterosexuality' is a significant part of heterosexism in which gay men, lesbians and bisexuals are regarded as deviant and inferior. This is exemplified by the assumption that homosexuals are not safe to work with children:

> It is commonly assumed by many people that homosexuals regard children as valid objects of sexual desire. This is reflected in, for example, the French use of the word pédéraste, which literally means 'lover of boys', to refer to homosexuals in general – and this is even confirmed in the dictionary definition (*Le Petit Robert*) . . . The irrational view of homosexuality as a threat is indicative of the paranoia which both reflects and reinforces heterosexist ideology.
>
> (Thompson, 2001a, pp. 143–4)

Such negative and prejudicial assumptions can be widespread in organizations, leaving many people facing a choice between discrimination as a result of 'coming out' and the pressures of keeping their sexual identity a secret.

The failure of most organizations in addressing inequality in relation to sexual identity can be recognized by the fact that so many do not include issues of sexual identity within the ambit of equal opportunities policies (Cooper, 1993).

Age

The setting of age limits in employment is a long-standing practice, and is not covered by anti-discrimination legislation. Occupational ageism is therefore an established feature of organizational life. However, in recent years, the need to challenge age discrimination in organizations has begun to be recognized.

The use of early retirement as a means of reducing the size of the workforce at times of labour surplus is, in itself, an example of age as a social division serving the interests of powerful groups. As Phillipson (1982) points out, retirement acts as a means of regulating the labour supply in accordance with the demands of the economy at any particular time. This very mechanism introduces a degree of inequality in so far as it utilizes age as a means of attributing value to members of the workforce, older workers representing an assumed lower level of value for money. The ageist ideology dominant in the wider society therefore reappears in the workings of employing organizations.

Disability

The social model of disability, as we noted in Chapter 1, conceives of disablement as the result of the special response to an individual's impairment. On this basis, organizations can be seen as the site of considerable disablist discrimination. This can arise in terms of:

- physical, environmental barriers to full involvement in the organization;
- attitudinal barriers in the form of personal prejudices and negative assumptions;
- an organizational culture that devalues the contribution that disabled people can make.

The implementation of the Disability Discrimination Act 1995 has made some impact on some aspects of this situation, although it would be naïve to assume that the Act will resolve the question of disability discrimination. The Act makes it unlawful, in certain circumstances at least, for an employer to:

- treat a disabled employee less favourably than non-disabled employees (unless this can be justified in some substantial and non-trivial way);
- fail to make 'reasonable adjustments' to the organization's physical environment or employment arrangements that substantially disadvantage one or more disabled employees.

As is the case with other Acts of Parliament, this Act relies heavily on what is deemed to be 'reasonable'. The Act's scope for challenging discrimination is therefore weakened by the likely difficulties involved in determining what is 'reasonable' for disabled people to have to accept in a society in which disablism is inherent in its cultural and structural patterns. However, it is important to note that what is 'reasonable' will tend to be determined by case law, and so it is important that opportunities for establishing precedents are taken in order to strengthen the anti-discriminatory potential of the Act.

Although these are the main forms of inequality to be found in organizations, they are, of course, by no means the only ones. What is needed, then, is not simply an understanding of specific forms of inequality within organizations, but rather an appreciation of inequality (and the concomitant discrimination and oppression) more broadly as a feature of the complex dynamics of organizational life.

These dynamics, and the patterns of inequality they engender, can again be understood in terms of PCS analysis:

P   Personal prejudices and negative attitudes towards particular groups of people can play an important part in the interpersonal relationships and inter-group dynamics.

C   Norms, values and stereotypes that form the basis of organizational culture often have much in common with the dominant cultural values and norms of the wider society (organizational culture will be discussed in more detail below).

S   Organizations do not operate in a sociopolitical vacuum. They are influenced by, and contribute to, the economy and the social order more generally.

The subtle intricacies of organizational dynamics form the basis of extensive academic interest (Mullins, 1996; Stacey, 1993). It is beyond the scope of this book to give them the attention they merit, and so I shall restrict myself to a more limited analysis of their significance, beginning with a consideration of continuity and change.

Continuity and change

The discussions so far in this chapter have, understandably, focused on issues of power and inequality. However, in order to understand the organizational context more fully, it is necessary to develop an appreciation of some of the deeper issues. It is for this reason that I shall now concentrate on seeking to clarify the significance of continuity and change. I shall do this by drawing on theoretical concepts already used in my analysis (structuration theory, for example) and introducing new concepts that cast some light on this area of study (autopoiesis, for example).

Stacey (1993) argues that organizational success relies on a degree of both stability and instability. He describes this as a paradox. However, this is a rather static term – a snapshot, rather than a dynamic process. I would therefore prefer to speak of a dialectic between the two, a process of conflict between conservative forces of continuity (stability) and forces of change (instability). This dialectic has much in common with Reed's (1992) notion of a 'dialectic of control':

> Thus, enshrined within all work organizations there lies a 'dialectic of control'; that is, a dynamic process of struggle between contending groups to secure and command the conditions through which collective action is made possible . . . The 'dialectic of control' is the dynamic process which underlies the changing balance of power experienced in all complex organizations and the crucial effect it has on the capacity to shape and reshape the structures and practices through which domination is simultaneously protected and challenged at the level of routine everyday life or at the level of strategic decision-making and corporate governance.
>
> (pp. 99–100)

This passage helps to paint a picture of the complex interactions and power struggles that are part and parcel of organizational life. Indeed, Marsden (1993) argues that: 'an organization isn't a thing, it's a process' (p. 119).

Other theorists have argued that organizations are not just processes, but rather a particular type of process – that of 'autopoiesis'. This is a term that originates in biology and refers to the way in which biological systems take on a life of their own through a process of 'self-production' (autopoiesis means literally 'self-production'). An autopoietic system is one in which a self-producing, or 'recursive' unity is formed, as in a particular biological life form.

This notion was introduced by Maturana and Varela (1978; 1980) who were keen to point out that the concept should be restricted to biology and not generalized to other forms of system. However, despite this, the concept has been extended to apply to social systems (Luhmann, 1990); the law (Teubner, 1993); the state (Jessop, 1990) and organizations (Marsden, 1993). It is this last example that interests us here. Hannan and Freeman (1989) argue that: 'organizations develop lives of their own, with action at least partly disconnected from ostensible goals, from demands of relevant environment, and often from the intentions of organizational leaders' (p. 5, cited in von Krogh and Roos, 1995, p. 83).

Organizational life, then, is not simply a matter of the rational pursuit of 'business objectives' or 'strategic aims'. According to this view, an organizational system which achieves autopoietic status ('autopoietic take-off', as Jessop, 1990, calls it) can lose sight of its goals and even its reason for existing. This would help to explain how and why supposedly 'caring' organizations can contribute to discrimination and oppression. Autopoiesis means that an organization can become so engrossed in its own processes of self-reproduction (maintaining its 'shape' and character, for example) that it loses track of what it is trying to achieve or how it is going to achieve it, thereby introducing the possibility/likelihood, of outcomes that are contrary to the organization's aims (see the discussion of 'systematic practice' in Thompson, 2002c). It is in this way that organizations that are ostensibly committed to equality, at a policy and strategy level at least, can actually be guilty of perpetrating significant acts of discrimination, by both omission and commission, thereby increasing oppression rather than challenging it.

◀ PRACTICE FOCUS 6.3 ▶

Sandra was very pleased to be appointed officer-in-charge of a residential home for older people, especially as she was committed to developing anti-ageist practice. However, on taking up her post, she was very dismayed and disappointed to discover that the regime at the home, although ostensibly committed to treating older people with dignity, was geared more towards the staff's interests and concerns than those of the residents. It was as if a culture had developed in which it had been forgotten that the purpose of the home was to provide standards of care that gave residents as high a quality of life as possible in the circumstances. Sandra decided she would have to make training in anti-ageist practice a priority.

Although the concept of autopoiesis is helpful in explaining how discriminatory outcomes arise from the nature of organizational life (due to cultural assumptions and power structures within the organization – C and S levels), rather than simply from the ill-will or incompetence of specific individuals (P level), it is also problematic. This is because, as Sibeon (1996) points out, the concept of autopoiesis rests on a reified conception of agency, especially as used by Luhmann:

Luhmann argues that systems are self-referencing (1988): he claims (1982: 265) systems are self-referential in that they are able to reflect and have consciousness of themselves as systems, and are able to take decisions. In other words, he is claiming that social systems are actors. Luhmann fails to adequately address the agency/structure debate. It is true that social systems have emergent structural properties that arise for reasons that cannot be 'reduced' to the agency exercised by actors (whether individual or social actors), but it is quite another thing to claim that social networks/social systems are themselves actors with capacities for reflection and with causal, decision-making powers.

(p. 42)

This is a reified conception in the sense that it treats a social system as if it were an entity that is able to exercise agency – to make choices or decisions.

The situation with regard to organizations is complex. On the one hand, an organization is a social system and we must therefore be wary of attributing agency where it does not or cannot apply. For example, an organization can be said to 'have' knowledge, as in the case of organizational culture (to be discussed below), but this is not to say that the organization in some way has consciousness or is a conscious entity. On the other hand, however, as organizations can make decisions and are therefore responsible for their consequences – they are what Harré (1981) refers to as 'supra-individuals' (Sibeon, 1996). However, the decisions made by organizations can be traced back to (but not 'reduced' to) the actions (or refusals to act) of particular individuals or groups. It should therefore be remembered that the notion of organizations 'having a life of their own' is to be understood at a metaphorical level only.

How, then, are we to understand organizational change and continuity? In brief, I propose two responses. First, it is important to return to Sibeon (1996) when he argues that:

it is entirely possible to acknowledge the importance of recursive (self-reproducing) tendencies in social systems and in social networks without having to also endorse reductionist and reified conceptions of recursion, such as Luhmann's.

(p. 43)

That is to say, the notion of autopoiesis (or 'recursion') has value within limits, as long as its use is not overextended to form the basis of a reductionist theory in which social systems are mistakenly attributed with agency or in which the restricted agency of organizations is exaggerated.

Kickert (1993) is similarly critical of one aspect of autopoiesis theory, namely the underlying construct that the maintenance or stability of a system arises from its 'closed' nature, its tendency to reproduce itself in a self-referential way – 'in its own image', as it were. Kickert counters this by suggesting that stability within a system derives from its response to disturbances outside the system, from its ability to adjust to them, rather than its 'closure' from them. He therefore prefers to refer to autopoiesis in terms of 'dynamic conservatism' (a concept I shall discuss in more detail below). By this he means a process of self-maintenance through 'interaction with a turbulent outside world' (p. 274). Thus recursion occurs *through* interaction between an organization and the wider sociopolitical environment, rather than as a result of closure from it.

Second, it is important to return to structuration theory in order to develop our understanding further. Structuration, as we saw in Chapter 2, refers to the process whereby human actions (agency) reproduce structural relations. While Giddens's analysis relates to structures at the sociopolitical level, it can also be brought to bear at an organizational level. Individuals within the organization are constrained by its parameters: the nature and purpose of the organization, its structures, power relations, rules and regulations, culture and common practices. However, as such individuals act and interact within these parameters, such actions have the effect of not only reflecting these factors, but also reinforcing them. The structures are reproduced in and by the actions of those working within them, as illustrated in Figure 6.1. Thus, the dialectic between agency and structure (or between subjective and objective, to use the existentialist terminology) operates not only at the macrostructural level of sociopolitical structures but also at the intermediary level of organizational life.

Organizational culture

A culture, broadly speaking, is a 'symbolic universe', a set of meanings, representations and values on which belief systems, norms and practices are based. A culture therefore provides a ready-made, albeit changing and evolving framework through which to make sense of the world and our own experience within it. Culture is not deterministic, in the sense that it ultimately determines our experience or the meanings we ascribe to it. Rather, it provides the context and parameters in which we operate. That is, the P level operates within the context of the C level but is not determined by it. The relationship is a dialectical one, rather than deterministic.

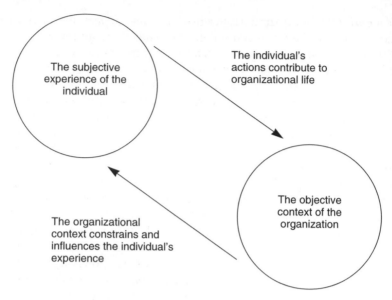

Figure 6.1   The subjective–objective dialectic within an organization

This analysis can be seen to apply in relation to organizations. An organization develops a culture (and a set of subcultures) through which people make sense of their experience of the organization and negotiate their positions, relationships and practices within it. The concept of 'organizational culture' is therefore an important one, and potentially useful for explaining:

- the development of norms and values within an organization: 'That's the way we do things round here';
- conflict and power struggles between groups (the interaction of subcultures vying for dominance);
- feelings of affiliation (feeling comfortable with the culture) and alienation (feeling at odds with the culture);
- organizational socialization – the process through which new recruits learn how to function and behave within the parameters of the culture;
- problems, tensions, conflicts and misunderstandings between organizations where their respective cultures are not compatible (as can occur in attempts to develop multidisciplinary collaboration); and
- the distinctive 'feel' or strong identity that many organizations display.

There are a number of factors that contribute to organizational culture, not least of which is management style (Johanssen and Page, 1990), as shown, for example, in relation to where the organization can be located on a continuum between autocratic controls and democratic approaches. Few, if any, organizations are entirely autocratic or entirely democratic, and so they can generally be located along a continuum between the two extremes.

Organizations that are closer to the autocratic end of the spectrum are likely to have a 'culture of compliance'. This refers to a set of expectations or cultural norms in which staff are subject to strong controls with little autonomy and are likely to face sanctions if they 'step out of line'. More democratically based organizations, by contrast, are likely to be characterized by a 'culture of commitment' in which staff identify with the aims of the organization and are prepared to commit time and effort above and beyond the basic level required as part of a commitment to the organization's success and the quality of work carried out.

At one level there are clear links between organizations within the helping professions and the notion of a culture of commitment in terms of:

- professional values and a sense of 'vocation' associated with the caring professions;
- the recognition, at a theoretical level at least, of the importance of valuing people and giving them the opportunity to participate and contribute; and
- the need for a degree of autonomy in decision-making. Much of the work involved in 'people work' cannot be carried out effectively by 'following orders' and requires a degree of independence of thought, and therefore professional discretion.

However, it would be naïve not to recognize that strong elements of a culture of compliance are also to be found in organizations within the helping professions. I am sure that staff in health authorities, local authority departments, schools, voluntary bodies and so on would have little difficulty in identifying examples of a culture of compliance in the form of expectations that they should 'do as they are told', in certain respects at least.

This illustrates the fact that organizational cultures are not simple, monolithic entities, but rather complex, subtle and intricate blends of expectations, norms, values and meanings. They are, of course, also subject to change over time as they develop and evolve in response to changes both within and outside the organization.

Organizational culture is therefore a good example of the concept of 'recursion', as discussed earlier. It is, in large part, through organizational culture that patterns and relationships (including power relations) are reproduced and sustained over time. It is for this reason that organizational culture is particularly significant in relation to inequality, discrimination and oppression.

The effect of organizational culture is a degree of stability, a maintenance of patterns and norms. Consequently, if an organization's culture is one in which inequalities are accepted and condoned, or even valued and promoted, then change in the direction of emancipatory practice will need to address changes at the level of organizational culture. That is, efforts towards change at the P level will be limited, undermined or even extinguished if the C level continues to tolerate or promote discrimination.

An important concept here is that of the 'centre of gravity' (Malahleka, 1992), a term which is used to refer to the crucial point at which a set of discriminatory assumptions and practices can be destabilized, and thus brought down. The greater the degree of resistance to inequality and oppression at the P level, the more difficult it becomes for assumptions and norms at the C level to go unchallenged. In this way, efforts to tackle inequality may well be thwarted by C level resistance or 'absorption' of such efforts, but there can also be situations where the 'centre of gravity' shifts to the point that change occurs at the cultural level. This is an important point to which I shall return below in my discussion of the 'organizational operator'.

◀ **PRACTICE FOCUS 6.3** ▶

Roy was a long-standing and respected member of the staff team and was often influential when it came to team decision-making. However, whenever he raised any concerns about equality issues, no one really took him seriously, preferring instead to make jokes about Roy being a 'trendy leftie'. This situation was to change, though, when a new member of the team was appointed. Sue was a very experienced worker and came with a reputation for being very competent and reliable. However, she was also very interested in equality issues, particularly in relation to gender. Having *two* team members interested in such matters was to prove significant in tilting the balance. Suddenly, the team started to listen more carefully to what Roy had been saying for a long time. A second voice saying very similar things was enough to convince team members that they should take the issues seriously.

Of course, we also need to understand the C level in the context of the S level. As Lawton and Rose (1994) put it:

> All organizations exist within some wider context and we would expect an organization's culture to reflect this. We would expect a match between the organizational culture and the wider culture of society at large. Thus it may be unrealistic to expect a democratically run workplace when the prevailing political and social ethos is authoritarian.
>
> (p. 69)

It is therefore important to recognize that the C level relates dialectically not only to the P level but also the S level (the 'double dialectic' of agency, culture and structure, as described in Chapter 1). To a certain extent at least, organizational culture is a reflection of, and contributor to, the broader macro-level of society, economy and polity. It is not surprising, then, as we noted earlier in this chapter, to find that patterns of inequality in the wider society (racism, sexism, ageism and so on) are also to be found within organizations and their cultures.

It is also important to note the significance of language in relation to organizational culture. Von Krogh and Roos (1995) use the term 'languaging' to refer to the process of 'coordinating behaviour' through speaking, and they argue that: 'Over time, organizations develop their own distinct domains of language . . . the obvious explanation is that languaging may be understood as the "stuff" that the organization is made of' (p. 97). That is to say, linguistic interactions are a primary medium though which organizational culture is transmitted, and through which a sense of unity and identity is maintained. Consequently, we must once again acknowledge the crucial role of language in constructing social reality, both in general and at the specific level of organizational culture (Thompson, 2003).

Another important aspect of organizational culture is the extent to which a particular culture is predominantly masculine in its orientation. As discussed earlier in this chapter, gender is a significant feature of organizational dynamics. This can particularly be the case in so far as organizational culture is concerned. This often manifests itself in 'be tough' attitudes which, as we shall see below, can play a key role in relation to stress. Strongly masculine cultures tend to be characterized by:

- a focus on toughness and a stoic approach;
- a reluctance to address, or even recognize issues relating to feelings;

- an emphasis on competitiveness, often at the expense of cooperation and collaboration;
- hierarchical power relations and channels of communication.

A strongly masculine culture can be very problematic in relation to issues of equality and discrimination. This is not only in terms of gender, where what many women have to offer is devalued or marginalized, but also with regard to other forms of discrimination. For example, a 'be tough' attitude can act as an obstacle to developing a sensitive approach to issues of culture, race, language, age, disability or sexual identity.

It should be clear from the discussions in the previous few pages that an understanding of organizational culture should be part of the knowledge base needed to underpin the development of effective equality strategies and practices.

Human resource management

In discussing organizational culture we can be seen to have entered the terrain of what has come to be known as human resource management (HRM). This is an approach to the 'people issues' within organizations, and the world of employment more generally, that has grown from traditional personnel practices.

Storey (1995a) defines HRM as:

> a distinctive approach to employment management which seeks to achieve competitive advantage through the strategic deployment of a highly committed and capable workforce, using an integrated array of cultural, structural and personnel techniques.
>
> (p. 5)

He then goes on to describe HRM in terms of four sets of features:

1. *Commitment*   As discussed earlier in this chapter, a culture of commitment is seen as more constructive and helpful for all concerned. This has implications for selection and recruitment, training, supervision, appraisal and other personnel-related issues. This is potentially a positive approach as far as equality is concerned, as an emphasis on commitment on the part of staff does not sit comfortably with an oppressive and disempowering organizational regime.

2. *Strategic integration*   This refers to the need to ensure that staff-related ('human resource') issues are taken into consideration in

formulating and implementing organizational strategy more broadly. Human resource issues should be integral to the strategy process, rather than an afterthought. Again this is potentially a positive development in relation to equality practice in so far as it places staffing issues high on the organizational agenda. This allows questions of equality and diversity to feature in strategic planning and thereby lessens the likelihood of these issues being marginalized or overlooked.

3. *The role of managers* HRM involves moving away from having specialist personnel and/or training departments and placing more emphasis on line managers taking responsibility for human resource issues. They are seen as having a crucial role to play in ensuring success at the human resource level (and therefore at the overall strategic level). The potential benefit of this development is that there should be a greater awareness of equality issues if line managers have greater levels of responsibility for human resource matters and 'people' issues generally.

4. *HR levers* 'Levers' refers to the techniques and processes available for maximizing human resource potential. These include selection, communication, training, restructuring and job redesign. These are to be seen as part of the broader process of 'managing' organizational culture, using such levers to influence culture with a view to creating as positive and constructive a culture as possible in line with the organization's strategic aims. This has the potential to make equality a primary focus within the organization and an inherent part of its culture, although it has to be recognized that cultural changes are generally very difficult to achieve and do not occur overnight.

It should be noted that, in each of these four cases, the positive changes in favour of promoting equality are *potential* changes. There is nothing inherent in HRM that makes it a guaranteed positive force for challenging discrimination and oppression. However, it is fair to say that the development of HRM as an approach to personnel issues in organizations does offer increased opportunities for promoting equality, although these can be blocked or even used to reinforce inequality if the political will is not present to use them positively.

Another important development associated with HRM is the concept of the 'learning organization' (Garvin, 1993; Schein, 1993). This refers to the type of organization in which learning becomes a central part of organizational life. This involves a number of factors, including the following:

- a focus on training and development as integral to the organization's activities, rather than peripheral to them;
- open and constructive channels of communicating to encourage opportunities for staff learning from each other;
- the removal, where possible, of barriers to learning at both a personal and on organizational level;
- a willingness to experiment and promote innovation; and
- the facilitation of learning in all aspects of the organization's activities, rather than simply within the context of formal training.

The development of a learning organization is once again a matter of culture change. The steps that need to be taken involve moving away from traditional cultural assumptions and values that can often stand in the way of learning:

> Developing a learning organization represents a strategy of culture change. It involves a concerted effort to change the values and assumptions dominant within an organization. Such a change of culture is not a simple matter and requires a major commitment of time and energy over an extended period of time. It is not an undertaking that can be taken lightly or one that can be entered into by only a minority of staff – it requires a whole-hearted commitment on a collective basis.
>
> (Thompson, 2000a, p. 133)

An emphasis on personal and organizational learning can be seen as an important step in the direction of promoting equality in so far as it encourages an open and reflective approach in which sensitive issues can be discussed and addressed positively and constructively, rather than being swept under the carpet. However, it should also be apparent that the establishment of a learning organization is a tall order that requires a very high level of commitment. The irony of this situation is that the sort of organization that could benefit most from this approach is perhaps the least likely organization to want, or be able, to make the necessary commitment to bring it about. Its potential as a strategy for promoting equality is therefore limited, but none the less important as an approach that can bear fruit where and when the circumstances are right.

Although clearly not a panacea as far as tackling inequality is concerned, HRM would appear to offer more than both traditional forms of management and more modern forms based on managerialism (Clarke and Newman, 1997) which owe more to producing compliance than generating commitment.

The diversity approach

The concept of 'managing diversity' is one that has grown out of HRM and is also a movement away from traditional equal opportunity policies and practices. It is premised on a recognition of diversity and differences as positive attributes of an organization rather than as problems to be solved. This approach, then, clearly has much in common with poststructuralism in terms of its affirmation of the value of difference. Baxter (2001a) comments as follows:

> There has been a tendency for equal opportunities policies to focus on the legal aspects and requirements to avoid discriminatory acts. Such a stance, in addition to being essentially defensive, can also limit initiatives to those areas which fall under the antidiscrimination legislation. Managing diversity, on the other hand, has a more positive message in relation to the overall organisational benefits of valuing and capitalising on the different backgrounds, characteristics and experiences of all employees.
>
> (p. 10)

This is a relatively new approach which is now beginning to become well established in a variety of organizations and organizational sectors. It can be seen, in some ways at least, as a response to feelings of dissatisfaction with conventional equal opportunities strategies. This new emphasis, then, is on building positives, rather than seeking simply to eradicate or reduce negatives. And, of course, this argument can be taken a step further by proposing that it is not only in terms of gender and race or ethnicity that difference can be valued, but also in relation to age, disability and so on. Diversity is not limited to gender and ethnicity.

As part of the move towards a managing diversity approach, Walker (1994) proposes what she calls a 'Valuing Differences' model. She goes on to explain that this is based on four key principles:

1. People work best when they feel valued.
2. People feel most valued when they believe that their individual and group differences have been taken into account.
3. The ability to learn from people regarded as different is the key to becoming fully empowered.
4. When people feel valued and empowered, they are able to build relationships in which they work together interdependently and synergistically. (p. 212)

As noted in Chapter 3, oppression arises as a result of negative discrimination, the process of attributing negative characteristics and stereotypes to particular groups of people. The diversity approach, then, seeks to intervene in this process by presenting differences between people as a positive asset rather than the basis of discrimination. Difference can be the basis of equality rather than inequality.

The advantages of the diversity approach include the following:

- less reliance on a legalistic approach which can easily become tokenistic;
- the involvement of all staff in maximizing their potential, rather than only those groups traditionally identified as disadvantaged;
- addressing issues at the level of organizational culture, rather than simply at a personal or individual level;
- a strategic, rather than ad hoc incremental approach; and
- doing more than 'tolerating' difference.

This final point is a particularly important one, in so far as it enables equality issues to be seen in more holistic terms, more closely linked to the purpose and objectives of the organization. As Blakemore and Drake (1996) comment:

> Having a more coherent and comprehensive equality strategy . . . means more than being able to coordinate separate 'equal opportunity' activities. According to a managing diversity perspective, it entails a strategic vision of where the organization is headed (Kandola *et al.*, 1995: 34). Thus it is argued that equality and diversity goals must be incorporated into the main vision or mission of the organization – a statement of 'what the company or organization is all about'.
>
> (p. 195)

For 'people work' organizations this notion of 'what the . . . organization is all about' is particularly relevant, as there is a significant overlap between their humanitarian concerns and the promotion of equality.

◀ **PRACTICE FOCUS 6.4** ▶

As a result of attending a training course on 'managing diversity', Martin decided to implement a programme of team development based on the principle of valuing difference. The idea behind it was not, as is often traditionally the case, to promote uniformity and consensus in the team, but rather to recognize the differences within the team in terms of people's background and to try and use these positively and constructively by using difference as an opportunity for learning and enrichment. He hoped that this would provide a good platform from which to challenge discrimination and oppression.

However, it is important not to adopt an uncritical approach to diversity. Lister (1997) makes a very telling point when she argues that:

> a preoccupation with and delight in diversity for its own sake, shorn of any political edge, runs the risk of losing sight of the power relations that shape the significance of diversity when it translates into divisions and their related axes of advantage/disadvantage and domination/subordination. Indeed, 'managing diversity' has become a management tool which effectively obscures the reality of discrimination (Bacchi, 1996).
>
> (p. 78)

While there are clearly benefits to a more positive approach (especially in view of my comments in Chapter 5 about defensiveness and dogmatism), we should not allow the positives to distract attention from the very real problems of discrimination and oppression. Valuing diversity can be seen as a contribution to promoting equality but this should not be at the expense of tackling discrimination and oppression. For example, we should be wary of comments such as:

- 'increasingly the "language of oppression" . . . has given way to terms reflecting less confrontational and inclusive ideology' (Baxter, 2001c, p. xxi) – As we noted in Chapter 5, an emphasis on oppression does not have to be confrontational, but there are very real dangers in allowing the focus on discrimination and oppression to become blurred.
- 'Managing diversity, however, adopts an inclusive approach, focusing on the individual rather than the group' (Baxter, 2001b, p. 11) – It has taken us a long time to go beyond the traditional liberal emphasis on the individual to recognize the significance of wider cultural and structural issues. There is therefore a very real danger that a narrow focus on diversity could become a backward step rather than a positive development.

Of course, it would be naïve to herald the diversity approach as 'the answer', especially in view of the fact that, as we have seen, it does not address power relations and the structural level, but it clearly has more to offer than many traditional aspects of equality practice which can be disjointed and tokenistic. However, given the entrenched attitudes, vested interests and structured inequalities that characterize modern organizations, it has to be recognized that the development of the diversity approach is likely to face obstacles and limitations. What is needed is a critical approach to valuing diversity which can be integrated with the progress made in promoting equality. In other words, we need valuing diversity to be seen as a contribution to promoting equality rather than as an alternative to it.

Stress and inequality

Occupational stress has long been recognized as a feature of some forms of organizational life. It is a problem that has significant costs for individuals, organizations and users of services (Thompson *et al.*, 1994b; 1996a; Thompson, 1999), including costs that relate to inequality, as we shall see below.

A common view of stress is one in which it is perceived as a failing or inadequacy on the part of the individual concerned. There are at least three problems associated with this approach:

- It 'pathologizes' the individual, blaming him or her for the situation.
- It fails to take account of the organizational context.
- It can lead to a vicious circle in which feelings of guilt and inadequacy add to the pressures of the situation and therefore increase the levels of stress.

All three of these can have the effect of making people reluctant to seek help or gain support, thereby reinforcing the focus on the individual and letting the organization 'off the hook'.

This approach can be characterized as two-dimensional, represented as a 'battle' between the pressures or 'stressors' one faces and one's ability to cope with them (see Figure 6.2). This simple model presents stress as the outcome of this battle where the stressors overpower the coping resources. A more appropriate model is a three-dimensional model in which stressors and coping resources are joined

Figure 6.2   The two-dimensional model of stress

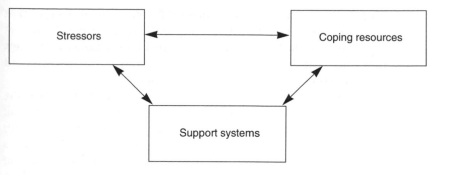

Figure 6.3   The three-dimensional interactive model of stress

by the key issue of support (Thompson *et al.*, 1994b). This model is a dynamic, interactive one in which support can reduce stressors and increase coping resources (through confidence, for example), and a lack of support can magnify stressors and undermine coping resources (Figure 6.3).

◀ **PRACTICE FOCUS 6.5** ▶

Pauline had been showing signs of stress for quite some time but she was adamant she did not need any help or support. She was determined to be strong enough to overcome the pressure she faced. However, the time came when she could no longer handle the immense weight of work and other pressures that bore down on her and she became quite ill. She was absent from work for over two months and, at the suggestion of the Occupational Health Unit, she received confidential counselling before returning to work. Fortunately, the counsellor was able to help her appreciate the important third dimension of support and to discourage her from the stoic approach that can leave people isolated and vulnerable.

Each of the three dimensions of this model can be seen to have close links with the organizational context:

* *Stressors* Many of the stressors people encounter are primarily organizational factors. These include role stress (ambiguity, incompatibility, conflict, overload); relations at work; unclear or unrealistic expectations; noise, overcrowding, poor facilities; excessive or inappropriate workload; lack of appreciation; discrimination and harassment.
* *Coping resources* Important factors in coping with pressures are a

positive attitude and high self-esteem (Totman, 1990), factors that can be undermined by a negative organizational culture (Thompson *et al.*, 1996b). Similarly, a feeling of control over oneself and one's circumstances can be very beneficial, but can again be discouraged or undermined in some organizational settings.

- *Support*   Here organizations can play a crucial role. In principle, organizations have a variety of support measures at their disposal: supervision; confidential counselling; training and development; appraisal; grievance procedures and so on. Some organizations have formal staff care policies. However, the measures available may not be used, may be ineffective or may even be counterproductive (for example, counselling may reinforce notions of individual blame or pathology – Murphy, 1991). Some organizations may, at a rhetorical level, profess a commitment to supporting staff, while their actions and attitudes may be less than supportive of employees undertaking complex and demanding duties.

Stress, then, is clearly an organizational concern, rather than simply a matter of individual failing or a low level of tolerance of pressure. It is therefore worth exploring the links between stress and inequality by reference to the organizational context. Once again the three dimensions of stressors, coping resources and support can provide a useful framework for helping us understand these issues:

- *Stressors*   Discrimination and oppression are, in themselves, significant sources of pressure. For example, black workers can find themselves exposed to racial abuse from service users and even from colleagues. In addition, the pressures arising from discrimination can be more subtle and less overt, but perhaps just as problematic and disempowering.
- *Coping resources*   A person's social location is likely to be a factor in their access to coping resources. For example, social class will be an important issue in relation to 'buying power' (Thompson *et al.*, 1994a). Similarly, there is evidence to suggest that men and women typically adopt different styles of coping (Weintraub *et al.*, 1989).
- *Support*   Access to support can be differential, again according to social location. Women staff may feel unsupported in male-dominated organizations (McDerment, 1988). Black workers may also feel unsupported in white-dominated organizations (Hutchinson-Reis, 1989; Ferns, 1987), as indeed may disabled members of staff in organizations which do not go beyond the minimum requirements of the Disability Discrimination Act 1995.

There are also parallels between stress and inequality in terms of the way the two issues tend, ideologically, to be individualized, with little or no attention paid to the wider contextual factors. They also have much in common in terms of what needs to be done to tackle the problems that they present:

- sensitivity and empathy, appreciating other people's situations and points of view;
- a willingness to look beyond the personal or individual level and take account of cultural and structural factors;
- a rejection of stereotypes and dogmatism;
- a recognition of the role of power and the ways in which it can be misused and abused, together with a commitment to empowerment;
- the need to develop a collective, collaborative approach; and
- an avoidance of simple answers to complex problems.

Both sets of issues also involve the challenge of making professional practice a more humanitarian endeavour by valuing people, recognizing their strengths and providing the support they need to make a positive contribution.

The organizational operator

'Organizational operator' is a term I use to describe the role an individual can play in seeking to have a positive influence on the organization in which he or she works, particularly in relation to challenging discrimination and oppression. This is a role that can be developed over time, and my intention here is to contribute to aiding that development by discussing some of the issues that relate to it. As Preston-Shoot (1996) comments, workers:

> need more sophisticated change agent skills in relation to organisations, based around: agenda building, problem defining, proposal making and policy assessing, based on issues which arise from cases, coupled with alliance constructing and skills of analysis, using power strategically, and group working.
>
> (p. 37)

In seeking to influence an organization, of course, we are using power. Clearly organizations are more powerful than individuals, but this is not to say that individuals or groups within an organization do not have the ability to influence processes and outcomes. An important issue here is the concept of 'resistance', or what is sometimes known as 'countervailing power'. This refers to the ability to work against dominant ideas and practices.

Organizations are generally seen to work on the basis of an assumed consensus, with managers engaged in attempts to prevent or marginalize conflicts, as much of the work on HRM and organizational culture demonstrates. However, the reality of conflicts and resistance is much more complex. As Collinson (1994) comments:

> Resistance and consent are rarely polarized extremes on a continuum of possible worker discursive practices. Rather, they are usually inextricably linked, often in contradictory ways within particular organizational cultures, discourses and practices. Resistance frequently contains elements of consent and consent often incorporates aspects of resistance.
>
> (p. 29)

An important point to deduce from this is that there are no grounds to justify the defeatist view of employing organizations as all-powerful monoliths that are beyond influence or change. Clearly, some organizations will prove more difficult to influence than others, particularly those with deeply ingrained or entrenched cultures that react strongly to attempts to innovate or make changes. However, it is important to note that some change is possible, even if we have to work to a longer-term timescale. If we adopt a defeatist attitude, we become part of the inertia that equality initiatives have to overcome. That is, we become part of the problem rather than part of the solution (Figure 6.4).

We should be careful not to confuse the notion of resistance with that of sabotage. The former is a constructive process while the latter is destructive. At times sabotage may well be an appropriate tactic to adopt, but the circumstances for this must be right, as the price to be paid in terms of a 'backlash' can be very high indeed. The broader process of resistance may include sabotage, perhaps as a last resort, but should not be equated with it.

It is both interesting and significant to note that the bulk of the literature on power in organizations addresses itself to strategies of control – that is, strategies for management to control and discipline (in Foucault's sense) the workforce (Thompson and McHugh, 1995). There is also a smaller, but none the less significant, literature on resistance in the sense of the workforce attempting to resist management's agenda and satisfy their own (Jermier et al., 1994). What appears to be

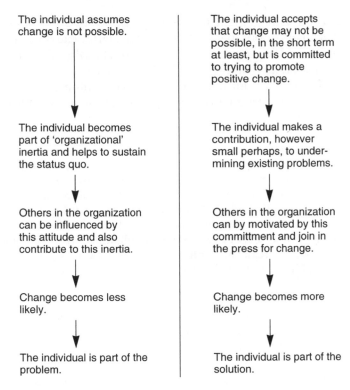

Figure 6.4   Promoting positive change in organizations

missing, however, is a significant literature and research base on attempts by the workforce to establish a common agenda of promoting equality. There are writings on how managers can 'incorporate' the workforce by convincing them that it is more productive for all to work together towards common ends. However, the question of how the workforce can seek to influence managers in the direction of equality has been addressed to a far lesser extent. That is, we need to look more closely at how resistance can be geared towards realizing the professional values of equality and the affirmation of difference – how resistance or countervailing power can become a positive, proactive force for change, rather than simply a negative, reactive force.

Ranson and Stewart (1994) regard management in the public sector as a process of realizing values, that is, of making values a reality. Perhaps it is time that we recognized that it is not only management but also professional practice that is about realizing values, and that it is an important management task to respond positively to staff influences rather than simply to seek to influence staff. Realizing the value of equality should be seen as a two-way street, with all participants having a responsibility, and a contribution to make.

How, then, can staff influence organizations? Collinson (1994) once again makes an important point when he comments on the importance of knowledge:

> Workplace resistance crucially draws upon various forms of knowledge. In practice subordinates have extensive knowledge which may not be shared with those in more senior positions, and which can be used as an important 'weapon of resistance' (Scott, 1986). Like resistance, knowledge itself can take multiple forms in organizational life. Oppositional practices are usually informed by the strategic exercise of particular knowledges which may be, for example, technical, bureaucratic and procedural, social, regional, cultural and historical, legal, economic, strategic/political and/or about self.
>
> (p. 49)

A well-informed 'organizational operator' can use his or her knowledge to good effect as, for example, in the case of the informal power relations discussed earlier in this chapter. Knowing who has an influence over what can be an important part of the repertoire needed to work effectively within the organizational setting towards equality goals.

A knowledge of the relevant law and policy can also be invaluable. For example, many organizations respect only the letter of the law rather than the spirit, while others may not even practise within the law. An understanding of what is required by law and policy can equip members of staff with the opportunity to point out shortcomings in current practices and procedures or to identify potentially beneficial changes. For example, the Children Act 1989 requires issues of race and culture to be taken into account, and so staff operating under the requirements of this act may be able to use it as a lever to promote the development of ethnically sensitive and anti-racist practice.

◀ PRACTICE FOCUS 6.6 ▶

Amelia had been concerned for quite some time about the lack of facilities for interpreting when working with people whose first language was not English. She felt strongly that non-English speakers were at a disadvantage as a result of the lack of attention paid to language issues. However, while attending a course on the requirements of the Mental Health Act 1983, she learned that there was a duty for a person being assessed under this Act to be interviewed 'in a suitable manner' and, for some people, this may mean via an interpreter. Amelia was delighted to hear this and returned to work the next day determined to use this newfound piece of information as a means of increasing pressure on managers to make interpreting facilities available.

Taking this argument a step further, we can see that *professional* practice in general can be an important focus for promoting equality in and through organizations. While a knowledge of the relevant law and policy is a fundamental expectation of professional practice, there are also other aspects that can be drawn upon. Primary among these is values, the value base of professional practice. The values of equality and the affirmation of difference can be made explicit and used as the basis of what Collinson (1994) calls 'resistance through persistence'. By repeatedly and consistently coming back to these core values, a theme of persistence is established, making it difficult for others, including managers, to ignore or marginalize them.

Professional practice is also premised on the notion of reflective practice, in so far as it is expected that staff should avoid unthinking, uncritical routines and act on the basis of a clear rationale that can be justified if challenged (that is, it should be accountable). Reflective, accountable practice therefore offers a firm basis for promoting equality and can be used to:

- challenge routinized, uncritical forms of practice and policies, pro-cedures or managerial/supervisory practices that encourage them;
- promote an ethos in which equality issues are openly and explicitly on the agenda;
- give a clear message to anyone in the organization who would wish to condone inequality and discrimination that they are likely to face conflict and resistance.

Moves in the direction of critically reflective practice can be instru-mental in tilting the balance in favour of equality. This can be an example of the process I mentioned earlier in this chapter, that of shifting the centre of gravity. Sometimes changes in a particular direc-tion can reach the critical point at which it becomes necessary for more far-reaching changes to take place. That is to say, an organization can absorb or rebuff a certain amount of resistance, but there often comes a time when this tactic has to be abandoned and further changes con-ceded. This is especially the case in relation to issues of equality where, in some respects at least, there is a legal duty to take seriously issues of inequality and discrimination – and therefore a reluctance to be seen as unreasonably resisting or blocking equality initiatives.

The notion of the 'centre of gravity' is therefore an important one to bear in mind, partly because it is a useful tactic to employ, or aim for, and partly because it is a source of hope and confidence – and therefore, potentially at least, a major resource to draw upon. Shifting the centre of gravity can also form the basis of further positive changes and developments. It can begin a 'roll' in which one element of progress stimulates another, and so on, thereby building up confidence and momentum. This, in turn, can form the basis of another key element in becoming an organizational operator – developing collective or collaborative approaches in which people are able to support each other.

Collaborative approaches have a number of benefits and advantages, not least the following:

- Groups of people generally have more impact and influence than individuals.
- People can learn from each other and develop a broader perspective on the situations they are seeking to influence.
- Working in a group is generally more enjoyable and rewarding and less stressful than working alone.
- Individuals are less vulnerable to recriminations when they are operating as part of a group.

An organizational operator, then, is someone who is able to work effectively in groups and, ideally, is able to recognize where a group is needed and take the necessary steps to promote the establishment of such a group.

The influence of both groups and individuals has to be understood in the context of our earlier discussion of continuity and change. Organizations are not static entities; they are constantly subject to change and development. The organization reproduces itself in and through the actions and decisions that are taken on a daily basis. This returns us to Kickert's (1993) notion of 'dynamic conservatism' – continuity is not something that just occurs naturally, it is something that has to be maintained through a constant process of reconstruction. Organizational continuity (conservatism) is therefore the outcome of a process (dynamic), rather than a natural state of affairs that cannot be changed or challenged. In this respect, conservatism is a form of handling change, rather than an alternative to change.

Once again we find ourselves in the domain of structuration theory. The structural relations of society generally, and of organizations more narrowly, are in dialectical relationship with the actions (agency) of those people located within such structures. That is, structure and agency shape and influence each other. Consequently, the actions of staff within organizations can have an effect on the structures and power relations of the organization. Whether or not such attempts are successful will depend on a range of factors, as I shall outline below, but the point needs to be emphasized that existing structures are not written in tablets of stone, and are subject to change. The nature, pace, extent and outcome of such change depend, in part at least, on the efforts and endeavours of staff within the organization – and their skills as organizational operators.

Given the pressures of the organization and its culture, it is often the case that the organizational operator requires support from someone outside the organization, as well as from within. Like-minded people outside the organization (colleagues elsewhere, former tutors or mentors) plus members and officials of professional associations can all play a part in the support systems that can be drawn upon in seeking to influence organizations for the better.

◀ PRACTICE FOCUS 6.7 ▶

In preparation for the forthcoming reorganization a set of proposals was circulated throughout the organization. However, many of the staff objected to these proposals, as they felt they would reduce the level of services, particularly for older and disabled people. They therefore set about putting forward their own set of proposals for how services should be reorganized. In order to maximize the chances of their proposals being accepted they put a lot of effort into thinking through the implications of the changes they had in mind and identifying the potential benefits. Although the senior management team did not accept the staff's plan in full, many elements of it were incorporated into the new organizational structure. The staff had therefore had a major influence on the organization.

Organizations are complex arenas with subtle, intricate and multi-level relations of power and influence. Promoting change is therefore likely to be a difficult, complex and lengthy process, but none the less a worthwhile one. Success or otherwise depends on a range of factors: the political climate both within and beyond the organizations; other pressures for change (large-scale reorganizations, for example); styles of management and managerial values; organizational culture; the charisma of particular individuals, and so on. Developing the skills of becoming an organizational operator will not guarantee success but will certainly increase the chances of achieving positive change.

In sum, then, being an organizational operator involves:

- having a good knowledge of the relevant law and policy, and of the formal and informal power relations within the organization;
- using such knowledge strategically to promote equality;
- promoting professional practice which is critically reflective;
- making the value base of equality and the affirmation of difference open and explicit;
- endeavouring to 'shift the centre of gravity' to the point where structures of inequality are replaced by equality initiatives;
- developing collective approaches and supporting others in their efforts; and
- not being defeatist; accepting that change may take time but is none the less worth pursuing.

Conclusion

Professional practice takes place within an organizational culture. This chapter has focused on some of the key elements of organizational life and some of the implications of the organizational settings in which we operate. What should be abundantly clear is the complexity of organizational life and the vast and intricate range of factors and issues that we face when we seek to understand, and work within, the organizational context.

Questions of power and inequality, organizational culture, management practices, diversity, stress and the skills of being an organizational operator have all been important issues to address, even though these have, for reasons of space, not been covered in the depth they merit. Similarly, these are not the only questions that have a bearing on the organizational context of professional practice. However, what has been covered should be sufficient to paint a picture of the challenges organizational life presents and the benefits that can be gained from developing the knowledge and skills required to work effectively within the organization with a view to promoting equality.

As I stated earlier, organizations can be dangerous places in which a lot of harm can be done. It is therefore vitally important that the issues discussed here are carefully thought through, rather than rushed into. Situations have to be weighed up and the implications of particular courses of action appreciated before decisions are made or actions taken. Challenging discrimination and oppression in organizations is a difficult and demanding task, and therefore one that has to be approached thoughtfully and cautiously.

This is one way in which a collaborative approach can pay dividends in terms of providing a forum for sharing ideas, supporting each other and identifying potential pitfalls. Indeed, perhaps the first and most important step towards becoming an organizational operator should be the step of becoming part of a network of people committed to the common aim of promoting equality.

7

CONCLUSION: STRATEGIES FOR PROMOTING EQUALITY

Introduction

In this concluding chapter, my aim is to present an overview of the various strategies that can be called upon in an effort to challenge discrimination and oppression and promote equality. This is not by way of providing a set of formulas to follow or definitive statements to close off the debate, as that would be both reductionist and dogmatic. My intention, rather, is to explore what I see as the basis of good practice in terms of the steps that can be taken to develop emancipatory practice and to incorporate equality issues into all aspects of professional practice.

The ideas presented are intended as a stimulus to further discussion, debate and analysis and as a starting point for practitioners seeking guidance on how to proceed. Note, though, that I use the term 'starting point'. There would clearly be problems involved in taking the suggestions here as rules to be followed or a blueprint to be adhered to. What this chapter offers is a set of ideas intended to facilitate and enhance reflective practice rather than act as a substitute for it.

However, before reviewing the strategies available to us, I first want to outline the main costs of discrimination and oppression so that it becomes clear just how important it is to develop emancipatory practice. Such costs include:

- *Violence* Violence against women owes much to sexism (Maynard, 1993), as does elder abuse to ageism (Thompson, 1995a).
- *Injustice* Inequality in the criminal justice and penal systems (Hudson, 1993) is just one example of how discrimination can lead to injustice.
- *Disenfranchisement* The exclusion and marginalization of particular groups and individuals can leave them without a voice.

- *Psychological pressures* Discrimination can be a significant factor in terms of undermining confidence and self-esteem as a result of 'internalized oppression' (Mullaly, 1993).
- *Detrimental effects on health* Inequalities in health have profound consequences for some groups, as we saw in Chapter 4.
- *Housing* Access to adequate and appropriate housing can be seen to follow distinctly unequal patterns (Mason, 2000).
- *Economic effects* Inequalities in pay, conditions of service, access to training, promotion, and employment itself have been extensively documented.

Inequality, discrimination and oppression, then, are not only unacceptable at the abstract level of moral values and principles but also at the practical level of the profoundly harmful effects of oppression on people's lives. We should therefore remember these costs and their very real impact on people's lives and well-being when considering strategies for promoting equality, and indeed when seeking to put them into practice. As Donnison (1998) puts it:

> The inequalities in British society are neither inevitable nor accidental. They are now severe enough to damage every citizen. They are most plainly damaging of our children and young people – preparing them for exclusion from the mainstream of what should be their society. We shall pay a heavy price for that. The price will be paid in money, in fear, in poorer health and shorter lives, in blighted hopes for the future, and in the loss of a political nerve which blight's a nation's capacity for creative innovation. Worse still follows when citizens unable to gain justice by constitutional means turn to violence.
>
> (p. 30)

Steps towards equality

The remainder of this chapter is devoted to outlining a range of strategies that can be used to promote equality by challenging discrimination and oppression. Needless to say, the list is neither comprehensive nor exhaustive. It is merely intended as a guide and a stimulus to further debate and development. I shall begin with what is perhaps one of the most important strategies, and one that incorporates a range of other issues and serves as a unifying theme – that of empowerment.

Empowerment

The term 'empowerment' is one that is used in a number of contexts, with different, but related meanings. As Clarke *et al.* (1994b) comment:

We can identify a multiplicity of empowerments which are current in the contemporary world of public services. One . . . is the empowerment of managers themselves in the creation of greater autonomy and the enhanced 'right to manage' services. A second is the commitment of the new managerialism to empower employees as participants in the process of change, to devolve greater responsibility within organizations to, or at least towards, the 'front line' in the search for more responsive working practices. A third is the empowerment of the service user in relation to public organizations, most characteristically in the form of increased 'choice' or personalized attention and the establishment of limited quasi-contractual rights concerning service delivery (for example, the citizen's charter and its variants). A fourth is the empowerment of communities, sometimes defined in terms of their geographical basis but more often as 'communities of interest' which involves more or less expansive views of redressing imbalance of power between the state and particular social groups or within the broader social structure.

(p. 237)

Empowerment is clearly a complex, multilayered concept, and it is no surprise that Clarke *et al.* go on to describe it as a 'loose cannon'. It is therefore important to be clear about what we mean by empowerment as a strategy for promoting equality. While recognizing that empowerment is a contested concept (Adams, 1996), we can identify its core element as a process of helping people gain greater control over their lives and the sociopolitical and existential challenges they face.

In this context, empowerment can be seen as a process geared towards achieving authenticity. It is not a question of 'enabling', in the sense of simply helping people adjust to their circumstances (Jack, 1995a), but rather a process of identifying the steps that need to be taken to remove obstacles to progress, steps that can involve both subjective elements (developing confidence and self-esteem, for example) and objective ones (advocacy or other changes at the social level, for example).

In an earlier work (Thompson, 1992a), I distinguished between ontological and sociopolitical freedom, between existential freedom and political liberty. The former refers to the need to choose that is fundamental to human existence – we cannot choose not to choose and we are therefore responsible for our actions (human agency). The latter refers to the sociopolitical context in which such actions take place, a nexus of structured inequalities (structure). In order to develop a greater degree of freedom and choice at the sociopolitical level, it is necessary to remove barriers at the ontological level of agency.

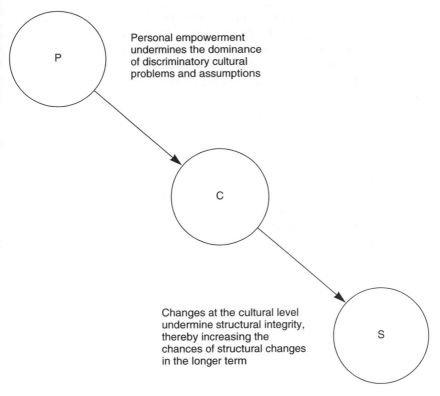

Figure 7.1   PCS levels of empowerment

Empowering people at the ontological level is therefore a basic starting point for tackling inequality, discrimination and oppression at the broader sociopolitical level. If people are not supported in casting off the shackles of socialization into disempowered roles and frames of reference, it is unlikely that they will be able to achieve empowerment at a broader sociopolitical level.

It would be naïve to assume that professional practice can make major changes at the structural level. However, empowerment, by assisting people to take greater control over their lives, can have a significant positive impact at the personal level, thereby making a contribution at the cultural level and, in turn, playing at least a small part in undermining inequality at the structural level (Figure 7.1).

Partnership and participation

Like empowerment 'partnership' has become something of a 'buzz-word' and runs the risk of being dismissed as a fad or fashion, and its significance as a practice principle lost in the process (Thompson, 2002b). Working in partnership involves moving away from a medical model in which the worker presents him- or herself as an 'expert', with the expertise to define what the problem is and what needs to be done. A partnership-based approach involves working together to:

- identify problems to be tackled, issues to be addressed, goals to be achieved;
- decide what steps need to be taken and who needs to do what;
- undertake the necessary work through a process of collaboration and consultation;
- review progress and agree any changes that need to be made to the agreed course of action;
- bring the work to a close if/when appropriate; and
- evaluate the work done, highlighting strengths, weaknesses and lessons to be learned.

Partnership entails reducing the power differential between professional workers and users of services. However, this is not to say that partnership work is not possible where a worker has to draw upon legal powers. The use of statutory powers may raise obstacles to the trust and respect that underpin partnership but this serves only to make partnership more difficult, not impossible, to attain. That is, it is still possible to work in partnership, even in situations where there is a conflict of interest or the need to use compulsory powers. For example, in child protection cases, even where it has become necessary to remove the child(ren) concerned under an Emergency Protection Order, it is still possible, and indeed desirable, for workers from all professional disciplines involved to:

- consult fully, and listen carefully to people's wishes, feelings and views;
- act unilaterally only where strictly necessary; and
- work carefully to rebuild trust and establish a basis for collaboration.

Of course, this is more easily said than done, but it none the less remains the case that it does not follow that partnership has to be abandoned in situations involving the use of legal powers.

'Participation', as a practice principle, can be seen as a broader form of partnership in which collaboration occurs not only at the micro-level of specific practice situations, but also at the wider levels of strategic planning; policy development and evaluation; training; and so on. It could be argued that, ultimately, the development of partnership must depend on a greater level of participation at all levels in organizations.

Developing approaches based on partnership and participation is a challenging task, and one that demands considerable skill and commitment. Indeed, it could be said that the process involves moving away from being an 'expert' who is expected to have the 'answers' towards having a degree of expertise in working collaboratively with people to help them to address their own needs, problems and aspirations.

◀ **PRACTICE FOCUS 7.1** ▶

The newly established community mental health team was keen to establish high standards of practice right from the beginning and so they paid a lot of attention to deciding how best to tackle the new challenges they faced. As part of their discussions they considered the importance of partnership and participation. Consequently, they decided to incorporate, as far as possible, a user perspective in all aspects of their work. It was only after many months of trying to put their intentions into practice that they realized just how little attention they had previously paid to the idea of working in partnership.

Conscientization and politicization

PCS analysis helps us to understand individual actions and circumstances in terms of the cultural context of shared values, meanings and norms, and the broader context of social and political structures. 'Conscientization' can be seen as the process of helping to make people aware of the broader context of the situations they face, and 'politicization', in turn, is the process of seeking to address problems at the broader sociopolitical level.

Conscientization is not intended to be a crude process of trying to win someone over to a particular political ideology. Rather, it is a question of 'deindividualization' (Thompson et al., 1994b) – helping people understand the extent to which their position is a reflection of broader cultural and political patterns. For example, a woman who feels depressed following an assault by her partner may gain some reassurance and succour by understanding that she is not alone in this, that her plight is part of a national problem of 'domestic' violence. Indeed, one of the distinct advantages of conscientization is that it can help to stop people blaming themselves, and thereby to develop a broader, more positive perspective.

Conscientization is also an important strategy for countering internalized oppression. For example, in working with older people, a situation commonly encountered is that characterized by comments such as: 'I don't want to be a nuisance', or 'There must be younger people who are more deserving than I am'. It may well be a difficult task to convince older people that such comments reflect an internalization of ageist ideology, but it is none the less an important task if professional practice is to be an emancipatory project, rather than a reinforcement of existing patterns of discrimination. Of course, this has to be done tactfully and sensitively and without using technical jargon. Conscientization is a skilled process that merits an investment of time and energy. It is not something that should be taken lightly, as a crude approach can undermine professional credibility and prove to be a source of alienation and mistrust.

While conscientization refers to raising awareness of the significance of wider issues, politicization involves seeking to address those wider issues. This can take a number of forms, including the following:

- *Lobbying politicians* – for example, by writing to MPs.
- *Community action* – for example, through people with common concerns coming together to form a pressure group.
- *Policy development* – for example, the development of health equality or anti-poverty strategies.

As with conscientization, this process needs to be handled in a skilful and sophisticated way. Crude forms of politicization can be dangerous, in so far as they can alienate key people; cause division and infighting; undermine credibility; divert energies in the wrong direction; undo previous good work done; and generally prove to be counterproductive.

It is therefore important that attempts at politicization should not be essentialist in assuming there is one right answer or definitive solution, or reductionist in seeking to find simple solutions to complex problems. None the less, although both conscientization and politicization are challenging and demanding, they can both play a key role in promoting equality.

Collaboration

While partnership relates to the process of professional workers and their clientele working together towards jointly agreed goals, I use the term 'collaboration' to refer to the strategy of like-minded workers within an organization or professional network supporting each other in pursuing equality aims. Individuals who challenge inequalities run the risk of being victimized – for example, by being labelled as 'troublemakers'. It is therefore important that people work together in order to prevent this problem from arising. A collective approach, of course, can also prove far more effective and influential than the isolated efforts of individuals.

Collaboration also provides opportunities for people to learn from each other, to develop their understanding of the complexities of inequality, discrimination and oppression, and generally to raise awareness of the significance of such issues. Similarly, mutual or group support in dealing with the pressures of developing emancipatory forms of practice is a further distinct benefit of approaches based on collaboration.

A collective approach can be developed through:

- teams or staff groups developing strategies together – for example, through regular discussion of equality within team or staff meetings, team philosophies and so on;
- the establishment of specific support or development groups, for example, a women's group or a black workers' group;
- involvement with relevant organizations and groups; and
- encouraging service users to work together and support each other, where appropriate.

Critically reflective practice

Reflective practice is a concept that has had a significant impact on at least some aspects of professional education and training. It is a term that has its roots in the work of Schön (1983, 1987, 1992). It refers to forms of practice in which the practitioner engages in a 'reflective conversation with the situation' (Schön, 1983, p. 163). That is, he or she integrates theory and practice through a process of 'reflection-in-action'. This can be seen as an important part of promoting equality in so far as:

- A non-reflective approach is likely to rely on ideological assumptions that are discriminatory and therefore potentially oppressive.
- A 'reflective conversation' allows scope for greater sensitivity to issues relating to power, inequality and disadvantage.
- Reflection avoids the need for reliance on dogma and orthodoxy.
- Reflective practice enables practitioners to take account of a range of factors at the personal, cultural and structural levels.

It can further be argued that good practice should be critically reflective practice. That is, it is not enough simply to reflect upon practice, as this too can become, ironically, a routine, uncritical form of practice. The reflection therefore needs to be critical, in the sense of not taking existing social arrangements for granted, not making assumptions that can legitimate, reinforce or accentuate existing patterns of inequality.

◀ **PRACTICE FOCUS 7.2** ▶

As part of her professional training course Val was involved in a reflective practice project in which she was asked to identify a 'critical incident', something that had happened that had a crucial bearing on what was to follow. The task then was to consider the incident, what had led up to it, what had flowed from it and, most significantly, what could be learned from it. Val found this a very useful technique as it helped her to learn not only about various aspects of her work but also about herself, her feelings and her approach to the work.

Elegant challenging

Promoting equality is, as we have seen, a matter for collective response, rather than simply a question of individual conscience or morality. One consequence of this is the need to challenge the actions and attitudes of others where these can be seen to be discriminatory or oppressive in their consequences.

It is not enough for individuals to be non-discriminatory in terms of their own personal behaviour. The need is for anti-discriminatory practice – that is, forms of practice that contribute more broadly to the promotion of equality. To condone discrimination in the actions and attitudes of others is not to promote equality. However, as we saw in Chapter 6, crude, unskilled or poorly thought-through forms of challenging can do more harm than good by creating unnecessary tensions and defensiveness.

If challenging is to be an effective part of an emancipatory strategy, it needs to be *elegant* challenging. That is to say, it should:

- be tactful and constructive, rather than a personal attack;
- avoid 'cornering' people and allow them to save face;
- pay attention to the appropriate time and place – a carefully chosen moment can be much more influential than an immediate challenge;
- not be punitive – the aim is to promote equality and not to create unnecessary tensions and hostilities;

- acknowledge explicitly or implicitly the vulnerability of the challenger to similar bad practice; and
- be undertaken in a genuine spirit of compassion and a commitment to social justice, rather than one of taking the moral high ground.

Such 'elegant' challenging is a skilful activity and one that draws on the resources of interpersonal and communication skills that 'people work' relies upon for its day-to-day effectiveness. The task, then, is to draw upon and develop these skills to serve as the basis of constructive forms of challenging. Challenging, if it is not to be counterproductive, needs to both tactical and tactful.

Sensitivity to language and image

I have already stressed the importance of language and its role in the construction of reality, rather than simply its representation. If we are to be successful in preventing the transmission of patterns of inequality from one generation to the next, we need to break down the patterns of language and imagery which subtly incorporate aspects of discrimination.

Discriminatory forms of language are so well established that they are generally taken for granted without their potential for oppression being recognized. We become so accustomed to such language forms that we tend not to recognize that:

- black and white are generally used to refer to negative and positive factors respectively, thereby reinforcing notions of white superiority;
- masculine linguistic forms are associated with positions of power and contribute to the 'invisibility' of women and therefore their subordinate role;
- disabled people are often described in unnecessarily negative and dehumanizing terms ('the handicapped', for example);
- older people are often patronized by the demeaning and overfamiliar terms used to refer to them or address them.

This is not to say that a simple list of 'taboo' words to be avoided is the way forward. Such a 'political correctness' approach oversimplifies – and trivializes – a complex set of issues. 'PC' is no substitute for developing a sensitivity to the various ways in which language, imagery and forms of communication generally can:

- reinforce unequal power relations;

- exclude or marginalize certain individuals or groups; and
- have the effect of stigmatizing and devaluing particular individuals or groups.

◀ PRACTICE FOCUS 7.3 ▶

When Li took over as deputy manager of the mental health resource centre on the retirement of her predecessor, she was largely happy with the standards of care provided but she did have some concerns about the language that was often used. Consequently, she arranged with the centre manager to devote a staff meeting to the subject of language. Li opened the meeting by saying why she thought language was so important and giving some examples of the 'medicalized' and infantilizing language that was often used. The discussion that followed proved to be very useful and helpful. Some staff clearly thought it was 'a lot of fuss over nothing', although for the majority it was a very good learning experience and made an important contribution to developing an increased level of sensitivity to language.

Gergen (1999) links the importance of language to reflective practice when he talks about:

reflexive inquiry, that is, forms of investigation that help us to reflect critically and appreciatively on our condition, our tradition, institutions, and relationships. If we create our worlds largely through discourse, then we should be ever attentive to our ways of speaking and writing. Through reflexive inquiry on our ways of constructing the world, and the practices these sustain, we open doors to emancipation, enrichment, and cultural transformation.

(p. 115)

Naming the process

Naming the process is an effective strategy not only for promoting equality but also for maximizing the potential of interpersonal interactions more generally. It refers to the tactic of making explicit a destructive or unhelpful process that is going on in an implicit or unacknowledged way. By bringing the process out into the open (in a tactful and 'elegant' way), its potency can be undermined.

If the process being used is a deliberate strategy on the part of the person concerned (abuse of power), naming the process makes it difficult for him or her to sustain its use in such a way. If the process reflects an aspect of learned behaviour (misuse of power), then naming it can help the person concerned appreciate the (potentially) oppressive impact of his or her behaviour.

An example of this strategy in use is to be found in the case of a male manager who, during staff meetings, tended to treat the men and women very differently – often seeking the men's views and opinions, while his comments to the women team members were generally of a protective nature, making sure that they were 'OK'. It was only when this tendency was gently pointed out to him that he realized what he had been doing and accepted the need to be more 'tuned in' to the gender dynamics of the team, and his own role within those dynamics.

As with any strategy, 'naming the process' is not guaranteed to work, but it can none the less be a powerful tactic that can play an important role in challenging discrimination and oppression and promoting equality.

Openness and demystification

Where machinations take place behind closed doors and where events, decisions and processes are shrouded in mystery, the scope for inequality and the abuse of power to flourish is greatly increased (Wineman, 1984). From an egalitarian point of view, therefore, it pays dividends for such matters to be transparent – that is, open and free from mystification.

This can be seen to apply in a number of ways:

- Interactions between staff and service users should be based on openness and honesty, with no collusion, hidden agendas, deceptions or withholding of information.
- Language used, both verbally and in writing, should be 'user-friendly', with no jargon or other possibilities for mystifying the process of communication.
- Interpreting facilities should be sought as and when required, so that fluency in English does not become a necessary condition for receiving an appropriate level of service.
- Decisions should be made jointly where possible, and where this is not possible, the situation should be explained fully and appropriately to the client or service user, and information should be given about complaints and representation procedures.

Such 'transparent' practice provides a basis for open and honest practice as a foundation for partnership-based emancipatory forms of work.

◀ PRACTICE FOCUS 7.4 ▶

Marge had been attending the hospital on a regular basis for many years, and she knew that there was not going to be a simple short-term solution to her problem. However, she wasn't entirely sure why she needed to keep going to the hospital or what exactly it was they were doing when she went there. She felt a little out of place in what she saw as the formal environment of the hospital and did not like to ask what was happening. She just had to trust that the doctors and nurses knew what was best for her. One day, however, she was greeted by a new member of staff she had not met before. She began by explaining to Marge what her role was, what they were trying to do and what the next steps were to be. She even went a step further by talking to Marge about what options were available to her. When Marge left the hospital that day she felt so much happier than she had after any previous visit there. This 'open' approach had made such a difference to her.

The revitalization of theory

Much of the theory underpinning contemporary practice was developed in times when awareness of issues of discrimination and oppression was at a much lower level than is the case today. Consequently, much of the knowledge base on which day-to-day practice draws pays little or no attention to inequality, and can often be seen to condone or exacerbate discrimination. For example, much of the developmental psychology literature on the life course can be seen to have distinct tendencies towards ageism, while a great deal of psychological work has an ethnocentric bias (Robinson, 1995).

However, this is not to say that the bulk of traditional theory should be rejected or dismissed out of hand. This would lead to the loss of a substantial and significant knowledge base, and one that holds many insights that can be of great value. The challenge that faces us, then, is to rework existing theories so that, as far as possible, they can be rendered compatible with emancipatory practice.

For some theories, or aspects of theories, this may not be possible. The discriminatory assumptions may be so ingrained that the theory falls apart without them. For many others, however, the revitalization of theory remains a very real possibility and one that can:

- allow the valuable parts of traditional theories to be 'disconnected' from the discriminatory assumptions incorporated within them;
- remove barriers to further theory development;
- help to avoid the tendency to reject theory in favour of practice in the name of promoting equality.

However, it should be noted that this 'revitalization' of theory is only one part of the broader project of developing new forms of theory that can play a positive role in promoting equality and making professional practice part of the solution rather than part of the problem.

In drawing on existing elements of the theory base, we should therefore be careful to ensure that we:

- consider the discriminatory potential of the ideas and frameworks we are drawing upon;
- identify what changes or adjustments are necessary to make the ideas compatible with emancipatory practice (for example, by recognizing and eradicating a gender bias);
- discuss these developments openly with colleagues so that learning can be shared and a collective approach to theory development be adopted.

One pointer that can or should help in this process is the use of dialectical reason. Traditional forms of theory often neglect a dialectical dimension. That is to say, they do not pay sufficient attention to (i) the importance of the interaction of conflicting forces and (ii) the significance of change, movement and flux – the dynamic nature of social and psychological phenomena. Understanding professional practice in the context of dialectical reason can be a major help in the development of both theory and practice.

Systematic practice

'Systematic practice' is a term I use to refer to forms of practice which involve the worker in keeping a clear focus on what he or she is doing and why (Thompson, 2002c). In a highly pressurized work setting it is relatively easy to lose sight of what we are doing, and to fall foul of 'drift'. Systematic practice therefore hinges on avoiding such drift by keeping a clear focus on:

- what we are trying to achieve;
- how we intend to achieve it; and
- how we will know when we have achieved it (What will success look like?).

This framework can be seen as a general guideline for good practice, but it is also particularly applicable to promoting equality. As we have seen, emancipatory practice involves a degree of self-awareness;

an awareness of stereotypes; a sensitivity to issues of power, injustice and inequality; and a commitment to positive change. However, all of these can be reduced or even lost altogether if we allow ourselves to lose our focus, and thus lose sight of what we are doing and why.

If we can lose track of what we are trying to achieve in general terms, then clearly we are also prone to losing track of what we are trying to achieve in terms of promoting equality. The efforts required to develop and sustain systematic practice are therefore a worthwhile investment in the development of emancipatory practice.

◀ **PRACTICE FOCUS 7.5** ▶

When his new line manager took up post, Andrew was pleased to find that she was very supportive. However, he was very taken aback when she told him that she wanted a summary of what work he was doing, including a definition of the identified problem, agreed action plan and proposed timescale for each individual or family that he was working with. At first, he found this highly systematic approach quite unsettling, threatening in fact. However, once he became used to it and accepted it as a constructive process, he found it very helpful indeed as a means of managing a heavy workload through maintaining a clear focus. This approach helped to increase his sense of security, confidence and job satisfaction. (Thompson, 2002c)

Using the law

Without going into fine detail relating to the specifics of the legal context of professional practice, we should none the less note that there are a number of Acts of Parliament that contain provisions for the promotion of equality in one form or another. In addition to the specific equality of opportunity legislation (the Equal Pay Act 1970, the Sex Discrimination Act 1975, the Race Relations Act 1976, the Disability Discrimination Act 1995, The Race Relations (Amendment) Act 2000), various Acts contain reference to matters relating to equality. For example, both the Children Act 1989 and the NHS and Community Care Act 1990 address issues of race and culture.

The law therefore presents us with the potential to develop aspects of emancipatory practice – the potential to use legal powers to challenge discrimination and thus prevent or lessen oppression. As Preston-Shoot (1996) comments:

> Legislation not uncommonly is characterised by vague drifting and, together with accompanying guidance, is expressed through concepts which are capable of different meanings. Need, empowerment, and part-

nership are three such examples. Demystifying these concepts, and using the room for manoeuvre which the vagueness of the law and guidance allows, may enable practitioners and service users to intervene within agencies to enhance the supportive aspects of the systems created. This represents a proactive use of the law, informed by dialogue with users.

(pp. 32–3)

However, it is also vitally important to recognize that:

- The law also has considerable potential to oppress – it is a two-edged sword (Dalrymple and Burke, 1995).
- The use of the law is not unproblematic. The relationship between law and practice is complex, and it is not simply a matter of 'applying' the law (Braye and Preston-Shoot, 1997).
- Using the law on its own is not a sufficient basis for challenging discrimination. A narrow, legalistic perspective can distract attention from the wider changes that are needed to promote equality.

Using the law, then, can be an important part of developing emancipatory practice, but it needs to be part of a broader programme of promoting equality, rather than a solution in its own right.

Professionalism

Professionalism is a term that has both positive and negative connotations. In negative terms, it is associated with elitism and distinct power differentials between professional and client. However, the positive connotations of professionalism include:

- a commitment to a set of values;
- the explicit use of a knowledge base and a commitment to developing that knowledge base through research and reflective practice;
- a commitment to high standards of practice;
- a recognition that we are accountable for our practice; and
- actions and decisions based on informed assessment rather than the uncritical following of regulations, routines or standardized practices.

While the negative version is clearly antithetical to emancipatory practice, the positive version offers a sound basis for promoting equality, particularly where the values and knowledge base owe more to anti-discriminatory theory and practice than to the traditional bases of professionalism. Without a commitment to (positive) professionalism, it is

233

unlikely that practice will be of a sufficiently high standard to make a positive difference to the lives of people who experience discrimination and oppression.

◀ PRACTICE FOCUS 7.6 ▶

The Anwar family had been experiencing problems for some time as a result of a small but persistent group of teenagers who were harassing them, calling them racist names and so on. Eventually, they decided to make a complaint to their local council and went to the office in town. However, they were appalled by the response they received. The man they spoke to seemed totally disorganized and had little or no idea as to how he should respond to the situation. Instead of going to seek help from a more experienced colleague, he continued to make a mess of responding to the family's concerns, continually giving them the impression that he was incompetent. Not surprisingly, then, the family left after a little time, convinced that, if that was the best they could do, then clearly the council had no commitment to tackling racism or racial harassment in the community.

Evaluation

Evaluation can be seen as the fifth stage in a systematic process of helping (Thompson, 2002c). It involves identifying the strengths and weaknesses of a particular piece of work and the lessons that can be learned from it. This occurs at the end of the process, but much can also be learned from an ongoing process of review.

The benefit of evaluation, from an emancipatory point of view, is that it provides an opportunity to look closely at the impact of our actions and to gauge the perceptions of others as to their efficacy and suitability. This provides a basis for assessing:

- the extent to which we took account of issues of social location and discrimination at a personal, cultural and structural level;
- the extent to which we acted in partnership and encouraged/facilitated involvement and partnership;
- whether our actions were appropriate in the circumstances; and
- the lessons to be learned in terms of potential pitfalls to be wary of in future, and the strengths and assets to be drawn upon.

As Shaw (1996) points out, evaluation does not have to be associated with positivism and precise (pseudo)scientific measurements. There are ways and means of evaluating practice that can be brought to bear in an effort to maximize the learning to be gained from practice.

Some may argue that they do not have time to evaluate their practice. However, in view of the benefits to be gained from evaluating practice (and the costs of failing to do so), neglecting to evaluate practice in order to save time is a false economy, and a dangerous one at that.

Staff care

Professional practice is fraught with a number of pressures that can easily overspill into stress, particularly where staff are not adequately supported in meeting the complex and demanding challenges of the work. The possibility of health-affecting levels of stress is therefore an ever-present one.

One possible consequence of stress is that we become so overloaded with pressure that we function far below our usual level of competence, possibly to the point where our practice becomes dangerous. One extreme outcome of prolonged exposure to stress is that of 'burnout', a psychological condition in which the person concerned functions 'on automatic pilot' – that is, in an unthinking, unfeeling way, cut off from the sensitive issues involved in his or her work. Clearly, both stress and burnout are antithetical to emancipatory practice – they pose serious barriers to the development of sensitive and informed practice.

Consequently, an important strategy for promoting equality is the development of staff care. This refers to the range of policies and practices geared towards supporting staff in terms of:

- preventing pressures from becoming excessive, to the point where they become stressful;
- being responsive to staff when they experience stress; and
- dealing constructively with the aftermath of stress, for example through debriefing.

It has to be recognized that to expect staff to respond positively to the pressures of promoting equality when they are already overwhelmed by other pressures amounts to a very unfair expectation. Emancipatory practice therefore has to be built on a sound foundation of staff care.

◀ PRACTICE FOCUS 7.7 ▶

Hugh had worked in an inner city area where there was a high proportion of people from ethnic minority communities. Although there were anti-discriminatory policies in place, the reality of the situation was that most white staff avoided issues of race and culture as far as possible because they saw them as complex issues fraught with difficulties, a political minefield in fact. Line managers seemed to collude with this and offered little or no support in trying to make equality practice a reality. When he moved to his new job, then, Hugh was delighted to find that equality issues were discussed openly and were explicitly part of the day-to-day agenda. He was also very relieved to find that the managers, especially his own line manager, were very supportive and recognized the demands and complexities of promoting equality.

Humility

One of the benefits of evaluation, as discussed above, is that it helps us to remain open to new learning, to recognize that our work, however good, is never perfect. There are always ways in which we can improve, ways in which we can go a step further. This is particularly important in relation to emancipatory practice. This is because issues of inequality, discrimination and oppression are so complex, and so prone to change over time, that we should never rest on our laurels and assume that we have 'arrived'.

It may seem trite to suggest that promoting equality is a never-ending journey, but there is clearly a danger of complacency in assuming that we have done all that we need to do, or all that we can do. Although there is considerable expertise in promoting equality to be found across the professional workforce, this is not to say that any one person is an 'expert', if by this we mean someone who has 'all the answers' and has nothing further to learn, no further mistakes to make.

The field of inequality is a constantly changing one, with new challenges arising all the time. What is needed, then, is a degree of humility, a recognition that, however skilled, experienced or well informed we are, there is always a margin for error, and always scope for learning – an important principle on which to base all our attempts to promote equality.

REFERENCES

Abberley, P. (1987) 'The Concept of Oppression and the Development of a Social Theory of Disability', *Disability, Handicap and Society*, 2(1).

Abbott, P. and Payne, G. (eds) (1990) *New Directions in the Sociology of Health*, London, Falmer.

Abbott, P. and Sapsford, R. (1988) *The Body Politic: Health, Family and Society*, Unit 11 of Open University course, D211 *Social Problems and Social Welfare*.

Abercrombie, N., Hill, S. and Turner, B. S. (1994) *Dictionary of Sociology*, 3rd edn, Harmondsworth, Penguin.

Acheson, D. (1998) *Independent Inquiry into Inequalities in Health Report*, London, Stationery Office.

Adams, R. (1996) *Social Work and Empowerment*, 2nd edn, Basingstoke, Macmillan – now Palgrave Macmillan.

Adams, R., Dominelli, L. and Payne, M. (eds) (2002) *Social Work: Themes, Perspectives and Critical Debates*, 2nd edn, Basingstoke, Palgrave Macmillan.

Aggleton, P. (1990) *Health*, London, Routledge.

Ahmad, B. (1990) *Black Perspectives in Social Work*, Birmingham, Venture Press.

Ahmad, W. I. U. (ed.) (1993a) *'Race' and Health in Contemporary Britain*, Buckingham, Open University Press.

Ahmad, W. I. U. (1993b) 'Promoting Equitable Health and Health Care: A Case for Action', in Ahmad (1993a).

Ahmad, W. I. U. and Atkin, K. (eds) (1996) *'Race' and Community Care*, Buckingham, Open University Press.

Ahmed, S. (1991) 'Developing Anti-Racist Social Work Education Practice', in CD Project Steering Group (1991).

Alcock, P. (1993) *Understanding Poverty*, Basingstoke, Macmillan – now Palgrave Macmillan.

Alder, H. (1994) *Neurolinguistic Programming: The New Art and Science of Getting What You Want*, London, Piatkus.

Althusser, L. (1971) *Lenin and Philosophy, and Other Essays*, London, New Left Books.

Althusser, L. (1976) *Essays in Self-Criticism*, London, New Left Books.

Anionwu, E. N. (1993) 'Sickle Cell and Thalassaemia: Community Experiences and Official Response', in Ahmad (1993a).

Antonovsky, A. (1979) *Health, Stress and Coping*, San Francisco, Jossey Bass.

Antonovsky, A. (1984) 'The Sense of Coherence as a Determinant of Health', in Matarazzo (1984).

Antonovsky, A. (1987) *Unravelling the Mystery of Health*, San Francisco, Jossey Bass.

Antonovsky, A. (1993) 'The Sense of Coherence as a Determinant of Health', in Beattie *et al.* (1993).

Arber, S. (1990) 'Opening the "Black Box"; Inequalities in Women's Health', in Abbott and Payne (1990).

Arber, S. and Ginn, J. (eds) (1995) *Connecting Gender and Ageing: A Sociological Approach*, Buckingham, Open University Press.

Archard, D. (1993) *Children: Rights and Childhood*, London, Routledge.

Argyle, M. and Colman, A. M. (eds) (1995) *Social Psychology*, London, Longman.

Armstrong, D. (1989) *An Introduction to Sociology as Applied to Medicine*, Bristol, Livingstone.

Bacchi, C. (1996) *The Politics of Affirmative Action*, London, Sage.

Bailey, D. (ed.) (2000) *At the Core of Mental Health Practice: Key Issues for Practitioners, Managers and Mental Health Trainers*, Brighton, Pavilion.

Baistow, K. (1995) 'Liberation and Regulation? Some Paradoxes of Empowerment', *Critical Social Policy*, Spring.

Banton, M. (1994) *Discrimination*, Buckingham, Open University Press.

Banton, M. and Harwood, J. (1975) *The Race Concept*, Newton Abbot, David & Charles.

Banton, R., Clifford, P., Frosh, S., Lousada, J. and Rosenthal, J. (1985) *The Politics of Mental Health*, Basingstoke, Macmillan – now Palgrave Macmillan.

Bardwick, J. (1971) *The Psychology of Women*, New York, Harper & Row.

Barker, C. and Galasiński, D. (2001) *Cultural Studies and Discourse Analysis: A Dialogue on Language and Identity*, London, Sage.

Barnes, C. (1991) *Disabled People in Britain and Discrimination*, London, Hurst & Co.

Barnes, C. (1992) *Disabling Imagery and the Media*, Halifax, Ryburn.

Bateson, G. (1980) *Mind and Nature*, London, Fontana.

Baudrillard, J. (1983a) *Les Stratégies Fatales*, Paris, Grasset.

Baudrillard, J. (1983b) *Simulations*, New York, Semiotext(e).

Baxter, C. (ed.) (2001a) *Managing Diversity and Inequality in Health Care*, Edinburgh, Baillière Tindall.

Baxter, C. (2001b) 'Diversity and Inequality in Health and Health Care', in Baxter (2001a).

Baxter, C. (2001c) 'Preface', in Baxter (2001a).

Bayne-Smith, M. (ed.) (1996) *Racism, Gender and Health*, London, Sage.

BCODP (1987) 'Comment on the Report of the Audit Commission', London, British Council of Organisations of Disabled People.

Beattie, A., Gott, M., Jones, L. and Sidell, M. (eds) (1993) *Health and Wellbeing: A Reader*, Basingstoke, Macmillan – now Palgrave Macmillan.

Beauvoir, S. de (1972) *The Second Sex*, Harmondsworth, Penguin.

Bell, V. (1993) *Interrogating Incest: Feminism, Foucault and the Law*, London, Routledge.

Bellin, W. (1994) 'Caring Professions and Welsh-Speakers: a Perspective from Language and Social Psychology', in Huws Williams *et al.* (1994).

Berger, P. L. and Luckmann, T. (1967) *The Social Construction of Reality*, Harmondsworth, Penguin.

Bernard, M., Itzin, C., Phillipson, C. and Skucha, J. (1995) 'Gendered Work, Gendered Retirement', in Arber and Ginn (1995).

Best, S. and Kellner, D. (1991) *Postmodern Theory: Critical Interrogations*, London, Macmillan – now Palgrave Macmillan.

Bevan, D. (2002) 'Poverty and Deprivation', in Thompson (2002a).

Billig, M. (2001) 'Discursive, Rhetorical and Ideological Messages', in Wetherell *et al.* (2001).

Birt, R. (1997) 'Existence, Identity and Liberation', in Gordon (1997).

Blakemore, K. and Drake, R. (1996) *Understanding Equal Opportunity Policies*, London, Prentice-Hall/Harvester Wheatsheaf.

Bland, R. (ed.) (1996) *Developing Services for Older People and Their Families*, London, Jessica Kingsley.

Blumenfeld, W. J. and Raymond, D. (1988) *Looking at Gay and Lesbian Life*, Boston, Beacon Press.

Bogue, R. (1989) *Deleuze and Guattari*, London, Routledge.

Bourdieu, P. (1988) *Language and Symbolic Power*, Cambridge, Polity Press.

Bowser, B. P. (ed.) (1996) *Racism and Anti-Racism in World Perspective*, London, Sage.

Boyers, R. and Orrill, R. (eds) (1972) *Laing and Anti-Psychiatry*, Harmondsworth, Penguin.

Boyle, M. (1990) *Schizophrenia: A Scientific Delusion*, London, Routledge.

Boyne, R. and Rattansi, A. (eds) (1990) *Postmodernism and Society*, Basingstoke, Macmillan – now Palgrave Macmillan.

Braham, P., Rattansi, A. and Skellington, R. (eds) (1992) *Racism and Antiracism: Inequalities, Opportunities and Policies*, London, Sage.

Braye, S. and Preston-Shoot, M. (1997) *Practising Social Work Law*, 2nd edn, Basingstoke, Macmillan – now Palgrave Macmillan.

Brechin, A., Brown, H. and Eby, M. A. (eds) (2000) *Critical Practice in Health and Social Care*, London, Sage.

Brisenden, S. (1986) 'Independent Living and the Medical Model of Disability', *Disability, Handicap and Society*, 1(2).

Bristow, J. and Wilson, A. R. (eds) (1993) *Activating Theory: Lesbian, Gay, Bisexual Politics*, London, Lawrence & Wishart.

Brown, A. (1992) *Groupwork*, 3rd edn, Aldershot, Ashgate.

Brown, C. (1992) '"Same Difference": The Persistence of Racial Disadvantage in the British Employment Market', in Braham *et al.* (1992).

Brown, H. C. (1992) 'Lesbians, the State and Social Work Practice', in Langan and Day (1992).

Brown, G. W. and Harris, T. (1978) *The Social Origins of Depression*, London, Tavistock.

Brownmillar, S. (1977) *Against Our Will: Men, Women and Rape*, Harmondsworth, Penguin.

Bryson, V. (1999) *Feminist Debates: Issues of Theory and Political Practice*, Basingstoke, Macmillan – now Palgrave Macmillan.

Burgoon, M., Hunsaker, F. G. and Dawson, E. J. (1994) *Human Communication*, 3rd edn, London, Sage.

Burke, B. and Harrison, P. (2000) 'Race and Racism in Social Work', in Davies (2000).

Burr, V. (1995) *An Introduction to Social Constructionism*, London, Routledge.

Busfield, J. (1983) 'Gender, Mental Illness and Psychiatry', in Evans and Ungerson (1983).

Busfield, J. (1996) *Men, Women and Madness: Understanding Gender and Mental Disorder*, Basingstoke, Macmillan – now Palgrave Macmillan.

Butler, I. and Williamson H. (1994) *Children Speak Out: Children, Trauma and Social Work*, Harlow, Longman.

Butler, J. and Scott, J. (eds) (1992) *Femininsts Theorise the Political*, London, Routledge.

Bywaters, P. and McLeod, E. (eds) (1996) *Working for Equality in Health*, London, Routledge.

Callinicos, A. (1990) 'Reactionary Postmodernism', in Boyne and Rattansi (1990).

Callon, M. and Latour, B. (1981) 'Unscrewing the Big Leviathan: How Actors Macro-Structure Reality and How Sociologists Help Them to Do So', in Knorr-Cetina and Cicourel (1981).

Cameron, D. (ed.) (1998) *The Feminist Critique of Language: A Reader*, London, Routledge.

Cameron, D. and Frazer, E. (1994) 'Masculinity, Violence and Sexual Murder', in Giddens *et al.* (1994).

Campbell, J. and Oliver, M. (1996) *Disability Politics: Understanding Our Past, Changing Our Future*, London, Routledge.

Carlen, P. (ed.) (2002) *Women and Punishment: The Struggle for Justice*, Cullompton, Willan Publishing.

Carmichael, S . and Hamilton, C . (1969) *Black Power: The Politics of Liberation in America*, Harmondsworth, Penguin.

Carniol, B. (1990) *Case Critical: Challenging Social Work in Canada*, 2nd edn, Toronto, Between the Lines.

Cashmore, E. (ed.) (1996) *Dictionary of Race and Ethnic Relations*, 4th edn, London, Routledge.

Cassell, P. (ed.) (1993) *The Giddens Reader*, Basingstoke, Macmillan – now Palgrave Macmillan.

CD Project Steering Group (eds) (1991) *Setting the Context for Change*, London, Central Council for Education and Training in Social Work.

Chavkin, W. (ed.) (1984) *Double Exposure*, New York, Monthly Review Press.

Chesler, P. (1972) *Women and Madness*, New York, Doubleday.

Clarke, J. (ed.) (1993) *A Crisis in Care? Challenges to Social Work*, London, Sage.

Clarke, J. (1996) 'After Social Work?', in Parton (1996).

Clarke, J., Cochrane, A. and McLaughlin, E. (eds) (1994a) *Managing Social Policy*, London, Sage.

Clarke, J., Cochrane, A. and McLaughlin, E. (1994b) 'Mission Accomplished or Unfinished Business? The Impact of Managerialization', in Clarke *et al.* (1994a).

Clarke, J. and Newman, J. (1997) *The Managerial State: Power, Politics and Ideology in the Remaking of Social Welfare*, London, Sage.

Clegg, S. R. (1989) *Frameworks of Power*, London, Sage.

Collier, R. (1995) *Combating Sexual Harassment in the Workplace*, Buckingham, Open University Press.

Collinson, D. (1994) 'Strategies of Resistance: Power, Knowledge and Subjectivity in the Workplace', in Jermier *et al.* (1994).

Connell, R.W. (2002) *Gender*, Cambridge, Polity.

Cooper, D. (1993) 'An Engaged State: Sexuality, Governance and the Potential For Change', in Bristow and Wilson (1993).

Coward, R. (1993) 'The Myth of Alternative Health', in Beattie *et al.* (1993).

Craib, I. (1992) *Modern Social Theory: From Parsons to Habermas*, 2nd edn, London, Harvester Wheatsheaf.

Crook, S. (1990) 'The End of Radical Social Theory? Radicalism, Modernism and Postmodernism', in Boyne and Rattansi (1990).

Cropley, A. J. (1977) *Life-Long Education: A Psychological Analysis*, Oxford, Pergamon.

Culley, L. and Dyson, S. (eds) (2001a) *Ethnicity and Nursing Practice*, Basingstoke, Palgrave Macmillan.

Culley, L. and Dyson, S. (2001b) 'Introduction: Sociology. Ethnicity and Nursing Practice', in Culley and Dyson (2001a).

Cumming, E. and Henry, W. (1961) *Growing Old: The Process of Disengagement*, New York, Basic Books.

Curtis, J., Grabb, E. and Guppy, N. (eds) (1993) *Social Inequality in Canada: Patterns, Problems, Policies*, 2nd edn, Scarborough, Ont., Prentice-Hall.

Dalrymple, J. and Burke, B. (1995) *Anti-Oppressive Practice, Social Care and the Law*, Buckingham, Open University Press.

Davey, B., Gray, A. and Seale, C. (eds) (1995) *Health and Disease: A Reader*, 2nd edn, Buckingham, Open University Press.

Davies, D. (1996a) 'Working with Young People', in Davies and Neal (1996).

Davies, D. (1996b) 'Homophobia and Heterosexism', in Davies and Neal (1996).

Davies, D. (1996c) 'Towards a Model of Gay Affirmative Therapy', in Davies and Neal (1996).

Davies, D. and Neal, C. (eds) (1996) *Pink Therapy: A Guide for Counsellors and Therapists Working with Lesbian, Gay and Bisexual Clients*, Buckingham, Open University Press.

Davies, M. (ed.) (1991) *The Sociology of Social Work*, London, Routledge.

Davies, M. (ed.) (2000) *The Blackwell Encyclopaedia of Social Work*, Oxford, Blackwell.

Dawson, S. (1996) *Analysing Organisation*, 3rd edn, Basingstoke, Macmillan – now Palgrave Macmillan.

Deetz, S. (1994) 'The New Politics of the Workplace: Ideology and Other Unobtrusive Controls', in Simons and Billig (1994).

Deleuze, G. and Guattari, F. (1983) *Anti-Oedipus*, Minneapolis, University of Minnesota Press.

Deleuze, G. and Guattari, F. (1984) *A Thousand Plateaus*, Minneapolis, University of Minnesota Press.

Derrida. J. (1976) *Of Grammatology*, Baltimore, Md., Johns Hopkins University Press.

Divine, D. (1990) 'Sharing the Struggle', *Social Work Today*, 22 November.

Dobash, R. E. and Dobash, R. P. (1992) *Women, Violence and Social Change*, London, Routledge.

Dominelli, L. (1989) 'An Uncaring Profession? Anti-Racist Social Work', *New Community*, 15(9).

Dominelli, L. and McLeod, E. (1989) *Feminist Social Work*, Basingstoke, Macmillan – now Palgrave Macmillan.

Donald, J. and Rattansi, A. (eds) (1992) *'Race', Culture and Difference*, London, Sage.

Donnison, D. (1998) *Policies for a Just Society*, Basingstoke, Macmillan – now Palgrave Macmillan.

Douglas, J. (1996) 'Developing with Black and Minority Ethnic Communities, Health Promotion Strategies which Address Social Inequalities', in Bywaters and McLeod (1996).

Dreyfus, H. L. and Rabinow, P. (eds) (1982) *Michel Foucault: Beyond Structuralism and Hermeneutics*, University of Chicago Press.

Eagleton, T. (1991) *Ideology: An Introduction*, London, Verso.

Ehrenreich, B. and English, D. (1978) *For Her Own Good: A Hundred and Fifty Years of the Experts' Advice to Women*, New York, Anchor Press.

Elliot, F. R. (1996) *Gender, Family and Society*, Basingstoke, Macmillan – now Palgrave Macmillan.

Engel, G. I. (1961) 'Is Grief a Disease?', *Psychosomatic Medicine*, 23(1).

Engel, G. I. (1981) 'The Need for a New Medical Model: A Challenge for Bio-medicine', in Kaplan *et al.* (1981).

Evans, M. and Ungerson, C. (eds) (1983) *Sexual Divisions: Patterns and Processes*, London, Tavistock.

Fawcett, B. and Featherstone, B. (1996) '"Carers" and "Caring": New Thoughts on Old Questions', in Humphries (1996).

Fawcett, B. and Featherstone, B. (2000) ' Setting the Scene: An Appraisal of Notions of Postmodernism, Postmodernity and Postmodern Feminism', in Fawcett *et al.* (2000).

Fawcett, B., Featherstone, B., Fook, J, and Rossiter, A. (eds) (2000) *Practice and Research in Social Work: Postmodern Feminist Perspectives*, London, Routledge.

Fennell, G., Phillipson, C. and Evers, H. (1988) *The Sociology of Old Age*, Milton Keynes, Open University Press.

Ferns, P. (1987) 'The Dangerous Delusion', *Community Care*, 8 January.

Field, D., Hockey, J. and Small, N. (eds) (1997) *Death, Gender and Ethnicity*, London, Routledge.

Field, N. (1995) *Over the Rainbow: Money, Class and Homophobia*, London, Pluto.

Finkelstein, V. (1980) *Attitudes and Disabled People: Issues for Discussion*, New York, World Rehabilitation Fund.

Finkelstein, V. (1991) 'Disability: An Administrative Challenge?', in Oliver (1991).

Fiske, J. (1996) 'Opening the Hallway: Some Remarks on the Fertility of Stuart Hall's Contribution to Critical Theory', in Morley and Chen (1996).

Flax, J. (1992) 'The End of Innocence', in Butler and Scott (1992).

Foley, P., Roche, J. and Tucker, S. (eds) (2001) *Children in Society: Contemporary Theory, Policy and Practice*, Basingstoke, Palgrave Macmillan.

Fook, J. (2002) *Social Work: Critical Theory and Practice*, London, Sage.

Foucault, M. (1972) *The Archaeology of Knowledge*, London, Tavistock.

Foucault, M. (1975) *The Birth of the Clinic: An Archaeology of Medical Perception*, New York, Vintage Books.

Foucault, M. (1977a) *Language, Counter-Memory, Practice*, Ithaca, NY, Cornell University Press.

Foucault, M. (1977b) *Discipline and Punish*, Harmondsworth, Penguin.

Foucault, M. (1980) *Power/Knowledge: Selected Interviews and Other Writings 1972–77* (ed. C. Gordon), Brighton, Harvester Press.

Foucault, M. (1981) *The History of Sexuality Volume 1: An Introduction*, Harmondsworth, Penguin.

Foucault, M. (1982) 'On the Genealogy of Ethics', in Dreyfus and Rabinow (1982).

Foucault, M. (1988) *Politics, Philosophy, Culture: Interviews and Other Writings 1977–1984*, New York, Routledge.

Fox, N. J. (1993) *Postmodernism, Sociology and Health*, Buckingham, Open University Press.

Fuss, D. (ed.) (1991) *Inside Out: Lesbian Theories, Gay Theories*, London, Routledge.

Garvin, D. A. (1993) 'Building a Learning Organization', *Harvard Business Review*, July–August.

Gergen, K.J. (1999) *An Invitation to Social Construction*, London, Sage.

Gerrish, K., Husband, C. and Mackenzie, J. (1996) *Nursing for a Multi-ethnic Society*, Buckingham, Open University Press.

Giddens, A. (1972) *Politics and Sociology in the Thought of Max Weber*, Basingstoke, Macmillan – now Palgrave Macmillan.

Giddens, A. (1984) *The Constitution of Society: Outline of a Theory of Structuration*, Cambridge, Polity.

Giddens, A. (1990) 'Modernity and Utopia', *New Statesman and Society*, 2 November.

Giddens, A. (1991) *Modernity and Self-Identity*, Cambridge, Polity.

Giddens, A. (ed.) (1992) *Human Societies: A Reader*, Cambridge, Polity.

Giddens, A. (1993a) *Sociology*, 2nd edn, Cambridge, Polity.

Giddens, A. (1993b) *New Rules of Sociological Method*, 2nd edn, Cambridge, Polity.

Giddens, A. (1995) *A Contemporary Critique of Historical Materialism*, 2nd edn, Basingstoke, Macmillan – now Palgrave Macmillan.

Giddens, A., Held, D., Hubert, D., Seymour, D. and Thompson, J. (eds) (1994) *The Polity Reader in Social Theory*, Cambridge, Polity.

Gill, D. (1977) *Illegitimacy, Sexuality and the Status of Women*, Oxford, Blackwell.

Gill, D., Mayor, B. and Blair, M. (eds) (1992) *Racism and Education: Structures and Strategies*, London, Sage.

Ginsburg, N. (1992) 'Racism and Housing: Concepts and Reality', in Braham *et al.* (1992).

Gittins, D. (1993) *The Family in Question*, 2nd edn, Basingstoke, Macmillan – now Palgrave Macmillan.

Gomm, R. (1993) 'Issues of Power in Health and Welfare', in Walmsley *et al.* (1993).

Gordon, L. (ed.) (1997) *Existence in Black*, London and New York, Routledge.

Grabb, E. (1993) 'General Introduction', in Curtis *et al.* (1993).

Grimwood, C. and Popplestone, R. (1993) *Women, Management and Care*, Basingstoke, Macmillan – now Palgrave Macmillan.

Guirdham, M. (1999) *Communicating Across Cultures*, Basingstoke, Macmillan – now Palgrave Macmillan.

Gurnah, A. (1984) 'The Politics of Racism Awareness Training', *Critical Social Policy*, 11.

Haber, H. F. (1994) *Beyond Postmodern Politics*, London, Routledge.

Hall, S. (1996) 'The Problem of Ideology: Marxism Without Guarantees', in Morley and Chen (1996).

Hall, S., Held, D. and McGrew, T. (eds) (1992) *Modernity and its Futures*, Cambridge, Polity.

Halsey, A. M., Heath, A. F. and Ridge, J. M. (1980) *Origins and Destinations: Family, Class and Education in Modern Britain*, Oxford, Clarendon Press.

Hamnett, C., McDowell, L. and Sarre, P. (eds) (1989) *The Changing Social Structure*, London, Sage.

Hannan, M. T. and Freeman, J. (1989) *Organizational Ecology*, Cambridge, Mass., Harvard University Press.

Harding, L. F. (1996) *Family, State and Social Policy*, Basingstoke, Macmillan – now Palgrave Macmillan.

Harré, R. (1981) 'Philosophical Aspect of the Macro-Micro Problem', in Knorr-Cetina and Cicourel (1981).

Hartmann, H. I. (1994) 'The Family as the Locus of Gender, Class, and Political Struggle: The Example of Housework', in Herrmann and Stewart (1994).

Hassard, J. (1993) 'Postmodernism and Organizational Analysis: An Overview', in Hassard and Parker (1993).

Hassard, J. and Parker, M. (eds) (1993) *Postmodernism and Organizations*, London, Sage.

Havighurst, R. J. (1968) 'Personality and Patterns of Aging', *The Gerontologist*, 8.

Healy, K. (2000) *Social Work Practices: Contemporary Perspectives on Change*, London, Sage.

Hearn, J. (1987) *The Gender of Oppression: Men, Masculinity and the Critique of Marxism*, Brighton, Wheatsheaf.

Hearn, J. and Parkin, W. (1993) 'Organizations, Multiple Oppressions and Postmodernism', in Hassard and Parker (1993).

Hearn, J. and Parkin, W. (1995) *'Sex' at 'Work': The Power and Paradox of Organisation Psychology*, 2nd edn, London, Prentice-Hall/Harvester Wheatsheaf.

Held, D. (1992) 'Liberalism, Marxism and Democracy', in Hall *et al.* (1992).

Helman, C. (1981) 'Disease Versus Illness in General Practice', *Journal of the Royal College of General Practitioners*, 31.

Herrmann, A. C. and Stewart, A. J. (eds) (1994) *Theorizing Feminism: Parallel Trends in the Humanities and Social Sciences*, Oxford, Westview Press.

Hill, M. (1993) *The Welfare State in Britain: A Political History Since 1945*, Aldershot, Edward Elgar.

Hockey, J. and James, A. (1993) *Growing up and Growing Old*, London, Sage.

Hocquenghem, G. (1978) *Homosexual Desire*, London, Allison & Busby.

Hollinger, R. (1994) *Postmodernism and the Social Sciences: A Thematic Approach*, London, Sage.

hooks, b. (1992) *Black Looks: Race and Representation*, Toronto, Between the Lines.

Howarth, G. (1996) 'Introduction', in Howarth and Jupp (1996).

Howarth, G. and Jupp, P. (eds) (1996) *Contemporary Issues in the Sociology of Death, Dying and Disposal*, Basingstoke, Macmillan – now Palgrave Macmillan.

Hudson, B. A. (1993) *Penal Policy and Social Justice*, Basingstoke, Macmillan – now Palgrave Macmillan.

Hughes, B. (1995) *Older People and Community Care*, Buckingham, Open University Press.

Hughes, B. and Mtezuka, M. (1992) 'Social Work and Older Women: Where Have Older Women Gone?', in Langan and Day (1992).

Hugman, R. (1991) *Power in Caring Professions*, Basingstoke, Macmillan – now Palgrave Macmillan.

Hugman, R. and Smith, D. (eds) (1995) *Ethical Issues in Social Work*, London, Routledge.

Humphries, B. (ed.) (1996) *Critical Perspectives on Empowerment*, Birmingham, Venture Press.

Husband, C. (1987) *'Race' in Britain: Continuity and Change*, 2nd edn, London, Hutchinson.

Hutchinson-Reis, M. (1989) '"And for Those of Us Who Are Black?" Black Politics in Social Work', in Langan and Lee (1989).

Huws Williams, R., Williams, H. and Davies, E. (eds) (1994) *Social Work and the Welsh Language*, Cardiff, University of Wales Press.

Illich, I. (1977) *Limits to Medicine*, Harmondsworth, Penguin.

Ingleby, D. (ed.) (1981) *Critical Psychiatry: The Politics of Mental Health*, Harmondsworth, Penguin.

Jack, R. (1995a) 'Empowerment in Community Care' in Jack (1995b).

Jack, R. (ed.) (1995b) *Empowerment in Community Care*, London, Chapman & Hall.

Jameson, F. (1984a) 'Periodizing the 60s', in Sayres *et al.* (1984).

Jameson, F. (1984b) 'Foreword' in Lyotard (1984).

Janis, I. L. (1972) *Victims of Groupthink*, Boston, Houghton Mifflin.

Jermier, J. M., Knights, D. and Nord, W. R. (eds) (1994) *Resistance and Power in Organizations*, London, Routledge.

Jessop, B. (1990) *State Theory: Putting Capitalist States in Their Place*, Pennsylvania, Penn State.

Johanssen, H. and Page G. T. (eds) (1990) *International Dictionary of Management*, 4th edn, London, Guild.

Johnson, J. and Slater, R. (eds) (1993) *Ageing and Later Life*, London, Sage.

Jones, C. and Novak, T. (1999) *Poverty, Welfare and The Disciplinary State*, London, Routledge.

Jones, L. J. (1994) *The Social Context of Health and Health Work*, Basingstoke, Macmillan – now Palgrave Macmillan.

Kandola, R., Fullerton, J. and Ahmed, Y. (1995) 'Managing Diversity: Succeeding Where Equal Opportunities Has Failed', *Equal Opportunities Review*, 59 (Jan–Feb).

Kaplan, A. L. Engelhardt, H. T. and McCartney, J. J. (eds) (1981) *Concepts of Health and Disease: Interdisciplinary Perspectives*, London, Addison-Wesley.

Kendall, G. and Wickham, G. (2001) *Understanding Culture: Cultural Studies, Order, Ordering*, London, Sage.

Kickert, W. J. M. (1993) 'Autopoiesis and the Science of (Public) Administration: Essence, Sense and Nonsense', *Organization Studies*, 14(2).

Kitwood, T. (1993) 'Frames of Reference for an Understanding of Dementia', in Johnson and Slater (1993).

Knights, D. and Vurdubakis, T. (1994) 'Foucault, Power, Resistance and All That', in Jermier *et al.* (1994).

Knorr-Cetina, K. and Cicourel, A. V. (eds) (1981) *Advances in Social Theory and Methodology: Towards an Integration of Micro- and Macro-Sociologies*, London, Routledge.

Krajeski, J. P. (1986) 'Psychotherapy with Gay Men and Lesbians: A History of Controversy', in Stein and Cohen (1986).

Kritzman, L. D. (ed.) (1988) *Michel Foucault: Politics, Philosophy, Culture*, New York, Routledge.

Krogh, G. von, and Roos, J. (1995) *Organizational Epistemology*, Basingstoke, Macmillan – now Palgrave Macmillan.

Laing, R. D. (1965) *The Divided Self*, Harmondsworth, Penguin.

Laing, R. D. and Cooper, C. (1964) *Reason and Violence: A Decade of Sartre's Philosophy*, London, Tavistock.

Lake, T. (1987) *Defeating Depression*, Harmondsworth, Penguin.

Langan, M. and Day, L. (eds) (1992) *Women, Social Work and Oppression: Issues in Anti-Discriminatory Practice*, London, Routledge.

Langan, M. and Lee, P. (eds) (1989) *Radical Social Work Today*, London, Unwin Hyman.

Law, J. (1986) 'On Power and its Tactics: A View from the Sociology of Science', *The Sociological Review*, 34(1).

Lawton, A. and Rose, A. (1994) *Organisation and Management in the Public Sector*, 2nd edn, London, Pitman.

Lešnik, B. (ed.) (1997) *Change in Social Work*, Aldershot, Ashgate.

Lešnik, B. (ed.) (1998) *Countering Discrimination in Social Work*, Aldershot, Ashgate.

Lindemann, E. (1944) 'Symptomatology and Management of Acute Grief', *American Journal of Psychiatry*, 101.

Lister, R. (1997) *Citizenship: Femininst Perspectives*, Basingstoke, Macmillan – now Palgrave Macmillan.

Littlewood, J. (1992) *Aspects of Grief: Bereavement in Adult Life*, London, Routledge.

Lonsdale, S. (1990) *Women and Disability*, Basingstoke, Macmillan – now Palgrave Macmillan.

Lovell, T. (2000) 'Feminisms of the Second Wave', in Turner (2000).

Luhmann, N. (1982) *The Differentiation of Society*, New York, Columbia University Press.

Luhmann, N. (1988) 'Tautology and Paradox in the Self-Descriptions of Modern Society', *Sociological Theory*, 6.

Luhmann, N. (1990) *Essays on Self-Reference*, New York, Columbia University Press.

Lukes, S. (1974) *Power: A Radical View*, Basingstoke, Macmillan – now Palgrave Macmillan.

Lund, D. A. (ed.) (2001) *Men Coping with Grief*, Amityville, NY, Baywood.

Lynn, E. and Muir, A. (1996) 'Empowerment in Social Work: The Case of CCETSW's Welsh Language Policy', in Humphries (1996).

Lyotard, J-F. (1984) *The Postmodern Condition*, Minneapolis, Minnesota University Press.

Mabey, C. and Iles, P. (eds) (1994) *Managing Learning*, London, Routledge.

Macpherson, W. (1999) *Report on the Inquiry into the Stephen Lawrence Murder*, London, Home Office.

Malahleka, B. (1992) 'Centre of Gravity', paper presented at the British Association of Social Workers Conference, Malvern.

Mares, P., Henley, A. and Barker, C. (1985) *Health Care in Multi-Racial Britain*, London, Health Education Authority/National Extension College.

Marlow, A. and Loveday, B. (eds) (2000) *After Macpherson: Policing after the Stephen Lawrence Inquiry*, Lyme Regis, Russell House Publishing.

Marsden, R. (1993) 'The Politics of Organizational Analysis', *Organization Studies*, 14(1).

Marshall, M. and Rowlings, C. (1998) 'Facing Our Futures: Discrimination in Later Life', in Lešnik (1998).

Marshall, T. H. (1963) *Sociology at the Crossroads and Other Essays*, London, Heinemann.

Maslach, C. and Jackson, S. (1981) *The Maslach Burnout Inventory*, Palo Alto, Calif., Consulting Psychology Press.

Mason, D. (2000) *Race and Ethnicity in Modern Britain*, 2nd edn, Oxford, Oxford University Press.

Matarazzo, J. P. (ed.) (1984) *Behavioral Health*, New York, Wiley.

Maturana, H. and Varela, F. J. (1978) 'Preliminary Remarks', in Zeleney (1978).

Maturana, H. and Varela, F. J. (1980) *Autopoiesis and Cognition: The Realizations of the Living*, London, Reidl.

May, M., Page, R. and Brunsdon, E. (eds) (2001) *Understanding Social Problems: Issues in Social Policy*, Oxford, Blackwell.

Maynard, M. (1993) 'Violence Towards Women', in Richardson and Robinson (1993).

McDerment, L. (ed.) (1988) *Stress Care*, Surbiton, Social Care Association.

McDowell, L. (1989) 'Gender Divisions', in Hamnett *et al.* (1989).

McLean, P. E. (1996) 'Mass Communication, Popular Culture, and Racism', in Bowser (1996).

McLellan, D. (1995) *Ideology*, 2nd edn, Buckingham, Open University Press.

Mead, M. (1935) *Sex and Temperament*, New York, Mentor.

Midwinter, E. (1991) *Out of Focus: Old Age, the Press and Broadcasting*, London, Centre for Policy on Ageing.

Miles, A. (1987) *The Mentally Ill in Contemporary Society*, 2nd edn, Oxford, Blackwell.

Miles, A. (1991) *Women, Health and Medicine*, Buckingham, Open University Press.

Mills, C.W. (1970) *The Sociological Imagination*, Harmondsworth, Penguin.

Minkler, M. and Estes, C. (1991) *Critical Perspectives on Ageing*, San Francisco, Baywood.

Mishra, R. (1981) *Society and Social Policy: Theories and Practice of Welfare*, 2nd edn, Basingstoke, Macmillan – now Palgrave Macmillan.

Montgomery, M. (1995) *An Introduction to Language and Society*, 2nd edn, London, Routledge.

Morgan, G. (1986) *Images of Organization*, London, Sage.

Morley, D. and Chen, K-H. (eds) (1996) *Stuart Hall: Critical Dialogues in Cultural Studies*, London, Routledge.

Morris, D. and Williams, G. (1994) 'Language and Social Work Practice: The Welsh Case', in Huws Williams *et al.* (1994).

Morrison, T., Erooga, M. and Beckett, R. C. (1994) *Sexual Offending Against Children*, London, Routledge.

Morrow, R. A. (1994) *Critical Theory and Methodology*, London, Sage.

Mullaly, R. (1993) *Structural Social Work*, Toronto, McLelland & Stewart.

Mullender, A. (1996) *Rethinking Domestic Violence: The Social Work and Probation Response*, London, Routledge.

Mullins, L. J. (1996) *Management and Organisational Behaviour*, 4th edn, London, Pitman.

Murphy, M. (1991) 'Pressure Points', *Social Work Today*, 13 June.

Navarro, V. (1986) *Crisis, Health and Medicine*, London, Tavistock.

Neal, C. and Davies, D. (1996) 'Introduction', in Davies and Neal (1996).

Newman, J. (1994) 'The Limits of Managment: Gender and the Politics of Change', in Clarke *et al.* (1994a).

Nolan, M. (2001) 'Acute and Rehabilitative Care for Older People', in Nolan *et al.* (2001b).

Nolan, M., Davies, S. and Grant, G. (2001a) 'Introduction', in Nolan *et al.* (2001b).

Nolan, M., Davies, S. and Grant, G. (eds) (2001b) *Working with Older People and Their Families: Key Issues in Policy and Practice*, Buckingham, Open University Press.

Norman, A. (1980) *Rights and Risk*, London, Centre for Policy on Ageing.

Novak, T. (1988) *Poverty and the State: An Historical Sociology*, Milton Keynes, Open University Press.

Nusberg, C. (1995) 'Preface' in Thursz *et al.* (1995)

O'Brien, M. (1990) 'The Place of Men in Gender-Sensitive Therapy', in Perelberg and Miller (1990).

O'Neill, D. (1996) 'Health Care for Older People: Ageism and Equality', in Bywaters and McLeod (1996).

O'Neill, J. (1995) *The Poverty of Postmodernism*, London, Routledge.

Oakley, A. (1981) *From Here to Maternity – Becoming a Mother*, Harmondsworth, Penguin.

Oliver, M. (1983) *Social Work with Disabled People*, Basingstoke, Macmillan – now Palgrave Macmillan.

Oliver, M. (1990) *The Politics of Disablement*, Basingstoke, Macmillan – now Palgrave Macmillan.

Oliver, M. (ed.) (1991) *Social Work, Disabled People and Disabling Environments*, London, Jessica Kingsley.

Oliver, M. (1996) *Understanding Disability: From Theory to Practice*, Basingstoke, Macmillan – now Palgrave Macmillan.

Oliver, M. and Sapey, B. (1999) *Social Work with Disabled People*, 2nd edn, Basingstoke, Macmillan – now Palgrave Macmillan.

Papadopoulos, I. (2001) 'Antiracism, Multiculturalism and the Third Way', in Baxter (2001a).

Parkes, C. M. (1980) *Bereavement: Studies of Grief in Adult Life*, 2nd edn, Harmondsworth, Penguin.

Parton, N. (1985) *The Politics of Child Abuse*, Basingstoke, Macmillan – now Palgrave Macmillan.

Parton, N. (1988) *Child Abuse*, Unit 16 of the Open University course, D211 *Social Problems and Social Welfare*.

Parton, N. (ed.) (1996) *Social Theory, Social Change and Social Work*, London, Routledge.

Pearson, G. (1975) *The Deviant Imagination*, Basingstoke, Macmillan – now Palgrave Macmillan.

Pease, B. and Fook, J. (1999) *Transforming Social Work Practice: Postmodern Critical Perspectives*, London, Routledge.

Perelberg, R. J. and Miller, A.C. (eds) (1990) *Gender and Power in Families*, London, Tavistock/Routledge.

Phillipson, C. (1982) *Capitalism and the Construction of Old Age*, Basingstoke, Macmillan – now Palgrave Macmillan.

Phillipson, C. and Walker, A. (eds) (1986) *Ageing and Social Policy*, Aldershot, Gower.

Phillipson, C. and Thompson, N. (1996) 'The Social Construction of Old Age: New Perspectives on the Theory and Practice of Social Work with Older People', in Bland (1996).

Phillipson, J. (1992) *Practising Equality: Women, Men and Social Work*, London, Central Council for Education and Training in Social Work.

Phizacklea, A. and Miles, R. (1992) 'The British Trade Union Movement and Racism', in Braham *et al.* (1992).

Pilgrim, D. and Rogers, A. (1993) *A Sociology of Mental Health and Illness*, Buckingham, Open University Press.

Preston-Shoot, M. (1996) 'W(h)ither Social Work? Social Work, Social Policy and Law at an Interface: Confronting the Challenges and Realising the Potential in Work with People Needing Care or Services', *Liverpool Law Review*, XVIII(1).

Pride, P. (2001) 'Mental Disorder', in May *et al.* (2001).

Rabinow, P. (ed.) (1986) *The Foucault Reader*, Harmondsworth, Penguin.

Ranson, S. and Stewart, J. (1994) *Management for the Public Domain: Enabling the Learning Society*, Basingstoke Macmillan – now Palgrave Macmillan.

Reed, M. I. (1992) *The Sociology of Organizations: Themes, Perspectives and Prospects*, London, Harvester Wheatsheaf.

Reid, I. (1992) 'Social Class and Education', in Giddens (1992).

Richardson, D. and Robinson, V. (eds) (1993) *Introducing Women's Studies*, Basingstoke, Macmillan – now Palgrave Macmillan.

Riches, G. (2002) 'Gender', in Thompson (2002a).

Ricoeur, P. (1984) *Time and Narrative, Vol. 1*, University of Chicago Press.

Roberts, C., Davies, E. and Jupp, T. (1992) *Language and Discrimination*, London, Longman.

Robinson, L. (1995) *Psychology for Social Workers: Black Perspective*, London, Routledge.

Rogers, A., Pilgrim, D. and Lacey, R. (1993) *Experiencing Psychiatry: Users' Views of Services*, Basingstoke, Macmillan – now Palgrave Macmillan.

Rojek, C., Peacock, G. and Collins, S. (1988) *Social Work and Received Ideas*, London, Routledge.

Rosenberg, M. G. (1984) 'The Home is the Workplace', in Chavkin (1984).

Rubinstein, D. (2001) *Culture, Structure and Agency: Towards a Truly Multidimensional Society*, London, Sage.

Ryan, W. (1971) *Blaming the Victim: Ideology Serves the Establishment*, London, Pantheon.

Salaman, G. (1979) *Work Organizations: Control and Resistance*, London, Longman.

Sapey, B., Stewart, J. and Harris, J. (2001) 'Disability: Constructing Dependency Through Social Policy', in Baxter (2001a).

Sardar, Z., Nandy, A. and Davies, M. W. (1993) *Barbaric Others: A Manifesto on Western Racism*, London, Pluto.

Sartre, J-P. (1948) *Existentialism and Humanism*, London, Eyre Methuen.

Sartre, J-P. (1958) *Being and Nothingness*, London, Methuen.

Sartre, J-P. (1976) *Critique of Dialectical Reason*, London, Verso.

Saunders, E. (1993) 'Theoretical Approaches to the Study of Women', in Curtis *et al.* (1993).

Sayer, A. (1992) *Method in Social Science: A Realist Approach*, 2nd edn, London, Routledge.

Sayres, S. *et al.* (eds) (1984) *The 60s Without Apology*, Minneapolis, University of Minnesota Press.

Schein, E. H. (1993) 'How Can Organisations Learn Faster?', *Sloan Management Review*, Winter.

Schön, D. A. (1983) *The Reflective Practitioner*, London, Temple Smith.

Schön, D. A. (1987) *Educating the Reflective Practitioner*, San Francisco, Calif., Jossey Bass.

Schön, D. A. (1992) 'The Crisis of Professional Knowledge and the Pursuit of an Epistemology of Practice', *Journal of Interprofessional Care*, 6(1).

Scollon, R. and Scollon, S.W. (2001) *Intercultural Communication: A Discourse Approach*, 2nd edn, Oxford, Blackwell.

Scott, J. C. (1986) *Weapons of the Weak: Everyday Forms of Peasant Resistance*, New Haven, CT, Yale University Press.

Scrutton, S. (1989) *Counselling Older People*, London, Edward Arnold.

Scrutton, S. (1992) *Ageing, Healthy and in Control: An Alternative Approach to Maintaining the Health of Older People*, London, Chapman & Hall.

Seale, C. (1995a) 'Society and Death', in Davey *et al.* (1995).

Seale, C. (1995b) 'Dying', in Davey *et al.* (1995).

Sedgwick, P. (1973) 'Illness – Mental and Otherwise', *The Hastings Centre*, 1(3).

Segal, L. (1999) *Why Feminism?*, Cambridge, Polity.

Shaw, I. (1996) *Evaluating in Practice*, Aldershot, Arena.

Sibeon, R. (1991) 'The Construction of a Contemporary Sociology of Social Work', in Davies (1991).

Sibeon, R. (1992) *Towards a New Sociology of Social Work*, Aldershot, Avebury.

Sibeon, R. (1996) *Contemporary Sociology and Policy Analysis: The New Sociology of Public Policy*, Eastham, Tudor Business Publishing.

Sidell, M. (1995) *Health in Old Age: Myth, Mystery and Management*, Buckingham, Open University Press.

Simon, G. (1996) 'Working with People in Relationships', in Davies and Neal (1996).

Simons, H. W. and Billig, M. (eds) (1994) *After Postmodernism: Reconstructing Ideology Critique*, London, Sage.

Skellington, R. (1996) *'Race' in Britain Today*, 2nd edn, London, Sage.

Smith, S. (1989) *The Politics of 'Race' and Residence*, Cambridge, Polity Press.

Sokal, A. D. (1996) 'Transgressing the Boundaries: Towards a Transformative Hermeneutics of Quantum Gravity', *Social Text* 46/47 (Spring/Summer).

Sokal, A. D. and Bricmont, J. (1999) *Intellectual Impostures*, London, Profile Books.

Solomos, J. (1993) *Race and Racism in Britain*, 2nd edn, Basingstoke, Macmillan – now Palgrave Macmillan.

Solomos, J. and Back, L. (1996) *Racism and Society*, Basingstoke, Macmillan – now Palgrave Macmillan.

Spender, D. (1990) *Man Made Language*, 2nd edn, London, Pandora.

Stacey, R. D. (1993) *Strategic Management and Organisational Dynamics*, London, Pitman.

Stein, T. S. and Cohen, C. J. (eds) (1986) *Contemporary Perspectives on Psychotherapy with Lesbians and Gay Men*, New York, Plenum.

Storey, J. (1995a) 'Human Resource Management: Still Marching On, or Marching Out?', in Storey (1995b).

Storey, J. (ed.) (1995b) *Human Resource Management: A Critical Text*, London, Routledge.

Stubbs, P. (1993) '"Ethnically Sensitive" or "Anti-Racist"? Models for Health Research and Service Delivery', in Ahmad (1993a).

Summers, A. (1975) *Damned Whores and God's Police: The Colonization of Women in Australia*, Harmondsworth, Penguin.

Swain, J., Finkelstein, V., French, S. and Oliver, M. (eds) (1993) *Disabling Barriers – Enabling Environments*, London, Sage.

Szasz, T. (1961) *The Myth of Mental Illness*, New York, Hoeber–Harper.

Tannen, D. (1992) *You Just Don't Understand: Women and Men in Conversation*, London, Virago.

Taylor, C. and White, S. (2000) *Practising Reflexivity in Health and Welfare: Making Knowledge*, Buckingham, Open University Press.

Taylor-Browne, J. (ed.) (2001) *What Works in Reducing Domestic Violence: A Comprehensive Guide for Professionals*, London, Whiting and Birch.

Teubner, G. (1993) *Law as an Autopoietic System*, Oxford, Blackwell.

Thomas, M. and Pierson, J. (eds) (1995) *Dictionary of Social Work*, London, Collins.

Thomas, N. (2000) *Children, Family and the State: Decision-Making and Child Participation*, Basingstoke, Palgrave Macmillan.

Thomas, N. (2001) 'Listening to Children', in Foley *et al.* (2001).

Thompson, J. (1994) 'Ideology and Modern Culture', in Giddens *et al.* (1994).

Thompson. N. (1989) 'Making Use of Beatnik Thinking', *Social Work Today*, 19 August.

Thompson, N. (1991a) *Crisis Intervention Revisited*, Birmingham, Pepar.

Thompson, N. (1991b) 'The Legacy of Laing: A Critique of the Medical Model in Social Work and Social Care', *Social Science Teacher*, 20(2).

Thompson, N. (1992a) *Existentialism and Social Work*, Aldershot, Avebury.

Thompson, N. (1992b) *Child Abuse: The Existential Dimension*, Norwich, University of East Anglia Social Work Monographs.

Thompson, N. (1995a) *Age and Dignity: Working with Older People*, Aldershot, Arena.

Thompson, N. (1995b) 'Men and Anti-Sexism', *British Journal of Social Work*, 25(4).

Thompson, N. (1997a) 'Masculinity and Loss', in Field *et al.* (1997).

Thompson, N. (1997b) 'Children, Death and Ageism', *Child and Family Social Work*, 2 (1).

Thompson, N. (1998) 'The Ontology of Ageing', *British Journal of Social Work*, 28 (5).

Thompson, N. (1999) *Stress Matters*, Birmingham, Pepar.

Thompson, N. (2000a) *Theory and Practice in Human Services*, 2nd edn, Buckingham, Open University Press.

Thompson, N. (2000b) *Understanding Social Work: Preparing for Practice*, Basingstoke, Palgrave Macmillan.

Thompson, N. (2000c) *Tackling Bullying and Harassment in the Workplace*, Birmingham, Pepar.

Thompson, N. (2001a) *Anti-Discriminatory Practice*, 3rd edn, Basingstoke, Palgrave Macmillan.

Thompson, N. (2001b) 'The Ontology of Masculinity', in Lund (2001).

Thompson, N. (ed.) (2002a) *Loss and Grief: A Guide for Human Services Practitioners*, Basingstoke, Palgrave Macmillan.

Thompson, N. (2002b) *Building the Future: Social Work with Children, Young People and their Families*, Lyme Regis, Russell House Publishing.

Thompson, N. (2002c) *People Skills*, 2nd edn, Basingstoke, Palgrave Macmillan.

Thompson, N. (2002d) 'Social Work with Adults', in Adams *et al.* (2002).

Thompson, N. (2003) *Communication and Language: A Handbook of Theory and Practice*, Basingstoke, Palgrave Macmillan.

Thompson, N. and Bates, J. (1996) *Learning from Other Disciplines: Lessons from Nurse Education and Management Theory*, Norwich, University of East Anglia Social Work Monographs.

Thompson, N., Murphy, M. and Stradling, S. (1994a) *Dealing with Stress*, Basingstoke, Macmillan – now Palgrave Macmillan.

Thompson, N., Murphy, M. and Stradling, S. (1996a) *Meeting the Stress Challenge*, Lyme Regis, Russell House Publishing.

Thompson, N., Osada, M. and Anderson, B. (1994b) *Practice Teaching in Social Work*, 2nd edn, Birmingham, Pepar.

Thompson, N., Stradling, S., Murphy, M. and O'Neill, P. (1996b) 'Stress and Organizational Culture', *British Journal of Social Work*, 26(5).

Thompson, N. and Thompson, S. (2001) 'Empowering Older People: Beyond the Care Model', *Journal of Social Work*, 1(1).

Thompson, P. (1993) 'Postmodernism: Fatal Distraction', in Hassard and Parker (1993).

Thompson, P. and McHugh, D. (1995) *Work Organisations: A Critical Introduction*, 2nd edn, Basingstoke, Macmillan – now Palgrave Macmillan.

Thornton, R, and Tozer, P. (1994) *Involving Older People in Planning and*

Evaluating Community Care: A Review of Initiatives, York, University of York Social Policy Research Unit.

Thunhurst, C. (1982) *It Makes You Sick: The Politics of the NHS*, London, Pluto.

Thursz, D., Nusberg, C. and Prather, J. (eds) (1995) *Empowering Older People: An International Approach*, London, Cassell.

Totman, R. (1990) *Mind, Stress and Health*, London, Souvenir Press.

Townsend, P. (1979) *Poverty in the UK*, Harmondsworth, Penguin.

Townsend, P. and Davidson, N. (1988) 'The Black Report', in Townsend et al. (1988).

Townsend, P., Davidson, N. and Whitehead, M. (1988) *Inequalities in Health*, Harmondsworth, Penguin.

Trenchard, L. and Warren, H. (1984) *Something to Tell You*, London, London Gay Teenage Group.

Turner, B. S. (1986) *Equality*, London, Ellis Horwood/Tavistock.

Turner, B. S. (1995) *Medical Power and Social Knowledge*, 2nd edn, London, Sage.

Turner, B. S. (ed.) (2000) *The Blackwell Companion to Social Theory*, 2nd edn, Oxford, Blackwell.

UPIAS (1976) 'Fundamental Principles of Disability', London, Union of the Physically Impaired Against Segregation.

Ussher, J. (1991) *Women's Madness: Misogyny or Mental Illness?*, London, Harvester Wheatsheaf.

Vivian, J. and Brown, R. (1995) 'Prejudice and Intergroup Conflict', in Argyle and Colman (1995).

Walby, S. (1994) 'Towards a Theory of Patriarchy', in Giddens *et al.* (1994).

Walker, B. A. (1994) 'Valuing Differences: The Concept and a Model', in Mabey and Iles (1994).

Walmsley, J., Reynolds, J., Shakespeare, P. and Woolfe, R. (eds) (1993) *Health, Welfare and Practice: Reflecting on Roles and Relationships*, London, Sage.

Walter, T. (1994) *The Revival of Death*, London, Routledge.

Walter, T., Littlewood, J. and Pickering, M. (1995) 'Death in the News: The Public Investigation of Private Emotion', *Sociology*, 29(4).

Ward, D. and Mullender, A. (1993) 'Empowerment and Oppression: An Indissoluble Pairing for Contemporary Social Work', in Walmsley *et al.* (1993).

Watters, C. (1996) 'Representations and Realities: Black People, Community Care and Mental Illness', in Ahmad and Atkin (1996).

Weber, M. (1968) *Economy and Society*, New York, Bedminster.

Weintraub, J. K., Carver, C. and Scheier, M. (1989) 'Assessing Coping Strategies: A Theoretically-Based Approach', *Journal of Personality and Social Psychology*, 56(2).

Westwood, S. (2002) *Power and the Social*, London, Routledge.

Wetherell, M., Taylor, S. and Yates, S. J. (eds) (2001) *Discourse Theory and Practice: A Reader*, London, Sage.

Wheen, F. (1996) 'A Fine Old Case of Humbug', *The Guardian*, 17 January.

White, A. (1990) *Within Nietzsche's Labyrinth*, London, Routledge.

White, S. (1991) *Political Theory and Postmodernism*, Cambridge University Press.

Whitehead, M. (1988) 'The Health Divide', in Townsend *et al.* (1988).

Williams, F. (1989) *Social Policy: A Critical Introduction*, Cambridge, Polity.

Williams, H. (1994) 'Social Work and the Welsh Language', in Huws Williams *et al.* (1994).

Wilson, A. (1993) 'Which Equality? Toleration, Difference or Respect', in Bristow and Wilson (1993).

Wilson, E. (1993) 'Is Transgression Transgressive?', in Bristow and Wilson (1993).

Wineman, S. (1984) *The Politics of Human Services*, Montréal, Black Rose Books.

Wise, S. (1995) 'Feminist Ethics in Practice', in Hugman and Smith (1995).

Zeleny, M. (ed.) (1978) *Autopoiesis: Theory of the Living Organization*, Amsterdam, North-Holland.

Zola, I. (1972) 'Medicine as an Institution of Social Control', *The Sociological Review*, 20(4).

INDEX